Know how to Get Government Jobs

Know how to Get Government Jobs

A must-read for career
information and guidance

K. P. Shashidharan

JAICO PUBLISHING HOUSE
Ahmedabad Bangalore Bhopal Bhubaneswar Chennai
Delhi Hyderabad Kolkata Lucknow Mumbai

Published by Jaico Publishing House
A-2 Jash Chambers, 7-A Sir Phirozshah Mehta Road
Fort, Mumbai - 400 001
jaicopub@jaicobooks.com
www.jaicobooks.com

© K. P. Shashidharan

KNOW HOW TO GET GOVERNMENT JOBS
ISBN 978-81-8495-668-9

First Jaico Impression: 2015

No part of this book may be reproduced or utilized in
any form or by any means, electronic or
mechanical including photocopying, recording or by any
information storage and retrieval system,
without permission in writing from the publishers.

This book is dedicated to millions of educated job seekers, their parents, guardians, teachers, mentors, well wishers and trainers, living in 29 States and 7 Union territories of the country, chasing a dream.

The book is so designed as an "I-Book" to provide right information at right time to right persons to guide the job seekers to make an informed decision about their career planning and job selection; because, the prime objective of education tends to be finding a satisfying career of one's liking rather than accidently ending up in some job one seldom likes

About the Author

K. P. Shashidharan is a visiting Professor to NIFM, LBSNAA, IIMs, ICISA, NAAA, NADT, Universities and other premier professional, academic, and administrative training institutions. He is former Director General in CAG of India, Member of IAAS, a premier Indian Civil Service, an alumnus from the London School of Economics, established author, poet, and freelance columnist in most of the leading English newspapers. He has functioned in various capacities in Government of India and Comptroller and Auditor General of India. As Director General (Commercial) DG (Autonomous Bodies), DG (Western Region), DG (Central Audit), he has been actively associated with all Central and State governments, ministries and departments, attached and subordinate offices, Central and State Public Sector Enterprises, Autonomous Bodies, various projects, programmes, schemes of Central, States and the third tier government organizations like Urban Local Bodies and Panchayati Raj Institutions.

As Director in the Ministry of Home Affairs in the Government of India, he discharged important responsibilities administering State Reorganization, States Police, Law and Order, Modernization of police, Prison Administration, Criminal Justice System, involved in organizing conferences of Chief Ministers, Governors, Chief Secretaries on Centre State and interstate relations.

As Director and Deputy Secretary (Finance) in the Ministry of Home Affairs he supervised preparation of budget, exercised expenditure control as well as rendered financial advice to Cabinet papers, plan and non plan projects of the Ministry including those of the attached and subordinate offices like IB, CBI and Central Police Organizations including CRPF, CISF, BSF, NSG, Bureau of Police Research Training and Research, National Crime Records Bureau and Central Forensic Laboratories.

The author had published more than 100 humorous articles known as middles and more than 100 articles on edit pages of leading Indian English national newspapers and professional journals. He had authored 2 Volumes of best selling poetry acclaimed by Indian Sahitya Akademy of English literature and celebrity writers titled 'Whispering Mind' and 'Painting Symphony' and also co-authored a business book titled 'BIG: Business India Guru'.

DISCLAIMER

This book is compiled based on information on recruitment notifications available to help those who want to be in government service. The information for different posts may change at the discretion of the authorized recruitment agency. The candidates are advised to check the latest notification relating to a particular job or position before applying. The objective of this book is to present relevant information systematically in a logical order at place to guide the job seekers effective career planning to choose the government jobs they are interested. While effort are made to guide the domains where government jobs Civil, Technical and Uniformed including Central and States Public Sector jobs, Autonomous Bodies, Societies and other government organizations, it is difficult to include everything and the contents are more illustrative than exhaustive.

Preface

What This Book Can Do for You

Choosing a career

As a student or one in search of a suitable job, it is most likely that you may want to pursue a career more in keeping with your educational qualifications or what you are trained to be. Deciding on a career is an important decision that needs proper forethought and planning.

The Indian Civil Service is considered as the steel frame and backbone of administration in the country. Will you enjoy working in the Indian Administrative Service (IAS) or Indian Foreign Service (IFS) or Indian Audit and Accounts Service (IAAS) or Indian Police Service (IPS) or Indian Revenue Service (IRS) or any of the distinguished premier civil services of the Government of India with a distinguished suffix like IAS, IFS, IAAS, IRS after your name? Do you dream to be part of the prestigious uniformed services in Army, Navy or Air force and lead the forces to victory? Do you visualize retiring as a Secretary to the Government of India or an Indian Ambassador or High Commissioner or Director General of Intelligence Bureau, DG, Central Bureau of Investigation, DG Police of any State or Paramilitary Force like CRPF, BSF, CISF or Head of a Government Organization or Department or Chairman of Railway Board? Will you like to be recruited to be a future Deputy Governor of Reserve Bank of India or Chairman & Managing Director of any public sector bank or public sector enterprises or such coveted powerful positions? If you are well informed, you can decide. If you like to be part of the government machinery, you can and you will and it's your choice depending on you.

Challenges

These exclusive services provide you highly esteemed job titles recognized by the society, branding you as member of a distinguished premier civil service, or uniformed service, guaranteeing timely promotions, impressive career graph and taking you to the top most positions in different spheres of the government functioning. These are the most powerful government jobs in the country offering enormous opportunities and challenges to prove your competence and decision making abilities at every stage and allow you to derive maximum job satisfaction. True, the government jobs are obviously not the highest paid positions; but what makes these jobs distinguished and unique? These jobs enable you to be a part of the robust government machinery, its powerful permanent executive, providing you an opportunity to make a positive difference to you, the people around you, and the public and in nation building by contributing towards better service delivery and good governance.

What you need to know about government jobs

If you want to join any of the government services, you must be armed with adequate data and relevant information about job opportunities available in government as a whole. You need to have a clear idea about - where are the job opportunities, which are the different jobs available at different wings of Central, State governments including municipalities, corporations, urban local bodies and panchayati raj institutions in India, who recruit for different government jobs from the lowest rung of the hierarchy of government structure - multi tasking service (MTS) and clerical services to Group B and Group A officers including All India Services like IAS, IPS and Indian Forest Service, how to get selected for armed services, Central Police Organizations, Central Universities, IIMs, IITs and other similar central and state autonomous bodies and organizations, public sector banks including rural banks, cooperative banks and public sector central and state companies.

Getting a job through recruitment agencies

Many of the central and state government companies or public sector banks or government autonomous bodies/societies/organizations under different central and state ministries carry out recruitment through authorized recruiting agencies. Who are the recruiting agencies? When do these agencies advertise the job opportunities? Which are their websites? What are the eligibility criteria for different jobs? What are the tests, interview and procedure for selection for different jobs? And most importantly how to map the jobs, select the jobs and begin systematic planning to get selected with the highest possible rank at the earliest opportunity for any of the service of your choice based on your planning, preparation, knowledge, hard work, your core competitive edge and capabilities? Answers to these questions, and much more is detailed in this book.

Job opportunities available

There are jobs in Central Government departmental undertakings like Railways, Post and Telecommunication, Defence offices, Central and State public sector undertakings, public sector banks including Reserve Bank of India, nationalized banks, important sectors like insurance sector, armed forces covering Army, Navy and Air Force, central police organizations like Central Reserve Police Force, Border Security Force, Assam Rifles, ITBP, NSG, Black Cat, CBI, IB, RAW, Income Tax, Customs, Central Excise.

Choosing the most suitable job

The book provides quintessential information about jobs available in government at different levels, from the lowest rung of multi task force and clerical services to the highest Indian civil services and uniformed services and other higher civil service jobs. Also, information about when are these jobs are likely to be advertised generally, where to find them, how to apply for them, who are the recruiting agencies, recruitment procedures, what are the eligible qualifications, criteria and conditions, what are the different willing to work hard to reach your goal, then this book can and will make a great, positive difference to you and the people around you. This book can empower you and help you in carving out a better tomorrow.

*****

CHAPTER

INTRODUCTION TO GOVERNMENT OF INDIA: HIERARCHICAL STRUCTURE & GOVERNMENT SERVICES

Where are the government services?
What are the various services?
How are the services organized?
What are the emoluments, entitlements and perks?
This chapter gives a bird's eye view of the entire spectrum of the government services. The job-seekers are taken for a jobs tour showing and explaining where are the government jobs, what are the government jobs and what are the qualifications required for most of the government jobs. The organization chart of the Government of India is presented with its three distinct wings Legislature, Executive and Judiciary and the hierarchical structure of the Union Government and the States. This is to familiarize the reader the extent of government domain, bureaucratic hierarchy, its pyramid structure, interlinking and basic functions, and also to mentally prepare the job aspirants to get ready for focused job hunting with a win-win-win mantra and strategy.

The chapter also highlights how the government services are classified into Group A, Group B and Group C along with specified pay bands, emoluments and entitlements. All the government jobs available are spread across this spectrum in the well defined hierarchy in the three functional wings of the government -- at the centre, and in the states and union territories. The reader is further exposed to various government jobs available from the topmost positions to the lowest rung of the pyramid with minimum level educational qualification starting with just pass in Matriculation Level, Intermediate Level and graduation or degree level. It is for the job seekers to locate the jobs of their qualifications and liking and getting ready for job hunting with a minimum mantra and strategy.

PART I: HIERARCHICAL STRUCTURE OF THE GOVERNMENT MACHINERY

The first thing one should know when searching for a suitable job is the government structure and various services at different levels. The Government of India (GOI) is a union of 29 States and 7 Union Territories. The preamble of the Constitution of India, which came into existence on 26th January 1950, defines India as a Sovereign, Socialist, Secular, Democratic, Republic which is headed by the President of India as the Chief Executive. The President is the de Jure Commander in Chief of the Indian Armed Forces. The Vice-President of India is the second-highest ranking government official in the Executive branch of the GOI and also has the legislative function of acting as the Chairman of the Rajya Sabha.

The Government of India has three wings:

Legislature: Parliament

Executive: President, prime minister and governor

Judiciary: Supreme court

Parliament has two Houses, upper house known as Rajya Sabha and lower house known as Lok Sabha.

The executive power is vested in the President, who acts with advice tendered by the Head of Government Prime Minister of India and the Cabinet and the Council of Ministers. The President is responsible for making important appointments including Governors of States, Chief Justices, other judges of the Supreme Court and High Courts of India, the Attorney General, the Comptroller and Auditor General of India, the Chief Election Commissioner and other Election Commissioners, the Chairman and other Members of the Union Public Service Commission, Indian Ambassadors and High Commissioners, President's Office and also the Cabinet Secretary and members of premier civil services.

The Prime Minister heads the Council of Ministers including the Cabinet. GOI allocates its functions to different Ministries and Departments, attached and subordinate offices to the

Ministries, Public Sector Companies, Autonomous Bodies and other organizations under different Ministries.

The Cabinet of India includes the Prime Minister and Cabinet Ministers. Each Minister must be a member of one of the Houses of Parliament. The Cabinet is headed by the Prime Minister, and Cabinet Secretary acts as advisor. Other Ministers head various Ministries. The Civil Services of India, the permanent bureaucracy of the Government of India and the executive decisions are implemented by the Indian civil servants. The civil servants are employees of the Government of India and not of the Parliament of India.

The Cabinet Secretary is the chief of the entire government bureaucratic structure, which functions as de-facto permanent executive despite changes in the political executive from time to time after general elections. The Cabinet Secretary heads the bureaucracy and facilitates smooth transaction of business in ministries and departments of the Government. He is assisted by Cabinet Secretariat in decision-making in government by ensuring inter-ministerial coordination and evolving consensus through standing committees headed by secretaries of different ministries and departments.

In the States, Governor is the Head of the Executive and Chief Minister heads the government and other ministers look after various ministries and departments and attached and subordinate offices, autonomous bodies, state government companies and other organizations. More or less the same pattern is followed in all the States and Union Territories having legislature with certain difference like states having unicameral or bicameral legislature.

The Judiciary consists of Supreme Court at the centre and High Courts and other courts in the states and at district levels with specific jurisdiction for civil and criminal justice system.

In all the wings of the Government of India and of the States and Union Territories, different services are functioning. The government civil jobs are classified into three Groups—Group A, Group B, Group C. Earlier Group D has now been converted to Multi Tasking Staff (MTS) since 2011. Group A jobs are the highest entry level recruitment in government. Group B jobs are the next higher level jobs and are of two major categories - Gazetted Officers and Non-Gazetted Officers. Gazetted Officers are higher level government officers, whose designations are notified in the government gazette and are authorized by government to attest copies of certificates and various other documents as true copies. Group C jobs are the third level jobs available in government and MTS (erstwhile Group D) is the lowest grade positions recruited in government.

Army, Navy and Air Force has distinct rankings.

The organization structure of GOI is graphically depicted in Figure 1.1 and Figure 1.2.

Preamble of the Constitution of India

"WE, THE PEOPLE OF INDIA, having solemnly resolved to constitute India into a SOVEREIGN SOCIALIST SECULAR DEMOCRATIC REPUBLIC and to secure to all its citizens:

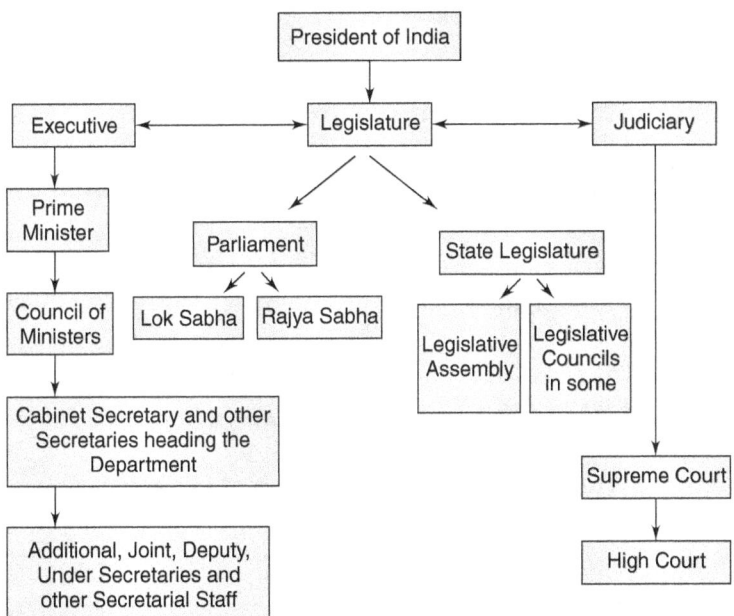

Fig. 1.1 *Government of India structure as per the Constitution*

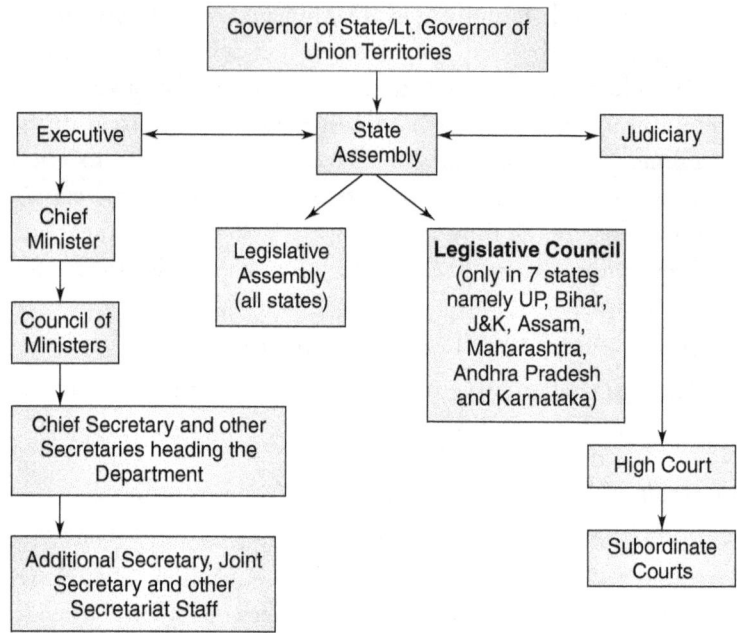

Fig. 1.2 *State Government structure as per the Constitution*

JUSTICE, social, economic and political; **LIBERTY** of thought, expression, belief, faith and worship; **EQUALITY** of status and of opportunity and to promote among them all **FRATERNITY** assuring the dignity of the individual and the unity and integrity of the Nation."

There can be minor variations from state to state in bureaucratic set up. Candidates interested in getting more information about a particular state must visit the website of the state. For example for the State of Maharashtra, you can visit the site cited below:

http://mdmu.maharashtra.gov.in/pages/State/pdf/chart.pdf

Sixth Pay Commission and Classification of Government Services

GOI appoints pay commissions once in 10 years for determining right pay to its services. The service conditions, emoluments, leave, pension, other perks and entitlements are regulated by the Pay Commission from time to time keeping in pace with changed economic environment. The last pay commission was the Sixth Pay Commission whose report came into effect in 2006. The Sixth Pay Commission Report reduced number of pay scales in the Central Government by harmonizing in different Pay Bands (PB) and the Grade Pay (GP) system. Most of the States and Union Territories also followed the system.

Currently, there are three categories of civil service jobs in the government i.e. Group A, Group B and Group C in the descending hierarchical order, with Group A topping the higher echelons of civil services.

The earlier existing Group D has been merged with Group C and re-designated as Multi Tasking Staff. The classification of various Groups and the corresponding Pay Band along with the various Grade Pays within the Pay Band is enumerated below. This classification is uniformly applicable to all Government jobs whether at Centre or State.

Table 1.1 Classification of various groups and corresponding pay band

Sr. No.	Classification of Posts	Description of Posts (After implementation of Sixth Pay Commission Report from 1.01.2006)
1(a)	Group A (Highest Civil Service posts where there is no direct recruitment and is filled through promotion)	A Central Civil Post in Cabinet Secretary's Scale (Rs 90000-fixed), Apex Scale (Rs 80000-fixed) and Higher Administrative Grade Plus Scale (HAG+) (Rs 75500-80000)
1(b)	Group A (Senior Administrative level including entry level for the Group A services. The entry level is PB-3 with a Grade Pay of Rs 5400)	a. **PB-4** – A Central Civil Post carrying the Grade Pay of Rs 12000, Rs 10000, Rs 8900 and Rs 8700 in the Pay Band of Rs 37400-67000. b. **PB-3** – A Central Civil Post carrying the Grade Pay of Rs 7600, Rs 6600 and Rs 5400 in the Pay Band of Rs 15600-39100.

2.	Group B (Gazetted) (Supervisory level which is mostly filled through promotion but certain posts are filled through direct recruitment)	**PB-2** – A Central Civil Post carrying the Grade Pays of Rs 5400 and Rs 4800 in the Pay Band of Rs 9300-34800.
3.	Group B (Non-Gazetted) (Mostly filled through promotion but some posts are filled through direct recruitment) (Clerical level)	**PB-2** – A Central Civil Post carrying the Grade Pays of Rs 4600 and Rs 4200 in the Pay Band of Rs 9300-34800.
4.	Group C (Mostly filled through direct recruitment)	**PB-1** – A Central Civil Post carrying the Grade Pays of Rs 2800, Rs 2400, Rs 2000 and Rs 1900 in the Pay Band of Rs 5200-20200.
5.	Multi-tasking Staff (MTS) (Supporting Staff level) (Through direct recruitment)	**PB-1** – A Central Civil Post carrying the Grade Pays Rs 1800 in the Pay Band of Rs 5200-20200. (Earlier Group D category has been abolished to introduce MTS since 2011.)

Pay and Emoluments

The pay includes the Basic Pay and Grade Pay and other allowances like Dearness Allowance flexible to compensate the inflationary trends in the economy, House Rent Allowance etc.

The Dearness Allowance is computed as a percent of Basic Pay and Grade Pay on the basis of the Consumer Price Index after taking inflation into consideration. The House Rent Allowance is also computed as a percent of Basic Pay and Grade Pay. Depending on the location of posting of the employee, the percent varies from metro cities to non-metro cities. The Travelling Allowance is linked to the Grade Pay in a Pay Band and the various entitlements (during tour and travel) are decided accordingly. The total emoluments of the Government employees comes to three times (approximately) of the Basic Pay and Grade Pay.

Apart from the salary there are certain other benefits in the form of Leave Travel Concession (two in a block of four years), Central Government Employees Group Insurance (CGEGIS), free medical facilities under the Central Government Health Scheme (CGHS) and pension benefits for self and dependents post retirement (or family pension as per rules).

There are certain other benefits in the form of Study Leave, Maternity Leave, and Paternity Leave (for two children) apart from the regular Earned Leave and commuted leave and recently introduced Child Care Leave for women.

The entitlements like leave including earned leave, half pay leave, study leave, maternity and paternity leave, provident fund, pension, travelling allowance, medical facilities, transfer grants allowances, leave travel concessions are regulated by specified rules. The Seventh Pay Commission is formed to study and recommend changes in the service conditions and entitlements of the government servants taking into account the changed circumstances and economic conditions of the country. The recommendations are expected by 2016 for implementation to enhance the status of government service vis-a-vis other service in the country.

The Government Bureaucracy Hierarchical Structure

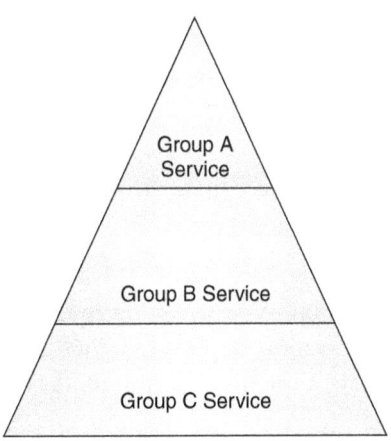

PART II: EDUCATIONAL QUALIFICATION FOR THE ENTRY LEVEL POSTS

The minimum qualification required for any entry level post in the Government is matriculation or equivalent qualification. There are certain posts for which the candidates should be Graduate in specified discipline according to the requirement of the post. Recruitment for most of the posts across Group A, Group B and Group C are open for candidates who have passed Graduation in any discipline. The following are the three entry level qualifications required for different jobs in the government:

1. Matriculation Level There is much recruitment in the Government where the basic qualification required for appearing is to have matriculation certificate from any recognized Board. The recruitment from this category is mainly for the Group C services across various Government Ministries and Department.

For example:
- The Multitasking Staff Exam conducted by the Staff Selection Commission
- Data Entry Operator and Lower Division Clerk recruited through Staff Selection Commission
- Security Assistant (Executive), Junior Intelligence Officer and Personal Assistant recruitment in Intelligence Bureau
- The post of commercial clerk, accounts clerk, ticket examiner, junior clerk cum typist and train clerk in the Indian Railways
- The recruitment of soldiers in Indian Army is also done at this level

2. Intermediate or 10+2 Level Various Group B and C services in the Government sector allows 10+2 passed candidates to appear for the entrance examinations.

For example:
- Entry for Group A services in the Indian Railways as Assistant Mechanical Engineer is done through the Special Class Railway Apprentice Exam conducted by the Union

Public Service Commission (UPSC) where the candidates are required to pass intermediate or equivalent exam
- Candidates can also appear for the Staff Selection Commission 10+2 level examinations for the recruitment of Data Entry Operators and Lower Division Clerk across various Government Ministries and Departments
- Candidates with certain specified qualifications can also apply for various posts in the Indian Army, Indian Air Force and Indian Navy
- The candidates can even apply for the post of Advisor in LIC, Postal Assistants and Sorting Assistants in the Postal Department
- Clerical level posts and certain technical posts in the State Governments and Public Sector Units
- The National Defense Academy Examination and Naval Academy Examination conducted by the UPSC for the 10+2 passed candidates gives plethora of opportunities to reach high ranks in the Indian Army and Indian Navy

3. Graduation or Degree Level Majority of the Government jobs across all groups are open for candidates having a pass degree in any discipline. Educational qualification for even the Indian Civil Services Examination, which selects the premier civil service officers of the country, is mere pass graduation degree in any discipline. Any degree is good enough for many of the Group A services to reach the highest rank in Government or the Group B services to enter the middle ranks or the Group C services for clerical level posts. The examination pattern, papers and the syllabus of the competitive examinations, methodology for selection and the standard of the examination changes based on the position for which the recruitment is conducted. Graduates from specified technical stream are eligible to apply for certain technical jobs. Most of the general competitive examinations are open for graduates from any stream without any discrimination. The selection is based on the score in the competitive examination including performance in the interview.

For example:

- For the UPSC civil service exam, graduates from any stream can apply. The candidates have absolute freedom to choose the optional subject without limiting to the subjects in which the candidate has graduated. The details of various other competitive examinations are discussed in the subsequent chapters.

CHAPTER 2

TYPES OF SERVICES AND RECRUITMENT IN GOVERNMENT

This chapter speaks about Group A, Group B and Group C services of the Government of India including the Indian Civil Services, considered as the crème de la crème or the steel frame of Indian bureaucracy and recruitment to premier uniformed services in Indian Army, Navy and Air Force services taking the job aspirants on a tour across various Ministries and Departments. The chapter provides vital information about the recruitment examinations, selection procedure, eligibility criteria, syllabus, and pattern of examination etc. for the entry level posts in different services. Most importantly, the job aspirants are briefed about the secret mantra and core win-win-win strategy and tips for succeeding in the competitive examinations. The job seeker is equipped with how to prepare a definite road map, demarcating important milestones for navigating and driving to reach the destination on time.

PART I: GROUP A SERVICES

The Civil services, forming the permanent executive in the government in India is given due importance by the framers of the Constitution of India by constituting a Public Service Commission for the Union - the Article 315 of the Constitution of India and a Public Service Commission in different states. UPSC and States PSCs are independent bodies created to function in fair and transparent manner for selection of suitable candidates.

UPSC consists of a Chairman and ten Members. The terms and conditions of service of Chairman and Members of the Commission are governed by the Union Public Service Commission (Members) Regulations, 1969.

Group A services constitute the highest entry level post in the Government. The recruitment is done by the Union Public Service Commission (UPSC) for the general Group A services and the Group A technical services, along with some Group B Gazetted posts and Premier Uniformed Services. For the details of the recruitment procedures, eligibility and pattern of examination candidates are advised to visit **www.upsc.gov.in**. Some of them are discussed subsequently.

Currently UPSC conducts the following 12 examinations given on its website including:
- Civil Services (Preliminary) Examination generally in May
- Civil Services (Main) Examination in October-November
- Indian Forest Service Examination in July
- Engineering Examination in June
- Geologist Examination in December
- Special Class Railway Apprentices' Examination in July

- National Defence Academy & Naval Academy Examination in April and September
- Combined Defence Services Examination in February and August
- Combined Medical Services Examination in January
- Indian Economic Service/Indian Statistical Service Examination in November
- Section Officers/Stenographers (Grade-B/Grade-1) Limited Departmental Competitive Examination in December
- Central Police Forces (Assistant Commandants) Examination in October.

The limited departmental examination conducted by UPSC is for serving employees and not open for fresh candidates. These examinations can be divided into following three categories:

1. General Group A services
2. Technical Group A services
3. Uniformed Group A/Premier services

1. GENERAL GROUP A SERVICES

The recruitment for the general Group A services is done through the Civil Service Exam which is open for the candidates having any graduation degree. The candidates are even free to choose subjects other than the subject in which degree has been obtained.

After selection, the candidates are allotted a state cadre where they have to serve initially. While most states have their own cadre of Officers, Arunachal Pradesh, Delhi, Mizoram, Goa and Union Territories like Andaman & Nicobar Islands, Chandigarh, Daman & Diu, Dadra & Nagar Haveli, Lakshadweep and Puducherry come under the same 'All Indian Service Officers' placed under the AGMUT cadre. As per the recruitment notification for 2014, following services and posts have been included for recruitment through the Civil Service Exam:

- Indian Administrative Service (IAS)
- Indian Foreign Service (IFS)
- Indian Police Service (IPS)

- Indian Post & Telecommunication Accounts and Finance Service, Group A
- Indian Audit & Accounts Service, Group A
- Indian Revenue Service (IRS)(Customs and Central Excise), Group A
- Indian Revenue Service (Income Tax), Group A
- Indian Civil Accounts Service, Group A
- Indian Defence Accounts Service, Group A
- Indian Postal Service, Group A
- Indian Ordnance Factories Service, Group A (Assistant Works Manager, Administration)
- Indian Railway Traffic Service, Group A
- Indian Railway Accounts Service, Group A
- Indian Railway Personnel Service, Group A
- Indian Defence Estate Service, Group A
- Indian Information Service (Junior Grade), Group A
- Indian Corporate Law Service, Group A
- Indian Trade Service, Group A (Grade III)
- Post of Assistant Security Commissioner in Railway Protection Force (RPF), Group A
- Armed Forces Headquarters Civil Service, Group B (Section Officer's Grade)
- Delhi, Andaman & Nicobar Islands, Lakshadweep, Daman & Diu and Dadra & Nagar Haveli Police Service, Group B
- Pondicherry Civil Service, Group B

The allocation of services of the successful candidates depends upon the rank attained in the exam and the preference indicated by the candidates while applying for the exam and the reservation policy of the Government.

Brief Introduction to some of the Group A services are provided below to guide the candidates:

The Group A services can be classified into-

1. All India Services There are three All-India Services and are common to the Centre and the States:

(i) **Indian Administrative Service:** In this service the candidates can be initially appointed as Sub-Collector and reach to the ranks of Chief Secretary in the States and Cabinet Secretary at the Centre. The IAS officers handle the general state of affairs of the government both at the state and central level which includes framing and monitoring of various developmental policies and its implementation. At the district level they look after the implementation of various developmental schemes. At the divisional level, the IAS officers look after law and order, general administration and various developmental works. At the time of initial appointed they are allotted a State Cadre. The recruitment to this service is done through Civil Service Exam conducted by the UPSC on the basis of the rank attained and the preference indicated while filling the form.

(ii) **Indian Police Service:** They serve the State Government in various capacities ranging from Assistant Superintendent of Police at the beginning of career to the Director General of Police at the stage of retirement. The major task assigned to this service is the maintenance of Law and Order. The services are availed by both the Central and State Governments. They can also serve the Central Government in various organizations like the Central Reserve Police Force, Border Security Force, Central Bureau of Investigation, Intelligence Bureau, Research and Analysis Wing (RAW) etc. At the time of initial appointed they are allotted a State Cadre. The recruitment to this service is done through Civil Service Exam conducted by the UPSC on the basis of the rank attained and the preference indicated while filling the form.

(iii) **Indian Foreign Service:** Though technically they do not belong to the 'All India Services' it is discussed here as this service has certain unique characteristic which differentiates it from other services. Members of this service primarily represent the country in the international arena. The Indian Foreign Service deals with the country's external affairs, including diplomacy, trade and cultural relations. It is responsible for the administration and activities of Indian missions abroad, and for the framing and implementation of the Government's foreign policy. The service offers immense exposure to different political, social, ethnic and cultural milieu. An I.F.S officer can be posted in 160 odd Indian Embassies and Missions abroad. They can also be deputed to institutions like United Nations, UNESCO, World Bank, SAARC, etc. Back home, they can be posted in various parts of the country as Passport Officers. The recruitment to this service is done through Civil Service Exam conducted by the UPSC on the basis of the rank attained and the preference indicated while filling the form. As per the trends, only top rankers have been part of this service.

2. Other Group A Civil Services The manpower for performing the functions of the Central Government is mainly provided by Central Services and cadres. The Central Group 'A' Services account for the bulk of the Group 'A' posts under the Central Government. The various services under this category are:

(i) **Indian Audit and Accounts Service:** The services are availed in the Office of Comptroller and Auditor General of India which is a Constitutional body and does not come under the control of any ministry or department. Though the post of C&AG of India is a constitutional post and not reserved exclusively for the members of IAAS, they can rise to the rank of Deputy C&AG (which is equivalent to the post of Secretary to Government of India). The initial appointment as Assistant Accountant General. The Indian Audit and Accounts service is under the Control of the Comptroller & Auditor General of India. The C&AG is the constitutional authority and is entrusted with the responsibility of maintenance and audit of accounts of Union and State. The services of officers of the IAAS are also lent to the Central and State Governments on deputation for functioning as Financial Advisers, Chief Accounts Officers, Chief Internal Audit Officers and so on. The entrants are trained at National Academy of Audit and Accounts, Shimla.

(ii) **Indian P&T Accounts and Finance Service:** After successful completion of training the officers are posted to work in the Department of Post or Department of Telecommunications as Assistant Chief Accounts Officers in the Junior Time Scale Grade. After recruitment through Civil Services Examination, the officers undergo a foundation course with the officers of other services (IAS, IRS, IFS & Central Services Group "A") lasting about 4 months at the National Academy of Direct Taxes at Nagpur. This is followed by a year of rigorous professional training in Financial Management at the National Institute of Financial Management, Faridabad which is a specialized training institute under the Ministry of Finance, Government of India. Thereafter, for further training in Telecom technologies and Postal procedures the officers are deputed for 10 months at National Institute of Communication Finance (NICF) at Ghaziabad (U.P.) In between this classroom training schedules, the officers are also deputed for on job field training in various areas. IP&TAFS has also a Group-B Cadre and Asst Accounts Officers, Accounts Officers and Sr. Accounts Officers are placed under this cadre with All India Service liabilities. These Officers are appointed on promotion selected through a Departmental Examination. The recruitment is done for Assistant Chief Accounts Officer and can rise up to Advisor (Finance) in the Ministry of Post and Telecommunications. The members can also get an opportunity to work in PSUs like MTNL and BSNL.

(iii) **Indian Revenue Service:** This service has been further sub-categorized into:

(a) **Indian Customs and Central Excise Service** This service comes under the direct control of Central Board of Excise and Customs (CBEC). The major difference in the functioning of Central Excise and Customs wing is that Customs duty is levied on the goods imported into the country and deals with the import and export of goods while on the other side the Central Excise deals with levy of tax on goods manufactured within the country. The members of this service can rise from the rank of Assistant Collector/Commissioner to Chairman CBEC. The entrants of the Customs wing are trained at Chennai while that in the Central Excise is trained at any of the Metros.

    (b) Indian Revenue Service (Income Tax) This service comes under the direct control of Central Board of Direct Taxes (CBDT). The services are availed in the Income Tax Department across the country. The members can rise through the ranks of Assistant Commissioner to Chairman CBDT. The entrants are trained at National Academy of Direct Taxes, Nagpur.

(iv) **Indian Defence Accounts Service:** The Indian Defence Accounts Service (IDAS) is responsible for maintaining the accounts of the Defence Services. The first position to be placed in after appointment is that of Assistant Controller of Defence Accounts. The defence accounts offices in cantonment, states and defence command headquarters are under the jurisdiction of the IDAS. IDAS officers are key advisers and financial managers during acquisitions, procurement, licensing, service warranties etc. of weapon systems/platforms, transfer of technology with foreign countries or under domestic-production. They are integral part of such processes & committees and render valuable advice and alternatives for meeting policy objectives and goals.

(v) **Indian Postal Service:** The entrants can become Superintendent in Post Offices and Railway mail services to the rank of Chief Post Master General in the HAG rank. They can also become member or Chairman of the Post and Telegraph Board.

(vi) **Indian Civil Accounts Services:** They are initially appointed as Assistant Controller of Accounts to the rank of Controller General of Accounts. Unlike the C&AG of India, it is not a statutory post and is controlled by Secretary (Expenditure) Ministry of Finance. The organization provides payment services, supports the tax collection system, performs government wide accounting, financial reporting functions, preparation of budget estimates and carries out Internal Audit in civil ministries of the Union Government.

(vii) **Indian Railway Traffic Service:** The entrants have to work in the Ministry of Railways as Assistant Superintendent Commercial Transportation or Operations and can reach up to Chief Commercial Manager to Member (Traffic) in Railway Board. The training is provided at Indian Railway Institute of Transport Management at Lucknow. The posting is in Operations or Commercial wing of Indian Railways have distinctive functions.

(viii) **Indian Railway Accounts Service:** The entrants can rise from Assistant Divisional Accounts Officers or Junior Accounts Officers to Financial Commissioner in the Indian Railways. They mainly deal with the financial matters and maintenance of Accounts of the Indian Railways.

(xi) **Indian Railway Personnel Service:** From the initial posting as Assistant Personnel Officer, the members can rise to the ranks of Chief Personnel Officer or Member (Staff) in the Railway Board. The functions mainly cover the human resource management of the staff of Indian Railways right from recruitment and training to salary.

(x) **Indian Railway Protection Force:** The entrants are initially posted as Assistant Security Commissioner or Assistant Commandant and can rise up to Director General. The initial training is imparted at Jagjivan Ram RPF Academy at Lucknow.

(xi) **Indian Defense Estate Services:** The recruitment is done as Cantonment Executive Officer or Defense Estate

Officer and can rise up to Director General Defense Estates.

(xii) **Indian Information Service:** The candidates can rise from Assistant Director/Assistant News Editor/Assistant Research Officer to Director General/Principle Information Officer in the Ministry of Information and Broadcasting. The primary function involves the dissemination of information of Government policies, press advisor etc.

Civil Services Examination

It is conducted in three stages:

(a) CS (Preliminary)

Notification of Examination - November/December of previous year
Conduct of Examination - May
Age limit - 21 to 32 years as on 1st August of the year of exam
Educational Qualification - Degree or equivalent
Maximum attempts - Six (earlier four) for General candidates and nine for OBC candidates since 2014
No limit for SC/ST candidate.

Scheme of CS (Preliminary) Examination

The Preliminary Examination consists of two papers of objective type (multiple-choice questions) carrying a maximum of 400 marks. It carries negative marking of 0.33. The Question Papers (Test Booklets) are set in English & Hindi. The number of candidates selected for Mains Examination is 12 to 13 times the number of vacancy available.

Paper – I (General Studies)	200 Marks
Paper – II (Aptitude Test)	200 Marks

(b) CS (Main)

Tentative date - October to November

Scheme - CS (Main)

Paper A	One of the Indian Languages to be selected by the candidate from the 18 languages included in the VIIIth Schedule to the Constitution (Qualifying Paper)	300 marks
Paper B	English (Qualifying Paper)	300 marks
Paper I	Essay	250 marks
Paper II	General Studies-I (Indian Heritage and Culture, History and Geography of world and society)	250 marks
Paper III	General Studies-II (Governance, Constitution, Polity, Social Justice and International Relation)	250 marks
Paper IV	General Studies-II (Technology, Economic Development, Bio-Diversity, Environment, Security and Disaster Management)	250 marks
Paper V	General Studies IV (Ethics, Integrity and Aptitude)	250 marks
Paper VI	Optional Subject - Paper I	250 marks
Paper VII	Optional Subject - Paper II	250 marks
Total Marks for Written Examination		1750 marks
Personality Test (Any language of candidate's choice)		275 marks
Grand Total		2025 marks

List of Optional Subjects - CS (Main) - (Total 25)

Agriculture	Management
Animal Husbandry & Veterinary Science	Mathematics
Anthropology	Mechanical Engineering

Botany	Medical Science
Chemistry	Philosophy
Civil Engineering	Physics
Commerce & Accountancy	Political Science & International Relations
Economics	Psychology
Electrical Engineering	Public Administration
Geography	Sociology
Geology	Statistics
History	Zoology
Law	Literature of any one of the following languages: Assamese, Bengali, Bodo, Dogri, Gujarati, Hindi, Kannada, Kashmiri, Konkani, Maithili, Malayalam, Manipuri, Marathi, Nepali, Oriya, Punjabi, Sanskrit, Santhali, Sindhi, Tamil, Telugu, Urdu and English

Note: Candidates can select any optional subject. There is no limitation to select the subjects from the candidates' stream of graduation.

Candidates can select either English or any language from VIIIth Schedule as a medium for writing the examination.

(c) Interview

The third and the last stage is interview which consists of 275 marks. Candidates declared successful in the Mains exam are called for interview.

2. TECHNICAL GROUP A SERVICES

The recruitment for certain technical Group A services are done through separate exams conducted by the UPSC.

- Indian Forest Service Exam is conducted for recruitment in Indian Forest Service
- Engineering Service Exam is conducted for Engineering Group A services in Civil, Mechanical & Electrical stream.
- Combined Medical Service Exam is conducted for some Group A medical services.

- Indian Economic & Statistical Service Exam is conducted for recruitment in Economic and Statistical Departments.
- Indian Geologist Examination is conducted for the Group A posts in Geological Survey of India and Central Ground Water Board.
- Special Class Railway Apprentice Exam is conducted for recruitment in Indian Railways as Assistant Mechanical Engineer.

(A) Indian Forest Service It is an "All India Service" with State Cadre allotment. The administrative hierarchy of Indian Forest Service in the Forest Departments in the States and Union Territories is in the following ascending order:

- Deputy Conservator of Forests
- Conservator of Forests
- Chief Conservator of Forests
- Additional Principal Chief Conservator of Forests, and finally as the
- Principal Chief Conservator of Forests

The Ministry of Environment and Forests is the cadre controlling authority for the Indian Forest Service and also the nodal ministry in respect of the Indian Forest Service. The IFS officer has been entrusted with protection, conservation, regeneration and development of forests. Recruitment to this service is through a separate exam conducted by the UPSC known as the Indian Forest Service Exam. **The only difference since the year 2014 is that the preliminary exam for the services is conducted along with the Civil Services Exam but the mains exam and interview is conducted separately as earlier.**

IFS probationers undergo professional training in forestry and allied subjects at Indira Gandhi National Forest Academy, Dehradun, the Foundation Course at Lal Bahadur Shastri National Academy of Administration, Mussoorie and one year "on the job" training in the cadre to which they are allotted. After successfully completing their probation period and on completing four years of service as per norms, the officers are appointed to the Senior Time Scale and are entitled to be posted as Divisional Forest

Officers or Deputy Conservators of Forests in charge of Forest Divisions.

Indian Forest Service Exam

Notification of Exam	- February/March every year
Exam date	- July
Age limit	- 21-30 years
Educational Qualification	- A Bachelor's degree with at least one of the subjects namely, Animal Husbandry & Veterinary Science, Botany, Chemistry, Geology, Mathematics, Physics, Statistics and Zoology or a Bachelor's degree in Agriculture or Forestry or Engineering of a recognized university or equivalent.
Scheme of Examination	- Preliminary test to be conducted along with Civil Service Exam (since 2014). Mains will be conducted separately.

I. Written Examination - Subjective

Paper I - General English	300 Marks
Paper II - General Knowledge	300 Marks
Paper III, IV, V & VI - Any two subjects to be selected from the list of optional subjects set out below. Each subject will have two papers.	200 Marks for each paper
Total marks for written examination	**1400 Marks**

List of optional subjects (in English)

• Agriculture	Forestry
• Agricultural Engineering	Geology
• Animal Husbandry & Veterinary	Mathematics
• Science	Mechanical
• Botany	Engineering
• Chemistry	Physics
• Chemical Engineering	Statistics
• Civil Engineering	Zoology

Provided that the candidates are not allowed to offer the following combination of subjects:
(a) Agriculture and Agricultural Engineering
(b) Agriculture and Animal Husbandry & Veterinary Science
(c) Chemistry and Chemical Engineering
(d) Mathematics and Statistics
(e) Of the Engineering subjects viz. Agricultural Engineering, Chemical Engineering, Civil Engineering, Mechanical Engineering - not more than one subject

II. Interview and Personality Test   300 Marks

(B) Engineering Service Examination There are certain technical services across various departments where degree in Engineering is required. The entrants can rise from the post of Assistant Executive Engineer/Assistant Works Manager/Assistant Director to the post of Director General/Managing Director/Chairman. The services are indicated below.

Civil Engineering Group A Services:
(i) Indian Railway Service of Engineers
(ii) Indian Railway Stores Service
(iii) Central Engineering Service
(iv) Indian Defense Service of Engineers
(v) Indian Ordnance Factories Service (IOFS)
(vi) Central Water Engineering
(vii) Central Engineering Service (Roads)
(viii) Border Roads Engineering Service
(ix) Survey of India Group 'A' service
(x) Indian inspection Service

Mechanical Engineering Group A Services:
(i) Indian Railway Service of Mechanical Engineers
(ii) Indian Railway Stores Service
(iii) Central Water Engineering
(iv) Central Power Engineering Service (Central Electricity Authority)

(v) Indian Ordnance Factories Service (IOFS)
(vi) Indian Naval Armament Service
(vii) Corps of Electrical and Mechanical Engineers (EME), a branch in the Indian Army
(viii) Indian Navy
(ix) Central Electrical & Mechanical Engineering Service (Central Public Works Department)
(x) Border Roads Engineering Service
(xi) Indian Supply Service (Directorate General of Supply and Disposals)
(xii) Indian Defence Service of Engineers
(xiii) Central Engineering Service (Roads)
(xiii) Indian Inspection Service

Electrical Engineering Group A Services:
(i) Indian Railway Service of Electrical Engineers
(ii) Indian Railway Stores Service
(iii) Central Electrical and Mechanical Engineering Service (Central Public Works Department)
(iv) Indian Naval Armament Service
(v) Indian Ordnance Factories Service (IOFS)
(vi) Central Power Engineering Service (Central Electricity Authority)
(vii) Indian Defence Service of Engineers
(viii) Indian Navy
(ix) Indian Supply Service (Directorate General of Supply and Disposals)
(x) Corps of Electrical and Mechanical Engineers (EME), a branch in the Indian Army
(xi) Indian Inspection Service

Engineering Service Examination

Notification of Exam	- January/February
Examination	- June/July
Categories	- Civil, Mechanical, Electrical, Electronics & Telecommunication

Age limit — 21-30 years as on 1st August

Educational Qualification — Degree in Engineering from a recognized university or equivalent. M.Sc degree or its equivalent with Wireless Communications, Electronics, Radio Physics or Radio Engineering as special subjects also acceptable for certain services/posts only.

Scheme of Examination

Written Examination		
Paper I (Objective type)	General Ability Test (Part A: General English) (Part B: General Studies)	200 marks
Papers II & III (Objective type)	Civil Engineering/ Mechanical Engineering/ Electrical Engineering/ Electronics & Tele-Communication Engineering	200 marks for each paper
Papers IV & V (Conventional Type)	Civil Engineering/ Mechanical Engineering/ Electrical Engineering/ Electronics & Tele-communication Engineering	200 marks for each paper
	Total marks for written examination	1000 marks
Personality Test		200 marks

(C) Combined Medical Services This exam is conducted by the UPSC for the recruitment of Medical Officers in the various Ministries of Government of India such as Indian Ordinance Factories in the Ministry of Defense, Assistant Divisional Medical Officer in Indian Railways, Medical Officers in Municipal Corporation of Delhi and General Duty Medical Officers in NDMC.

Combined Medical Services Examination

Notification	- August
Examination	- January
Posts recruited	- Assistant Divisional Medical Officer in Railways
	- Junior Scale Posts in Indian Ordinance Factory (health)
	- Junior Scale Posts in Central Health Services
	- Medical Officers in Municipal Corporation of Delhi
	- General Duty Medical Officers in NDMC
Age limit	- Below 32 years on 1st January
Educational Qualification	- MBBS passed/appearing

Scheme of Examination

Written Examination (2 papers of 200 marks each, both of objective type)	Weightage
Paper I (200 marks)	
(i) General Medicine including Cardiology, Neurology, Dermatology and Psychiatry	60%
(ii) Surgery including ENT, Ophthalmology, Traumatology and Orthopaedics	40%
Paper II (200 marks)	
(i) Paediatrics	20%
(ii) Gynaecology and Obstetrics	40%
(iii) Preventive, Social and Community Medicine	40%
Total marks for written exam 400	

(D) Indian Economic Services/Indian Statistical Services The Indian Statistical Service and the Indian Economic Service are career opportunities for those who have a keen interest to be a part of the Indian economic policy formulation team. They get an opportunity to be a part of planning commission and other government owned bodies in the country. The UPSC conducts the Indian Economic/Statistical Services Examination to recruit officers in the planning commission, planning board, ministry of economic affairs, national sample survey and other allied offices where specialists in economics and statistics are required. Selected candidates are also placed in the Labour Bureau, Central Electricity Authority, as Economic Advisers to many ministries, Forward Market Commission, Tariff Commission, Planning Board, Tariff Commission National sample survey, etc. Candidates may even go on deputations to different agencies of United Nations. The members can rise from Assistant director to the Chief Economic Advisor. The eligibility and pattern of examination has been discussed in the subsequent section.

Indian Economic/Statistical Services Examination

Notification — June
Examination — November
Posts recruited — Assistant Director
Age limit — 21-30 years on 1st January
Educational Qualification
Indian Economic Service — PG Degree in Economics/Applied Economics or Business Economics/ Econometrics
Indian Statistical Service — PG Degree in Statistics/Applied Statistics/Mathematical Statistics

Scheme of Examination

Part-I : Candidates are required to appear in the following papers of conventional type	
(i) For Indian Economic Service	
(a) General English	100 marks
(b) General Studies	100 marks
(c) General Economics-I	200 marks
(d) General Economics-II	200 marks
(e) General Economics-III	200 marks
(f) General Economics	200 marks

(ii) For Indian Statistical Service	
(a) General English	100 marks
(b) General Studies	100 marks
(c) Statistics-I	200 marks
(d) Statistics-II	200 marks
(e) Statistics-III	200 marks
(f) Statistics-IV	200 marks
Part II : Interview for Personality Test	200 marks

(E) Indian Geologist Examination The Union Public Service Commission (UPSC) holds a competitive Examination named Geologists Examination for recruitment to the posts of:

Category I - (i) Geologist (Junior), Group A (ii) Assistant Geologist, Group B in the Geological Survey of India.

Category II - (i) Jr. Hydrogeologist, Group A (ii) Assistant Hydrogeologist, Group B in the Central Ground Water Board (CGWB).

Candidates selected under category I are appointed on probation for two years. During this period they have to undergo training and pass test or examination prescribed by the competent authority.

Geologist Examination

Notification — June

Examination — November

Age limit — 21-32 years as on 1st January

Educational Qualification — Master's degree in Geology/Applied Geology or Marine Geology from a recognized university; or

Master's degree in Geology/Applied Geology or Marine Geology from a recognized university; or

Diploma of Associateship in Applied Geology of Indian School of Mines, Dhanbad; or

Master's degree in Mineral exploration from a recognized university (for posts in GSI); or

Master's degree in Hydrogeology from a recognized university (for posts in CGWB)

Scheme of Examination

Part I		Written Examination
Candidates competing for both categories have to appear in the following papers		
(i)	General English	100 marks
(ii)	Geology Paper-I	200 marks
(iii)	Geology Paper-II	200 marks
(iv)	Geology Paper-III	200 marks
(v)	Hydrogeology	200 marks
For **Category I** candidates have to appear in **Papers (i) to (iv)** above only and for **Category II** in **Papers (i) to (iii) and (v)** above only.		
Part II: Interview for Personality Test		200 marks

(F) Special Class Railway Apprentice Exam As already discussed, this exam is conducted by the UPSC for 10+2 passed candidates. This is the only exam which gives the 10+2 passed candidates direct entry into the Group A services after successful completion of the training at Jamalpur, Bihar. They are initially posted as Assistant Mechanical Engineer and can reach up to the ranks in senior railway administration like Divisional Railway Manager.

Special Class Railway Apprentices' Examination (SCRA)

Notification   - February
Examination   - July
Age limit   - 17-21 years as on 1st August
Educational Qualification - Must have passed in the first or second division, the Intermediate

or an equivalent examination of a university or board approved by the Government of India with Mathematics and at least one of the subjects Physics and Chemistry as subjects of the examination.

Scheme of Examination

Paper	Subject	Code Number	Time Allowed	Maximum Marks
Paper-I	General Ability Test (English, General Knowledge and Psychological Test)	01	2 hours	200
Paper-II	Physical Sciences (Physics and Chemistry)	02	2 hours	200
Paper-III	Mathematics	03	2 hours	200
			Total	600

Part I: Written Examination carrying a maximum of 600 marks in the subjects as shown below:

Part II: Personality Test carrying a maximum of 200 marks in respect of only those candidates who are declared qualified on the results of written examination.

Note Erstwhile Section Officer (Audit), Section Officer (Commercial) exam conducted by Staff Selection Commission will henceforth be conducted by UPSC as per the Government Resolution No. 18 dated 10th January 2013. The erstwhile eligibility and pattern of examination has been discussed in the subsequent section.

3. UNIFORMED GROUP A/PREMIER MILITARY SERVICES

The premier Group A uniformed service is Indian Police Service which is an "All India Service" and recruited through the Civil Service exam conducted by the UPSC. The details have already been discussed in the earlier section. The other examinations

Types of Services and Recruitment in Government **35**

conducted by UPSC for recruitment to Uniformed Group A services and premier Military Uniformed services are:
1. Central Police Forces (Assistant Commandants) Examination
2. National Defence Academy and Naval Academy Examinations
3. Combined Defence Services Examination

1. Central Police Forces (Assistant Commandants) Examination This examination is conducted by UPSC for the recruitment to the post of Assistant Commandants CISF (Central Industrial Security Forces), CRPF (Central Reserve Police Force), SSB (Sahashtra Seema Bal), ITBP (Indo-Tibetan Border Police) and BSF (Border Security Forces).

Notification   - May
Examination   - October
Age limit   - 20-25 years as on 1st August
Educational Qualification   - Graduation or equivalent

Scheme of Examination

Written Examination

PAPER-I	General Ability and Intelligence (Objective Type)	250 marks
PAPER-II	Essay, Précis writing and comprehension (Conventional Type)	150 marks
	PHYSICAL AND MEDICAL STANDARDS TEST	To be conducted only of candidates who qualify the written examination.
	Interview for Personality Test	200 marks

2. National Defence Academy / Naval Academy Examination This examination is conducted for the entry level premier posts in Indian Army, Indian Air Force and Indian Navy. The details have been covered under the subsequent chapter.

Notification	- October – November and April – May
Examination	- April – May and September – October
Age limit	- 16-1/2 – 19 years

Educational Qualifications	
For **Army Wing** of NDA	12th Class pass of the 10+2 pattern of school Education, or equivalent.
For **Air Force and Naval Wings** of NDA and for 10+2 (Executive Branch) Course at Naval Academy	12th Class pass of the 10+2 pattern of school Education with Physics and Mathematics, or equivalent

Candidates appearing at the 12th Class Examination are also eligible to compete. Such candidates will be required to submit the proof of passing the 12th Class Examination by a date to be specified in the Commission's Notice for the Examination.

Scheme of Examination

Written Examination	1. Mathematics (Objective type)	300 Marks
	2. General Ability Test (Objective type)	600 Marks
	Total marks for written examination	900 Marks
Marks for SSB Interviews		900 Marks

3. Combined Defence Services Examination It is conducted for recruitment in Indian Military Academy, Naval Academy, Air Force Academy and Officers' Training Academy. To ensure that appropriate candidates are chosen, a comprehensive selection process is adopted by the armed forces through Service Selection Board (SSB) interview. This system of selection is based on the "trait theory" of leadership which assumes that every leader must have some specific and pre-determined leadership traits. The present system of selection takes four to five days and based on an objective assessment of each candidate in which the qualities like initiative, alertness, judgment, courage, physical fitness endurance, cooperation, group planning, decisiveness, knowledge, etc. are judged. In addition, psychological and mental robustness of the candidate vis-a-vis requirements of the Armed Forces is judged and finally an overall assessment of the personality of a candidate is made by way of an exhaustive personal interview. The details have been discussed in the subsequent chapter.

Notification — August and March
Examination — April and August

Age-limits

19-24 Years	Indian Military Academy
19-22 Years	Naval Academy
19-23 Years	Air Force Academy
19-25 Years	Officers' Training Academy

(C) Educational Qualifications:

IMA & OTA	Degree of a recognized University or equivalent
Naval Academy	B.Sc. with Physics & Mathematics or Bachelor of Engg
Air Force Academy	B.Sc. with Physics and/or Mathematics or Bachelor of Engg

Candidates appearing at the degree or equivalent examination are also eligible to compete. Such candidates will be required to submit the proof of passing the requisite qualifying examination by a date to be specified in the Commission's Notice for the Examination.

Scheme of Examination:

Written Examination		
(a) For Indian Military Academy Naval Academy and Air Force Academy	1. English (Objective type)	100 marks
	2. General Knowledge (Objective type)	100 marks
	3. Elementary Mathematics (Objective type)	100 marks
	Total	**300 marks**
(b) For Officers' Training Academy	1. English (Objective type)	100 marks
	2. General Knowledge (Objective type)	100 marks
	Total	**200 marks**
Marks for SSB Interviews		
IMA, NA and AFA		**300 marks**
OTA		**200 marks**

Win-Win Win Strategy for preparation of competitive examinations with special reference to UPSC's Indian Civil Services Examination

A. WWW = Win-Win-Win Core Strategy to Reach the Destination

1. First things first, write down your career goal.
2. Map your path with milestones with definite time frame to reach the destination.
3. List out all the examinations you intend to take in the year with systematic schedule of preparation.
4. Place your goal, strategy, schedule of preparation etc on the wall in front of your study table.

5. Also keep some inspiring quotes, role model, symbols you believe which can inspire you and conscientiously remind you of your goal and enable you to drive towards the goal.
6. Spend some time daily for evaluating where you stand before the goal and think over how to achieve the goal.
7. Once the goal is decided, meditate on the ways and means to achieve your goal and then think how to prepare with right resources with absolute focus and mindfulness.
8. Remember in competitive examinations many of the general competitive papers are common with minor variations. Important thing to note is that like general crust of a pizza you will find the basic papers and topics to cover for most of the competitive examinations are the same with minor variations and certain additional special toppings in a pizza. The strategy demands to know these differences and select as many competitive examinations you feel you should take to evaluate you in real examination environment continuously and build your expertise and skills over the period to achieve your prime goal like UPSC Indian Civil Services Examination.
9. If you are preparing for UPSC Indian Civil Services Examination and say a Bank Probationary Officers' Examination you are practically preparing for many of the central and states competitive examinations because there are common papers like General Studies or General Knowledge, Essay, Logical Reasoning, Arithmetic etc in most of the competitive examinations. The level of preparedness will enable you to score very high marks in many competitive examinations. Even if you have not reached the standard of ICS examination, if you are taking lower level central or state examinations, there is very high likelihood of getting selected.
10. Now the question is, have you finalized a roadmap indicating important milestones, with definite time frame to reach the destination on right time? What is your strategy to drive to the destination with maximum possible speed

with highest possibility to reach the final destination on right time?

11. You can apply International Quality Management Standards for your preparation. The core strategy is to follow the PDCA Cycle of Plan-Do-Check-Act cycle continuously for the competitive examination strategy. Success depends on effective planning, systematic execution, timely and periodical review, objective evaluation, monitoring and taking definite positive steps for continuous improvement till the expected quality standards are achieved to realize the objectives. Enhancing the possibility of success solely depends on reducing the errors and omissions practically to NIL by incessant practice of solving the earlier year question papers in examination environment and improving the scores till achieving the expected quality standard.

12. The only maxim to reach the destination in right time is driving at maximum possible speed with absolute control and confidence with a clear roadmap that indicates important milestones. Once destination is selected, milestones are identified driving becomes safe and the possibility of reaching the destination safe on time is the highest.

13. The most powerful secret is that success in the competitive examinations guarantees that you will be offered the job you have rightly competed for. The only magic or mantra is you can and you will come out in flying colours in any competitive examination, provided you have confidence and determination to build the requisite competitive edge by firm commitment to work hard continuously.

14. Most importantly you should and must have blazing fire in you to excel your CQ or Competitive Quotient by systematic planning, consistent focused preparation, self assessment, objective evaluation by solving earlier question papers, reviewing your strengths and weaknesses and continuously improving till you come to the expected standards in knowledge, skills and performance till you reach the final destination.

15. Once you have firm resolution to take the competitive examination of your choice, please visualize yourself as achieving the goal and functioning as an officer of your dreams and keep the visualization before your mind as often as possible to guide you till you reach the destination.

B. WWW General Tips

Here are some of the general tips which will help the job aspirant to achieve success:

1. First and foremost understand the government job landscape by going over a pleasant tour of the book.
2. You must be then equipped to select the type of exams you are prepared to battle for based on your commitment, the level of preparation and over all knowledge, competence level and the Competitive Quotient (CQ).
3. Visit the concerned websites; go through the latest updated notification relating to the job of your interest. Familiarize with the essentials like the eligibility criteria, examination procedure, pattern, syllabus, papers, past question papers till you are absolutely familiar and comfortable.
4. Select the subjects as per one's own assessment and comfort level which can obtain the highest possible scores. UPSC does not insist at all that the candidate should choose the optional subjects in which they have completed graduation/ post graduation for ICS. Candidates are free to choose any subject but select the subjects after proper evaluation.
5. Familiarity with the syllabus is of utmost importance. Get yourself well informed about the content of the syllabi and the topics it covers.
6. Review past few years' examination question papers and solved model answers and conduct detailed Google search, extensive and intensive market survey, consultation with students who have already qualified the examination and coaching centres and guide books in the market to have clear understanding of your road map and to prepare well for the journey and driving to the destination with full zeal,

preparedness and focus. It is important to consult to have complete idea about the exam you are interested, conduct elaborate market survey and search to fetch the right books, guides, study material for the examination.

7. Subscribe to a popular, established daily newspaper and current affairs magazine to keep update about the latest happenings about the surroundings. The competitive magazines are specially designed for the examinations covering the essential subjects and past solved question papers, possible questions and test papers for self evaluation.

8. Go through the complete syllabus and past question papers of ten years to identify the pattern and important topics which are asked very frequently. Simultaneously, identify those topics which are particularly useful for conventional essay type questions.

9. For selection of books it is advisable not to go through a lot of books, instead go through one standard book on the topic which clarifies basic concept. Standard books not only save precious time but also guide you like a perfect GURU.

10. Always make it a habit to comprehend and remember what you have read and prepare brief self contained notes. Use always an analytical approach to study with why-why questions till you reach the root cause of the issue and all possible analytical aspects to get a full picture by asking all the 5W questions (Why, What, When, Who, Where) and the evidence searching How questions on the issue.

11. It is always advisable to make notes of the related topics. Well crafted notes help in many ways; make you familiar with the updated syllabus, in the process you are revising, continuously learning, improving comprehension, and developing analytical approach, communication skills, writing capabilities with pros and cons of an issue. In the process you are manufacturing the most valuable customized examination capsules for you to save you on the D-Day of the eve of the examination.

C. WWW Important Points to Remember

1. Always rely on self-prepared notes. Go through the short notes and continuously update when you come across any update, new dimension on the topic or any new argument or point of view till the exam.
2. Prepare short notes on as many topics you need based on important topics to be covered with key points that can be re-visited many times especially just before the examination.
3. Keep improving your Competitive Quotient by revising continuously and consistently.
4. Mock examination and tests help you to gain confidence and time management. Try to find time out of your schedule to remember and organize your thoughts logically and analytically.
5. Instead of trying to finish a chapter in one go, break it into small components and systematically approach to understand the issues as per schedule. Whether it is General Studies or Optional subject, follow the right methodology, pick up the right book, read one or two paragraphs; write the crux in the margin, leave.
6. Pick up the book again whenever free and repeat the procedure.
7. Study maximum required quality hours you need based on your confidence and level of preparation. Spend quality time with absolute focus in the morning, during the day or late in the evening based on your comfort level, free time and listening to the rhythm of your body clock.
8. Put as many hours you need for the preparation till you gain the confidence and reach the expected standard.
9. Once you are fully prepared for the best outcome, there is no need to get worried, confused or restless. Once you have absolute control over the subjects, you can enjoy a good sleep on the eve of the examination for gearing up fully for the best performance in the exam.

10. Avoid going through nervously any extra book or new material on the eve of examination.
11. Don't read any new topic in the last days to avoid confusion and lack of confidence.
12. Don't get baffled by others' intimidation or engaged with any last minute questions or problem resolution as it may ruin your mental balance, nullifying entire efforts and hard work. Remember, it is only the past investments that can only reap a better dividend.
13. Do not lose confidence, read all the questions properly before choosing the questions to answer.
14. Attempt all questions required within the time allotted.
15. Plan and write down the broad structure of the answer, giving pros, cons with arguments and finally derive your conclusions based on evidence, documentation and logical and coherent presentation of relevant facts, figures, different perspectives and lines of arguments
16. Keep your road map on your study table with milestones and time schedule to remind you every day about your goal.

D. Sources of Material for the preparation

No battle can be won without a proper selection and effective utilisation of the latest arms and ammunitions. The battle in this case is the exam conducted by the UPSC and to achieve the goal, assembling the resources like proper selection of books, study material, guides, journals, magazines, practice work books etc. are the arms and ammunitions which are to be properly used. Though it is very difficult to list out the books and study materials available in the market, an attempt has been made to highlight some of the most popular amongst them. The list is not exclusive and candidates are recommended to undergo a proper market research from the various available resources to select the right list of books and authentic study material.

List of Civil Services Books for General Studies

Preliminary UPSC ICS (General Studies)
- History books of Classes XI and XII – NCERT
- Any Standard Text Book on India's Freedom Struggle like one authored by Bipin Chandra

World Geography – including Indian Geography Good books
- Principles of Geography (Class XII-Part I, II)
- General Geography of India (Class XII) Part I – NCERT
- Geography of India – Resources and Regional Development Part II (Class XII) – NCERT
- Physical Geography – Leong
- A good Atlas
- Keep a globe on the study table
- Also hang maps of India and the world on the walls near the study table for ready reference

Indian Polity
- Introduction to Indian Constitution – D.D. Basu Related

Indian Economy
- Evolution of Indian Economy – NCERT
- Indian Economy – Dutt and Sundharam
- Indian Economy – Mishra and Puri

General Science
- NCERT books on Science.
- Science and Technology supplements in the newspapers and magazines.

Current Events of National and International importance
- One major National Daily – either *The Times of India* or *The Hindu*.
- News weeklies like *India Today* or/and *Outlook*
- Current Events – *Spectrum*

General Mental Ability
- No special preparation is required in this area. But some practice may be done from any exercise books or quantitative aptitude. In fact, an intelligent calculation is the basic requirement for this topic.

Main (General Studies)
History of Modern India
- India's struggle for Independence – Bipin Chandra and others.
- Modern India – NCERT.
- Freedom Struggle (NBT) – Bipin Chandra
- Modern India – IGNOU

Indian Culture
- Art and Culture portions of history books and Gazetteer of India.
- Culture Chapter (s) in the India Year Book.
- Encyclopedia of Indian Culture. A good library invariably has more than one encyclopedia on Indian Art and Culture selected notes may be taken from it.
- Books on culture/cultural topics brought out by Publications Division of Ministry of Information and Broadcasting and National Book Trust.

Current Affairs
- At least one major national newspaper – either The Times of India or The Hindu
- Newsweeklies like India Today or/and Outlook
- Current Affairs and News Analysis of news channels.
- Current events – Spectrum

Statistics
- Book on Statistics (Class XI) – NCERT

Indian Polity and Constitution
- Introduction to the Constitution of India – D.D. Basu.
- Our Parliament – S.C. Kashyap

Indian Geography and Economy
- Indian Geography (Class XI and XII) – NCERT
- Yozna
- Indian Economy – Dutt and Sundharam/Mishra and Puri
- The editorial page of the *Economic Times*.

Science and Technology
- Science and Technology section of the Wednesday edition of the newspaper 'The Hindu'.
- Science and Technology Published by the Spectrum.
- Yozna contains science and environment related topics.

1. Indian History – *India Struggle for Independence* by Bipin Chandra; NCERT Books (XI & XII)
2. Geography – *Spectrum*
3. Indian Polity – *Constitution of India* by Bakshi
4. Indian Economy – *Pratiyogita Darpan*
5. General Science – Tata McGraw Hill Guide
6. Mental Ability – *Quantitative Aptitude* by R.S. Aggarwal
7. Current Affairs – Some magazines and newspapers
    i. *The Hindu/The Times of India*
    ii. *Frontline*
    iii. *Civil Service Chronicle*
    iv. *Chanakya*
    v. *Competition WIZARD*
    vi. *Civil Services Today*
8. Guides
    i. Tata McGraw Hill
    ii. Spectrum
    iii. Unique

Books on Indian History & Culture:
- NCERT (+ 2 level): *Ancient India, Medieval India, Modern India*

- Publication Division : Gazetteer of India (Vol 2 : History & Culture)
- Gandhi Nehru Tagore & Ambedkar : Gopal Krishna
- Bipin Chandra – *Modern India*
- A.C. Banerjee – *History of Modern India*
- Raghavan Aiyer : *Mahatma Gandhi*

Books on Geography:
- NCERT: Physical Geography of India for X – XII Std
- A Good School Atlas
- Sharma & Coutinho: *Economic and Commercial Geography of India*
- Khullar: *India- A Comprehensive Geography*
- Charles Farro: *General Principles of World Geography*
- Charles Farro: *Monsoon Asia Reports* published by Centre for Science and Environment And Tata Energy Research Institute
- National journal – *Kurukshetra, Yojana* etc.
- Down to earth

Books on Indian Economy:
- NCERT (+1 level): *Evolution of Indian Economy* (I.C. Dhingra).
- Mishra & Puri or Dutt & Sundaram – *Indian Economy*
- *Economic Survey*
- *The Economic Times, Business Standard*
- *Yojana*

Books on Social and National Issues:
- *Social Problem* – Ram Ahuja
- *Social Welfare Magazine* – Published by ministry of social welfare
- *Yojana/Kurukshetra*
- IIPA Journal

Books on Indian Polity:
- NCERT (+1 level) : *Indian Political System*

- N.L. Madan: *Bhartiya Rajya Vyavastha*
- D.D. Basu: *Indian Constitution*
- Kashyap: *Constitution of India*
- Publication Division: Subhash C. Kashyap: *Our Parliament*
- P.M. Bakshi: *Indian Constitution*
- Subhash C. Kashyap: *Our Constitution*
- S.C. Kashyap: *Perspective on Constitution*
- Frontline Magazine
- IIPA Journal

Books on Science & Technology:
- NCERT: (10 level): Science, (+2 level):
- Popular Science Series (CSIR)
- Reports of the Ministry of Science and Technology in Yojana
- Science Reporter
- *Science and Technology in India* – Spectrum

Books on Statistics:
- (NCERT +1 level) Elementary Statistics
- S.C. Gupta: *Statistical Methods*

Books on India and the World:
- *Journal of Peace Studies*
- *World Focus*
- *Strategic Analysis*
- *South Asian Journal*

Other Books for General Studies:
1. India Year Book latest
2. One competitive Magazine
3. Guides like Tata McGraw Hill, Spectrum or Unique for General Reference
4. The Pearson General Studies Manual
5. Manorama Year Book

Recommended books for optional subjects have not been included in this list.

E. List of some websites which help in preparation:

Some Exclusive Websites for Civil Service Preparation:
1. www.jagranjosh.com
2. www.civilserviceindia.com
3. www.iaspreparationonline.com
4. www.iasaspirants.com
5. www.ClearIAS.com
6. www.Mrunal.org
7. www.UPSCPortal.com
8. www.gktoday.in
9. www.UPSCguide.com

Useful Government Websites for Civil Service Preparation
10. www.ncert.nic.in – Download NCERT Texts as PDF.
11. www.nios.ac.in – Download NIOS Online Materials.
12. www.egyankosh.ac.in – Download IGNOU Books.
13. www.yojana.gov.in – Download Yojana and Kurukshetra Magazines.
14. www.pib.nic.in – Press Information Bureau Website, for government updates.
15. www.prsindia.org – PRS Website for tracking bills in Parliament.
16. www.idsa.in – IDSA website for Defense and Foreign relations.
17. www.gatewayhouse.in – Indian Council for Global relations.
18. www.envfor.nic.in – Ministry of Environment and Forests.
19. www.mea.gov.in – Ministry of External Affairs.
20. www.indiabudget.nic.in – Download Budget and Economic Survey.
21. www.ptinews.com – Press Trust of India.
22. www.pdgroup.upkar.in – Pratiyogita Darpan Magazine.

PART II: GROUP B SERVICES

In this part, the job-seeker is exposed to middle level jobs in the Government Ministries and Departments.

A. TYPES OF GROUP B SERVICES

Group B services form the mid level of the Government Ministries and Departments. Some of these services also get an opportunity to enter into Group A services either through promotion or deputation on seniority-cum-merit basis. Some posts are filled through direct recruitment where the minimum qualification required is graduation passed. As per the DOPT notification the pay band PB-2 having Grade Pay from Rs. 4200 to Rs. 5400 is classified as Group B services and can be sub-divided into two categories:

1. **Gazetted Group B Services** The posts belonging to this category form the upper level of Group B services and are placed just below the Group A services. The posts are notified in the Gazette published by the Government and are empowered to attest the documents as true copies. The Grade Pay of Rs. 4800 and Rs. 5400 in the pay band of PB2 are notified as Gazetted Group B services. In most of the cadre, the Gazetted rank is filled through promotion or deputation but for some posts there is direct recruitment.

2. **Non-Gazetted Group B Services** The Grade Pay of Rs. 4200 and Rs. 4800 in PB2 are classified as Non-Gazetted Group B services. These are mostly clerical level posts across various ministries and departments of the Government and assist the Gazetted rank officers in discharging the official duty.

B. RECRUITMENT TO GROUP B SERVICES

The Group B services form the bulk of posts in various Ministries and Departments. The recruitment to these services is done through specified recruiting agencies of the Government. Some of them are:

1. **UPSC** The UPSC through its Civil Service Exam does recruitment for the following Group B services:
   a. **Armed Forces Headquarters civil service** Armed Forces Headquarters Civilian Staff is a group B service. The Armed Forces (Army, Navy, and Air Force) Headquarters and other inter-service bodies under the defence ministry have civilian staff that is responsible for administration. Such staff is chosen from the civil service exams held by the UPSC.
   b. **Union Territory Police service** Pondicherry, Andaman & Nicobar, Lakshadweep, Daman & Diu, Dadra & Nagar Haveli, Delhi Police Service are centrally administered. Selected officers are appointed to police departments of union territories and also to Pondicherry Civil Services.
   c. **Union Territory Civil Services** The selected candidates are also posted to the administrative post in the Union Territories.

   The details of qualification and pattern of examination has already been discussed in the earlier chapter.

2. **Staff Selection Commission- (www.ssc.nic.in)**

This commission is an attached office of the Department of Personnel and Training (DoPT) under the Ministry of Personnel, Public Grievances & Pension. The Staff Selection Commission has its headquarters at New Delhi. At present, there are seven Regional Offices at Allahabad, Mumbai, Delhi, Kolkata, Guwahati, Chennai, Bangalore and two Sub-Regional Offices at Raipur and Chandigarh. Each Regional Office is headed by a Regional Director and each Sub-Regional office is headed by a Deputy

Director. Staff Selection Commission (SSC) conducts exams to make recruitments to non technical groups 'C' and non-gazetted posts of group 'B'.

The Staff Selection Commission issues vacancies for the Group B and Group C posts in various Ministries and Departments. Some posts are filled through the common entrance examinations conducted on the basis of specified qualification required for the post. Some of the Common Entrance Tests conducted by the Staff Selection Commission are indicated below:

a. **Combined Graduate Level Examination** This exam is conducted for the recruitment of various posts like Assistants in Central Secretariat/Armed Force Headquarters/ Ministries etc., Inspectors in Central Excise/Income Tax, Preventive Officers in Excise and Customs, Inspector in Central Bureau of Investigation, Divisional Accounts and Auditors in C&AG and Upper Division Clerks in various Ministries and Departments on the basis of available vacancy.

Details of various posts recruited: Applications are invited by SSC for following posts:-

I. **Posts for which Interview cum Personality Test is prescribed:**

Pay band II: 9300-34800

Post	Ministries/Departments/Offices/Cadre
Assistant	Central Secretariat Service
Assistant	Central Vigilance Commission
Assistant	Intelligence Bureau
Assistant	Ministry of Railway
Assistant	Ministry of External Affairs
Assistant (Cypher)	Ministry of External Affairs
Assistant	AFHQ
Assistant	Other Ministries/Departments/Organisations
Assistant	Other Ministries/Departments/Organisations

Inspector of Income Tax	CBTD
Inspector (Central Excise)	CBEC
Inspector (Preventive Officer)	CBEC
Inspector (Examiner)	CBEC
Assistant Enforcement Officer	Directorate of Enforcement, Department of Revenue
Sub Inspectors	Central Bureau of Investigation
Inspector of Posts	Department of Post
Divisional Accountant	Offices under CAG
Statistical Investigator Gr. II	M/Statistics & Prog Implementation
Inspector	Central Bureau of Narcotics

III. Posts for which Interview cum Personality Test is NOT prescribed:

Pay Band-I: 5200-20200

Post	Ministries/Departments/Offices/Cadre
Auditor	Offices under C&AG
Auditor	Offices under CGDA
Auditor	Offices under CGA & others
Accountant/Junior Accountant	Offices under C&AG
Accountant/Junior Accountant	Offices under CGA & others
Upper Division Clerk	Central Govt. Offices/Ministries other than CSCS cadres.
Tax Assistant	CBDT
Tax Assistant	CBEC
Compiler	Registrar General of India
Sub-Inspector	Central Bureau of Narcotics

SSC Graduate Exam Eligibility Criteria

Age: The age of a Candidate must lie between
- (A) 20 to 27 years for Assistant Grade & SIs in CBI
- (B) 18 to 27 years for inspectors of CE/IT & Div. Acts/Auditors/UDCs, etc.
- (C) 20 to 25 years for SIs in CPOs on the first day of August of the year of Examination.

The upper age limit may be relaxed in case of Scheduled Castes, Scheduled Tribes, Other Backward Classes and few such other reserved categories.

Educational Qualification: Degree of a recognized University or equivalent.

Physical Standards: For the posts of Inspector of Central Excise and Preventive Officer, candidates have to satisfy the minimum physical standards as specified in the examination notifications. They would also be required to undergo a physical test.

SYLLABUS for TIER-I Exam

Currently there are four sections of 50 marks each which have to be covered within two hours.

- A. General Intelligence & Reasoning
- B. General Awareness
- C. Quantitative Aptitude
- D. English Comprehension

SYLLABUS FOR TIER-II OF THE EXAM: (2 sections, Total time - 2 hours for each section)

Paper I: Quantitative Ability (200 marks)

Paper II: English Language & Comprehension (200 marks)

Paper III: Statistics (200 marks)

Paper I and II is common for all while Paper III is compulsory for the post of Statistical Investigator and Compiler.

(C) PERSONALITY TEST/INTERVIEW

For posts for which Interview cum Personality Test is prescribed, the Personality Test/interview will carry a maximum of 100 marks.

(D) SKILL TEST

Computer Proficiency Test (CPT) for post of Assistant in CSS (Central Secretariat Services) only. This test is of qualifying nature.

b. Section Officer (Audit) Exam The recruitment to the post of Section Officer (Audit) in the Civil Audit branches of the Comptroller & Auditor General is conducted by a separate exam. Earlier the Post of Section Officer (Audit) was a non-gazetted post in the pay scale of 6500-10500. After the implementation of 6th CPC, various posts have been merged and now there is recruitment for Assistant Audit Officer (Gazetted) in PB2 having Grade Pay of Rs. 4800. As per the Government Resolution No. 18 dated 10th January 2013, the recruitment to the AAO post will be done through UPSC. The vacancy notification is yet to be issued.

Eligibility - Graduation from recognized university having 50% marks.

Part A Written Paper:

	Subject	Marks	Total Marks	Time
Paper I	General Awareness	100	300	2 Hours
	General English	100		
Paper II	Maths	200		2 Hours

B - Part II: Personality Test/Interview (100 Marks)

c. Section Officer (Commercial) Exam A separate exam is conducted on the earlier mentioned lines for recruitment into commercial wings of C&AG.

Eligibility - Graduation in Commerce/CA/ICWA/CS

Part A Written Paper:

	Subject	Marks	Type	Total Marks	Time
Paper I	General Awareness	75	Objective	200	2 Hours
	Arithmetical Ability	50			
	English	75			
Paper II	Commerce	200	Conventional	200	2 Hours

B - Part II: Personality Test/Interview (100 Marks)

The details of some other Group B services have been discussed under the chapter dealing with Uniformed Services.

C. WWW: WIN-WIN-WIN CORE STRATEGY TIPS FOR GROUP B POSTS

Note: Please follow the WWW Win-Win-Win Core Strategy given in case of UPSC Indian Civil Services Examination with necessary specialization and modification for all competitive examinations.

a. First things first, are you keeping the expected standard? If not, please obtain all the NCERT/School prescribed text books on the subjects you need to update from the class standard you are not sure of till you master the 10+2 text books.

b. Please do consult candidates who have cleared the examination, coaching centres, Google search of important websites and tips for preparation and extensive and intensive market survey to get the right resources, text books, guides, study notes solved previous years papers etc for preparation.

c. Please do familiarize the subjects, topics to be covered as per the syllabi and pattern of questions asked by reviewing previous years solved question papers and continuously practicing them till you achieve the expected standard.

d. For most of these examinations including Banks' Clerical and Probationary Officers' Examinations, topics covered include (a) General Studies or General Knowledge or General Awareness (b) English Grammar and Vocabulary; (c) Quantitative Aptitude & Logical Reasoning (d) Computer Awareness etc.

e. Going over the syllabi and past question papers will surely familiarize the topics you need to be through to succeed in the examination. Next important thing is extensive and intensive consultation and market research to find and obtain the right study resources, text books guides, study notes and material to begin detailed focused examination preparation strategy.

f. Once the subjects are covered and past question papers are resolved by continuous practice within the time frame in examination environment you are ready to take the examination.

Most of the competitive examinations for the recruitment of Group B and C post have question papers which include multiple choice questions. Advantage of such examination is that it is objective oriented and the candidates do not have to write lengthy notes. Also, due to Optical Mark Reader answer sheets, they can be evaluated quickly. The common subjects for all these examinations are:

1. **Maths** The level is mostly up to 10th standard and involves application of basic concepts. Several books are available in the market for preparation of this paper. Quantitative Aptitude by Shri R.S. Agarwal is one of the most popular books among them. For shortcuts, a book by Shri M. Tyra published by Banking Services Chronicle is also handy.

2. **Reasoning** This part involves verbal as well as non-verbal reasoning. The emphasis on non-verbal reasoning is mostly in banks recruitment. "A modern approach to analytical reasoning" by Shri R.S. Agarwal and "Analytical Reasoning" by M.K. Pandey are good for understanding the basics.

3. **English** English paper mostly involves grammar, vocabulary and reading comprehension. English grammar can be covered from various elementary level grammar books available in the market. Book by Wren and Martin is good book. Vocabulary has to be build over a period of time by reading and writing practice in English. It needs consistency and strategic planning. Books by Norman Lewis help to build vocabulary but the overall success depends on the candidates own efforts. Reading Comprehension is all about understanding lengthy paragraphs in less time. The

habit of reading has to be developed at the adolescent age. Reading novels, newspapers and magazines can be handy for this purpose. Though in some competitive exams the English paper is merely qualifying candidates tend to ignore it. But it is important to remember that marks in other papers will be of no use if the candidate does not achieve the qualifying marks in this paper.

4. **Current Affairs and General Knowledge** Candidates have to make a habit of perusing the leading news papers daily and make short notes of important developments. Read the editorial pages to understand the various events around the world. In addition subscription to monthly competitive magazines like *Competition Success Review*, *Pratiyogita Darpan* etc. are of great help. These magazines also contain information about various notifications of vacancies and test papers for practice for different competitive exams.

D. SOURCES OF MATERIAL FOR PREPARATION

Apart from the books mentioned in the previous section there are several books available which the candidates may refer to based on their choice and understanding. But, it is always suggested to reduce the burden of more and more books and emphasize on the extensive coverage of the topics. At the same time there are several websites which provide study/preparation material. Some of them are indicated below:

1. www.gr8ambitionz.com
2. www.wiziq.com
3. www.careerleaps.com
4. www.tcyonline.com

PART III: GROUP C SERVICES

A. Types of Group C Services

As already stated Group C services form the base of Government Ministries and Departments. The posts mostly belong to the clerical cadre and there are multiple recruiting agencies for different posts. There are certain posts in this cadre where some additional qualification is required. The Group C services can be divided into:

1. Clerical Cadre: All the post in PB1 with a pay band of 5200 to 20200 with a Grade Pay of Rs 1900, Rs 2000, Rs 2400 and Rs 2800 belong to the Group C cadre. They can be further sub-divided into:

  a. Technical Post There are many posts in the Group C cadre where some additional qualification is required to perform the job. The details of qualification required can be seen from the notification issued.

  b. Non-Technical Post The recruitment to this category of posts are open to the candidates from general stream.

2. Multitasking Staff (MTS): Prior to the year 2011, there was a separate Group D class which has been abolished since then and a new category of post has been included at the entry level in Group C itself. This category is in PB1 with a Grade Pay of 1800. There is a separate recruitment exam conducted by the Staff Selection Commission for the recruitment of MTS. Though recruited as a separate class they are assigned the duties on the basis of individual skill. They have been provided a better prospect of further promotion.

B. Recruitment to Group C Services

The details of the recruitment in Group C services can be discussed on the basis of the specialized recruitment exams conducted by the recruiting agencies:

1. Combined Higher Secondary Level (10+2) examination conducted by SSC SSC has introduced the Matric level Exam with a new name SSC Combined Higher Secondary Level (10+2) Examination. The qualification required for appearing this examination has also been elevated to higher secondary level. Through this examination the recruitment is done for the post of Lower Division Clerk, Data Entry Operator, Grade C & D Stenographers etc. in the offices of Armed Force Headquarters, Election Commission of India, Intelligence Bureau, Central Bureau of Investigation, Controller General of Accounts, Ministry of Parliamentary Affairs, President's Secretariat, Central Vigilance Commission, Comptroller and Auditor General of India and other subordinate and attached offices of Government of India.

The Examination comprises of a Written Objective Type Examination followed by Data Entry Skill Test/Typing Test.

Part	Description	Max Marks	Time Allowed
1	General Intelligence and Reasoning	50	2 hrs.
2	Quantitative Aptitude	50	
3	General Knowledge	50	
4	English	50	

The syllabus is broadly the same as Combined Graduate Level (CGL) Examination, though, the standard and coverage of the questions are limited as compared to CGL.

SKILL TEST for DATA ENTRY OPERATOR:

Data Entry Speed prescribed for the post is 8,000 Key Depressions per hour on Computer. The 'Speed of 8000 key depressions per hour on Computer' will be adjudged on the basis of the correct entry of words key depressions as per the given passage. Duration of the said Test will be 15 (fifteen) minutes and printed matter in English containing about 2000-2200 strokes/key-depressions are given to test the candidates.

Typing Test for LDCs:

Typing Test will be conducted for those candidates who qualify in the Written Examination. Such Typing Test will be conducted in English or Hindi and candidates while applying for the Examination, will have to indicate his/her choice/option for Skill

Test Medium in the Application Form. The choice of language in the application will be final and no change will be allowed.

2. SSC Multitasking staff:

Staff Selection Commission holds SSC Multitasking exam every year.

Eligibility:

Educational Qualification: Job hunters must have passed Matriculation from any recognized Board.

Age Limit: Candidates must be in between 18 years to 25 years of age. Relaxation in age will be given as per Govt. rules.

Selection process: Selection will be made on the basis of written test as follows:

Paper I   Duration - 2 Hours

Subject	Questions	Maximum marks
General Intelligence & Reasoning	25	25
Numerical Aptitude	25	25
General English	50	50
General Awareness	50	50

Paper II

Subject	Maximum marks	Duration
Short Essay/Letter in English or any language included in the 8th Schedule of the Constitution	50	30 minutes

C. Railway Recruitment Board

With 1.4 million people on their roster, the Indian Railways is the eighth largest recruiter in the world. The Indian railways are broadly divided and sub-divided into zones, divisions and departments, each controlling a particular function. Every division has a certain number of technical and non-technical departments, which form the base structure on which the railways function. Technical departments include civil, technical and mechanical engineering, signalling and telecom, and several others dealing with similar disciplines, while the non-technical departments include general services such as accounts, personnel management, Railway Protection Force (RPF) or security and traffic services, among others. Each department has staff at various levels. The recruitment to Group A services in the Railways is done by various exams conducted by the UPSC as already discussed. For the recruitment to the remaining Group B and C services there are 21 Railway Recruitment Boards which function under the Ministry of Railways to facilitate recruitment in the respective area.

Websites of the 21 Railway Recruitment Boards (RRBs):

Name of RRBs	Website
Ahmedabad	http://www.rrbahmedabad.gov.in
Ajmer	http://www.rrbajmer.gov.in
Allahabad	http://www.rrbald.gov.in/
Bangalore	http://www.rrbbnc.gov.in/
Bhopal	http://www.rrbbpl.nic.in/
Bhubaneshwar	http://www.rrbbbs.gov.in/
Bilaspur	http://www.rrbbilaspur.gov.in/
Chandigarh	http://www.rrbcdg.gov.in/
Chennai	http://www.rrbchennai.gov.in/
Gorakhpur	http://www.rrbgkp.gov.in/
Guwahati	http://www.rrbguwahati.gov.in/
Jammu	http://www.rrbjammu.nic.in/
Kolkata	http://www.rrbkolkata.gov.in/
Malda	http://www.rrbmalda.gov.in/
Mumbai	http://www.rrbmumbai.gov.in/

Muzaffarpur	http://www.rrbmuzaffarpur.gov.in/
Patna	http://www.rrbpatna.gov.in/
Ranchi	http://www.rrbranchi.org/
Secunderabad	http://rrbsecunderabad.nic.in/
Siliguri	http://www.rrbsiliguri.org/
Trivandrum	http://www.rrbthiruvananthapuram.gov.in/

Mostly, the Group B services in the Indian Railways are filled through promotion.

The various recruitment exams conducted by the RRBs on the basis of the regional requirements are as follows:

1. **COMMERCIAL APPRENTICE**

    Minimum Educational Qualification: A Degree in any discipline or its equivalent.

    Age Limit: 18 - 33 years

    Exam Pattern: Two stage written exam, followed by verification of documents. No Interview.

2. **TRAFFIC APPRENTICE**

    Minimum Educational Qualification: A Degree in any discipline or its equivalent

    Age Limit: 18 - 33 years

    Exam Pattern: Two stage written exam, followed by verification of documents. No Interview.

3. **ENQUIRY cum RESERVATION CLERK**

    Minimum Educational Qualification: A Degree in any discipline or its equivalent

    Age Limit: 18 - 33 years

    Exam Pattern: Two stage written exam, followed by verification of documents. No Interview.

4. **GOODS GUARD**

    Minimum Educational Qualification: A Degree in any discipline or its equivalent.

    Age Limit: 18 - 33 years

    Exam Pattern: Two stage written exam, followed by verification of documents. No Interview.

5. JUNIOR ACCOUNTS ASSISTANT cum TYPIST

Minimum Educational Qualification: A Degree in any discipline or its equivalent.

Typing proficiency @ 30 wpm in English or @ 25 wpm in Hindi.

Age Limit: 18 - 33 years

Exam Pattern: Two stage written exam, Qualifying Typing Test, followed by verification of documents. No Interview.

6. SENIOR CLERK cum TYPIST

Minimum Educational Qualification: A Degree in any discipline or its equivalent.

Typing proficiency @ 30 wpm in English or @ 25 wpm in Hindi.

Age Limit: 18 - 33 years

Exam Pattern: Two stage written exam, Qualifying Typing Test, followed by verification of documents. No Interview.

7. ASSISTANT STATION MASTER

Minimum Educational Qualification: A Degree in any discipline or its equivalent.

Desirable Qualification: Diploma in Rail Transport & Management, Transport Economics, Multimodal Transport.

Age Limit: 18 - 33 years

Exam Pattern: Single stage written exam, followed by Aptitude Test & verification of documents. No Interview.

8. TRAFFIC ASSISTANT

Minimum Educational Qualification: A Degree in any discipline or its equivalent. Desirable Qualification: Diploma in Rail Transport & Management, Transport Economics, Multimodal Transport.

Age Limit: 18 - 33 years

Exam Pattern: Single stage written exam, followed by Aptitude Test & verification of documents. No Interview.

9. COMMERCIAL CLERK

Minimum Educational Qualification: Matriculation or its equivalent with not less than 50% marks. SC/ST/Ex.S/PWD candidates who have passed matriculation can apply irrespective of marks obtained by them. Candidates who possess higher qualification can apply irrespective of marks obtained by them in matriculation.

Age Limit: 18 - 30 years

Exam Pattern: Two stage written exam, followed by verification of documents. No Interview.

10. ACCOUNT CLERK cum TYPIST

Minimum Educational Qualification: Matriculation or its equivalent with not less than 50% marks. SC/ST/Ex.S/PWD candidates who have passed matriculation can apply irrespective of marks obtained by them.

Candidates who possess higher qualification can apply irrespective of marks obtained by them in matriculation.

Age Limit: 18 - 30 years

Exam Pattern: Two stage written exam, followed by typing test & verification of documents. No Interview

11. TICKET EXAMINER/TICKET COLLECTOR

Minimum Educational Qualification: Matriculation or its equivalent with not less than 50% marks. SC/ST/Ex.S/PWD candidates who have passed matriculation can apply irrespective of marks obtained by them.

Candidates who possess higher qualification can apply irrespective of marks obtained by them in matriculation.

Age Limit: 18 - 30 years

Exam Pattern: Two stage written exam, followed by verification of documents. No Interview.

12. JUNIOR CLERK cum TYPIST

Minimum Educational Qualification: Matriculation or its equivalent with not less than 50% marks. SC/ST/Ex.S/PWD candidates who have passed matriculation can apply irrespective of marks obtained by them.

Candidates who possess higher qualification can apply irrespective of marks obtained by them in Matriculation.

Typing proficiency @ 30 wpm in English or @ 25 wpm in Hindi.

Age Limit: 18 - 30 years

Exam Pattern: Two stage written exam, followed by typing test & verification of documents. No Interview

13. TRAINS CLERK

Minimum Educational Qualification: Matriculation or its equivalent with not less than 50% marks. SC/ST/Ex.S/PWD candidates who have passed Matriculation can apply irrespective of marks obtained by them.

Candidates who possess higher qualification can apply irrespective of marks obtained by them in Matriculation.

Age Limit: 18 - 30 years.

Exam Pattern: Two stage written exam, followed by verification of documents. No Interview.

D. Strategy for Group C Services

There is not much difference between the strategy for preparation of Group B and Group C services. Mostly the syllabus for the recruitment examinations for both the categories of services are same and questions are generally of multiple question type. The only difference is that the standard of questions varies from one exam to the other. Even the books suggested for Group B Services are handy for the entrance examinations of Group C services. The ideal maxim for preparation of competitive examination is to prepare for similar type of examinations to gain familiarity, time management and accuracy.

CHAPTER 3

UNIFORMED SERVICES IN THE CENTRAL GOVERNMENT

This chapter provides information about the various uniformed services in the country and their recruitment procedures. The chapter has been divided into two parts to cover the civil side of uniformed services and military side of the uniformed services separately. The civil uniformed services include Central Paramilitary Forces covering Central Police Organizations (Tier-I) & (Tier-II) like CRPF, CISF, BSF, NSG and investigative agencies like RAW, IB & CBI. The chapter also provides information regarding various Military Uniformed Services in Indian Army, Navy and Air Force.

Civil Uniformed Services

1. Indian Police Service

As already discussed in chapter 2, the Indian Police Service is an all India service and the recruitment is done through the Civil Service Exam conducted by the UPSC on the basis of rank attained and the preference of the candidate. The entrants are initially posted as Assistant Commissioner/Superintendent of Police and can rise up to the ranks of Director General of Police. After selection for the IPS, candidates are allocated to a State cadre. There is one cadre in each of the Indian states, except three joint cadres viz. Assam-Meghalaya, Manipur – Tripura, and Arunachal Pradesh – Goa – Mizoram - Union Territories (AGMUT). Two-thirds of the strength of every cadre is filled directly by IPS officers and the remaining is promoted from the respective States' cadre officers. Apart from clearing the UPSC Civil Service examination, the candidates have to fulfill prescribed physical requirements for getting selected as an IPS officer.

2. Paramilitary Forces

The Paramilitary forces (PMF) ensure the internal security of the country. Most of these forces generally perform counter-insurgency or anti-terrorist missions. All branches of the PMF function under purview of the Ministry of Home Affairs.

Indian Paramilitary forces have several components with different rules. Overall it has a two tier structure, the Central Police Organizations (CPO), which forms the first tier, and the second tier known as Central Paramilitary Forces (CPF).

A. Central Police Organizations (Tier 1): The Central Police Organizations (CPO) work independently or in coordination with the Indian Federal Agencies and State Police Forces.

- **Railway Protection Force (RPF)** ensures the safety, security and boosts the confidence of the traveling public in the Indian Railways.
- **Central Reserve Police Force (CRPF)** -The role of Central Reserve Police (CRPF) Force being multifaceted, the Force is

being employed for variety of tasks varying from providing aid to the State Administration in maintenance of Law and Order, Static guard duties to protect vulnerable areas and very important persons, to actively fighting insurgents and anti-social elements in different parts of the country.

- **Other CPOs**
    - **Special Protection Group (SPG)** The Special Protection Group provides proximate security to the Prime Minister of India and the members of his immediate family.
    - **Home Guard** The Indian Home Guard is tasked as an auxiliary to the Indian Police.
    - **Commando Battalion for Resolute Action (COBRA)** Commando Battalion for Resolute Action (COBRA) battalion of the CRPF is specially raised to tackle Maoists.

B. Central Paramilitary Forces (Tier 2): The Central Paramilitary Forces (CPF) forms the second tier of Paramilitary Forces. The CPF works in cooperation with the Indian Armed Forces.

- **Border Security Force (BSF)** The specialized centrally controlled Border Security Force (BSF) guards the borders of the country.
- **National Security Guard (NSG)** As a Federal Contingency Deployment the primary role of the National Security Guard is to combat terrorism in whatever form it may assume in areas where the State Police and other Central Police Forces cannot cope up with the situation.
- **Central Industrial Security Force (CISF)** The Central Industrial Security Force (CISF) is a premier multi-skilled security agency of the country, mandated to provide security to major critical infrastructure installations of the country in diverse areas. CISF is currently providing security cover to nuclear installations, space establishments, airports, seaports, power plants, sensitive Government buildings and ever heritage monuments.

CISF has seven Training Institutions as under:
- Recruit Training Centre Arakkonam (T.N.)
- Recruit Training Centre Barwaha (M.P.)
- Recruit Training Centre Bhilai (Chattisgarh)
- Recruit Training Centre-I Deoli (Rajasthan)
- Recruit Training Centre-II Deoli (Rajasthan)
- Recruit Training Centre RTC Mundali (Odisha)
- National Industrial Security Academy at Hyderabad (A.P.)

- **Sashastra Seema Bal (SSB)** promotes sense of security among the people living in the border area, prevents trans border crimes and unauthorized entries into or exit from the territory of India and prevent smuggling and other illegal activities
- **Defence Security Corps (DSC)** The Defence Security Corps of the Army and its personnel are subjected to Army Act under Army. The Corps is a Security Force maintained and organised on the Army model. The role of Defence Security Corps (DSC) is to protect Defence units/installations where DSC cover is sanctioned under specific orders of the Government of India against minor sabotage and pilferage. To fulfill this role the DSC provides armed security staff, static guards, searchers, escorts and mobile patrols by day and night. The personnel are armed so as to afford a higher degree of protection.
- **Indo-Tibetan Border Police (ITBP)** The Indo-Tibetan Border Police is deployed on border guarding duties from Karakoram Pass in Ladakh to Diphu La in Arunachal Pradesh covering 3488 KM of India-China Border and manning Border Outposts on altitudes ranging from 9000' to 18500' in the Western, Middle & Eastern Sector of the India-China Border. ITBP is basically a mountain trained Force and most of the personnel are professionally trained Mountaineers and Skiers. Being the first responder for natural Disaster in the Himalayas, ITBP has been carrying out numerous rescue and relief operations.

3. Recruitment to Uniformed Services

As already discussed the recruitment to the Indian Police Service is done through the Civil Service Examination conducted by the UPSC. The recruitment in Paramilitary Forces is done for the Constable, Sub-Inspector, Assistant Sub Inspector, Assistant Commandant etc.

Recruitment to the post of Sub-Inspector/Assistant Sub-Inspector:

Recruitment to the post of Sub-Inspectors in CAPFs (Central Armed Police Forces), CISF (Central Industrial Security Force), ITBPF (Indo Tibetan Border Police Force), CRPF (Central Reserve Police Force), BSF (Border Security Force) and SSB (Sahastra Seema Bal) in the pay scale of Rs. 9300-34800 in Pay Band 2 with Grade Pay of Rs. 4200 and for the post of ASI (Assistant Sub-Inspector) in CISF in the scale of Rs. 5200-20200 in PB-2 with Grade Pay of Rs. 2800/- is done through a common entrance test conducted by the Staff Selection Commission based on the vacancy position available. The candidates have to indicate the preference of post at the stage of application itself. Recruitment to other posts is done through special notifications based on the available vacancies.

The examination for recruitment is held in two stages:

Part A consists of 200 marks (50 each from the following four sections)
- General Intelligence and Reasoning
- General Knowledge and General Awareness
- Quantitative Aptitude
- English Comprehension

Part B consists of English language and Comprehension of 200 marks

PET (Physical Endurance Test) based on the defined parameters is mandatory for the final selection.

Recruitment to the post of Assistant Commandant

Recruitment to the post of Assistant Commandant in the Central Armed Police Forces (CAPF) viz. BSF, CRPF, CISF, ITBP and

SSB etc is done by an entrance exam conducted by the UPSC. The examination details have already been discussed in Chapter 2.

Pay - Pay scale of Rs.15600-39100 with Grade Pay Rs. 5400.

4. Research & Analysis Wing (RAW), Central Bureau of Investigation (CBI), Intelligence Bureau (IB)

There is no direct entry to RAW (Research and Analysis Wing). Top ranking police officers with exceptional track record are sent on deputation to work with RAW. One can enter police service through UPSC (Union Public Service Commission) Civil Services examination or State Public Service Commission examinations.

Recruitment to the post of Sub-Inspector in Central Bureau of Investigation (CBI) is done through the Combined Graduate level Exam conducted by the Staff Selection Commission depending on the vacancy position.

Recruitment in Intelligence Bureau (IB)

1. IB Assistant Central Intelligence Officer ACIO Executive

Educational & Other Qualification (i) Essential:- Graduation or equivalent from a recognised University (ii) Desirable:- Knowledge of Computers.

Age limit Not exceeding 27 years as on the closing date for receipt of application. Upper age limit is relaxable by 5 years for SC/ST and 3 years for OBC.

Written Exam Pattern The written examination for the post of ACIO-II/Exe contains two papers namely Paper I (Objective type) and Paper II (Descriptive type on English language only). The total duration for both the Papers is 1 hour and 40 minutes.

How To Apply Applications should be submitted only through ON-LINE registration by logging on to the website www.mha.nic.in

2. IB Security Assistant (Executive) Scale of pay:- Rs. 5200-20200/- and Grade pay Rs. 2000/- plus allowances at Central Govt. rates. Age:- Not exceeding 27 years as on closing date of application. Upper age limit is relaxable for SC/ST/OBC, Ex-Serviceman as per Government of India rules. Also relaxable for departmental candidates up to 40 years in accordance with the instructions/orders issued by the Central Government from time to time.

Eligibility Conditions (A) Essential: (i) Matriculation (Class X) or equivalent from a recognized Board. (ii) Knowledge of local language/Dialect as specified. (B) Desirable: Field Experience in intelligence work.

Selection of Candidates The candidates who come up to a specific standard following a preliminary screening of applications based on knowledge of the local language(s) of the Centre concerned, academic qualification, marks obtained in the examinations and depending upon the number of vacancies, would be called for an Objective Type test on General Knowledge, Current awareness, aptitude, reasoning, general arithmetic and English for 100 marks to be held at the respective centres of examination where the candidates have applied for. Those candidates who meet specific standard in the objective type test will be further called for local language test (50 marks) and personality test (50 marks).

3. Recruitment for Personal Assistant in Intelligence Bureau

Educational Qualification Matriculation from a recognized Board with proficiency in Stenography (100 words per minute)

Desirable – Knowledge of computer operation.

Pay Scale:- Rs. 9300-34800/- (Pay Scale) + Rs. 4600/- (GP) + allowance as per Central Govt. rates.

Junior Intelligence Officer Grade-II (Wireless Telegraphy)

Educational Qualification Matriculation in Physics and Mathematics with two years Industrial Training Institute pass certificate in any of the following trades:-

   (i) Electronic, Mechanic
   (ii) Information Technology and Electronic System maintenance
   (iii) Electrician
   (iv) Mechanic Computer Hardware
   (v) Mechanic (Radio & TV)

(vi) Mechanic cum operator of Electronic Communication system.

Pay Scale Rs. 5200-20200/- (Pay Scale) + Rs. 2400/- (GP) + allowance as per Central Govt. rates

4. Intelligence Bureau: Junior Intelligence Officer Recruitment Grade-II (Electronics Data Processing)

Educational Qualification

(i) 12th Standard pass or equivalent

(ii) Training in computer operations for, at least, three months from recognised Institutions and possess a speed of not less than 8000 key depressions per hour for Data Entry work. Note: Speed of 8000 key depressions per hour for Data Entry work would be judged by conducting a speed test on EDP Machines by the Competent Authority.

Pay Scale Rs. 5200-20200/- (Pay Scale) + Rs. 2400/- (GP) + allowance as per Central Govt. rates.

Age limit

i. Between 18-27 years as on closing date of application for all post. Upper age limit is relaxable by five years for SC/ST and by three years for OBC candidates.

ii. For JIO-II/WT, the upper age limit is relaxable for Departmental candidates up to 40 years in accordance with the instructions or orders issued by the Central Government.

iii. Similarly, for JIO-II/EDP, the upper age limits is relaxable for Government servants up to 35 years in accordance with the instructions or orders issued by the Central Government.

iv. However, for Personal Assistant (PA) the upper age limit is relaxable for Government Servants up to five years in accordance with the instructions or orders issued by the Central Government.

v. The age limit is also relaxable for Ex-Serviceman as well as residents of J&K in terms of government instructions issued from time to time.

Recruitment process:

Candidates can apply for any or more of the three posts provided he/she fulfils the prescribed eligibility conditions. There will be a common written test (objective type multiple choice) for the posts of JIO-II/WT, JIO-II/EDP and PA. The written examination (descriptive type) for the post of PA will be held separately. Depending upon the number of vacancies in these posts, the candidates, who are short listed on the basis of their performance in the written examination, would be called for skill test and practical test-cum-interview separately for each post.

A. MILITARY UNIFORMED SERVICES

There are three types of Military services in India viz. Indian Army, Indian Navy and Indian Air Force. Considering the divergence in the type of services to be rendered in these services, the recruitment methodology for these services also varies. The recruitment for the premier posts in all the three wings are done through the National Defence Academy & Naval Academy Examinations and Combined Defence Services Examination conducted by the Union Public Service Commission. After clearing the examination the candidates are posted as Lieutenant and can reach the highest rank on the basis of performance and seniority.

1. Indian Army

Ranks and Insignia

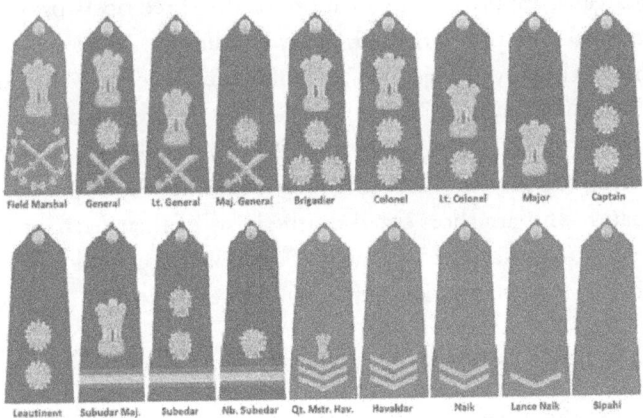

There are two types of services in Indian Army:

A. Permanent Commission

A Permanent Commission means a career in the Army till one retires. For a Permanent commission one has to join the National Defence Academy (NDA) or the Indian Military Academy (IMA).

The National Defence Academy, Pune

One can take the NDA entrance exam right after class XI. Clear the UPSC exam along with a 5-day Service Selection Board interview and medical tests. Apart from providing graduation degrees, NDA has the finest infrastructure for professional training.

Indian Military Academy, Dehradun

Indian Military Academy is yet another cradle of leadership. There are four main entries to get into IMA. In the final year of Graduation, one needs to pass the Combined Defence Services Exams, clear the SSB, be medically fit and join IMA as a Direct Entry.

The other entries are 10+2 Tech Entry where one can apply after your 12th Exams. University Entry Scheme is for those of who wish to apply for Army in Pre-Final/Final Year of Engineering. Those who have completed their BE/B Tech in notified streams can also join IMA in the Technical Graduate Course.

The selection procedure is same as for IMA (Direct Entry) accepting that there are no written exams. The duration of training is 1½ years for IMA (DE), five years (one year at IMA and four year at Cadet Training Wings) for 10+2 TES (incl. one year after commissioning) and one year for all other entries.

B. Short Service Commission

One also has the option of joining the Army and serving as a Commissioned Officer for 10 years. At the end of this period one has two options. Either elect for a Permanent Commission or opt out. Those not selected for Permanent Commission have the option of a 4 years extension. They can resign at any time during this period.

Officers' Training Academy, Chennai

Once selected for Short Service Commission, candidates go to the Officers Training Academy at Chennai. The selection process is a written exam followed by the SSB interview and medicals. For Technical (Engineering) graduates it is direct SSB interview and medicals. If one has done NCC Senior Division (Army) and obtained 'C' certificate with minimum 'B' grade, they can apply through their NCC Branch HQ/Zonal HQ to Recruiting Directorate for direct SSB interview. SSB qualified candidates undergo a medical examination. The duration of training is 49 weeks. OTA training provides you with opportunities to broaden the perspective and widen the horizon. Women officers also receive training at OTA, Chennai. One should be a Graduate/Post-Graduate to apply. After the written exam, there is the SSB interview followed by a medical examination.

Other categories of selection:

Category	Education	Age
Soldier General Duty	SSLC/Matric with 45% marks in aggregate. No % required if higher qualification.	$17^{1/2}$ – 21 Years

Soldier Technical	10+2/Intermediate exam passed in Science with Physics, Chemistry, Maths and English. Now eight age for higher qualification.	$17^{1/2}$ – 23 Years
Soldier Clerk / Store Keeper Technical	10+2/Intermediate exam passed in any stream (Arts, Commerce, Science) with 50% marks in aggregate and min 40% in each subject. Weightage for higher qualification.	$17^{1/2}$ – 23 Years
Soldier Nursing Assistant	10+2/Intermediate exam passed in Science with Physics, Chemistry, Biology and English with min 50% marks in aggregate and min 40% in each subject. No weightage for higher qualification.	$17^{1/2}$ – 23 Years
Soldier Trades man		
(i) General Duties (ii) Specified Duties	Non Matric Non Matric	$17^{1/2}$ – 20 Years $17^{1/2}$ – 23 Years
Havildar Education	Graduate with BEd/Post Graduate with BEd	20 – 25 Years
Religious Teacher (JCO's)	Graduate in any discipline In addition, qualification in his own religious denomination	27 – 34 Years
JCO (Catering)	10+2, Diploma/Certificate Course of a duration of one year or more in Cookery/Hotel Management and Catering Tech recognized by AICTE	21 – 27 Years
Surveyor Automated Cartographer	BA/BSc with Maths having passed Matric & 12th (10+2) with Maths & Science	20 – 25 Years

2. Indian Navy

Indian Navy

Rank Insignia
Shoulder and Sleeve

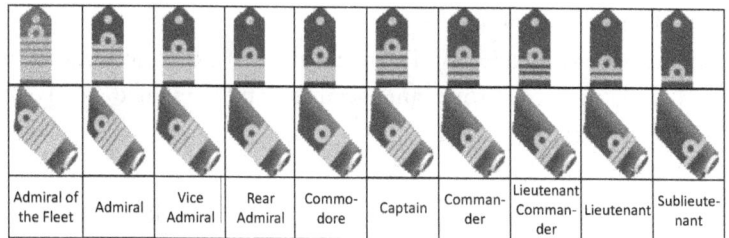

| Admiral of the Fleet | Admiral | Vice Admiral | Rear Admiral | Commo-dore | Captain | Comman-der | Lieutenant Comman-der | Lieutenant | Sublieute-nant |

A. Executive level

- **General Service Officer**

    As an Executive Officer, one will be both dealing with the ship as well as fighting on the ship. It means one will be a vital part of the complex system that manages the ship and also uses the ship as an instrument of tactical warfare. One will learn to have a good understanding of ship's capabilities and limitations and be able to turn them to one's advantage. It is for this reason that an Executive Officer alone can aspire for the command of a naval ship.

Executive Officers are trained in specializations like anti-submarine warfare, navigation, communications, gunnery, logistics, diving and hydrography. One could also opt for the air or submarine arm. Within the branch, promotional chances are not affected by the choice of specialization.

- **Hydrographic Officer**

  Executive Officers can specialize in hydrography. Hydrographic Officers are responsible for collecting information required for making the nautical charts used by the Indian Navy and other Navies around the world.

- **Naval Armament Inspection Officer**

  These specialist officers inspect the armaments supplied to the Navy by various agencies. While they ensure the quality, safety and reliability of naval armament and stores, they are also responsible for in-house research & development leading to indigenization. Both Permanent as well as Short Service Commissioned officers serve in this cadre.

- **Provost Officer**

  A separate cadre of Provost Officers exists to deal with policing, regulatory, and security and vigilance needs of the Navy.

- **Pilot Officer**

  For those with an aspiration to fly in the skies, the navy needs Pilots who act as airborne tactical coordinators of marine warfare. While most Navy pilots fly ship-borne helicopters and shore based maritime reconnaissance aircraft, some elite pilots also fly fighter aircraft such as Sea Harrier or Mig 29K. Naval aircraft locate and attack enemy surface ships and submarines and take part in amphibious warfare, search and rescue, casualty evacuation etc. For this, specialized training is imparted at various places on shore and afloat units.

- **Observer Officer**

  For those with a yearning for the skies, navy needs observers who act as airborne coordinators of maritime warfare.

Observer officer operates various state of the art equipment including sonics, sonars, radars and communication equipment. Observer officer gets an opportunity to participate in all facets of naval operations onboard the "eyes" of the fleet: the maritime Patrol aircraft.

- **Submarine Officer**

  For others who enjoy the challenge of new frontiers, meet the medical standards and have an exceptional record, this is the right specialization. These new hi-tech war machines have awesome firepower, state-of-the art weapon control systems, computer controlled machinery and a high standard of habitability. In peace time, one major responsibility of the submarines is to train for war as effectively as possible in the knowledge that will contribute to its prevention. After successful completion of the rigorous training, which is conducted at Visakhapatnam, the officer will be the proud possessor of the 'Dolphin Badge' and a member of a very elite arm of the Navy.

- **Diving officer**

  A Diving Officer's job ranges from under water inspection and repair of ships to defence of Indian Navy maritime assets. This is yet another elite and challenging task specialization wherein being in the parent professional arm with sub specialization such as Gunnery, Navigation, Anti-submarine warfare or else Logistics, Hydro, Aviation etc. One can become ships diver. Alternatively one may opt to become a Diving Officer wherein one would be required to undertake a Clearance Diving Officers course and/or a marine Commando course.

- **Law Officer**

  A separate cadre of Law Officers also exists to deal with the legal needs of the Navy. Both Permanent as well as Short Service Commissioned officers serve in this cadre.

- **Logistics Officer**

  A modern warship is not only a complex fighting unit, but also a mini township and community of several hundred people. These personnel have to be fed, clothed and paid, whatever may be the ship's role. A modern warship has also to be constantly supplied with fuel, water and spares for the vast array of sophisticated equipment and machinery. At sea or on shore the Logistics Officer has a vital part to play in the technical and human aspects of the ship's organisation. It is a job that requires exceptional managerial skills and the ability to deliver under pressure.

- **Information Technology**

    Indian Navy provides excellent career opportunities in the field of IT. Personnel gain hands-on experience in operations, maintenance and administration of core IT infrastructure applications. They are exposed to R & D functions as part of standard growth profile. Naval IT setup is unique since it involves not only shore based establishments but also afloat units, which require to maintain connectivity and synchronized operations.

Type of Entry	Unmarried Men/Women	Age Limit	Educational Qualification
EXECUTIVE BRANCH			
National Defence Academy (NDA) (Through UPSC)	Men	16½ – 19	10+2 or equivalent with Physics & Maths
(10+2) Indian Naval Academy, Ezhimala (Through UPSC)	Men	16½ – 19	10+2 or equivalent with Physics & Maths
Graduate Special Entry Scheme (GSES) Indian Naval Academy, Ezhimala (Through UPSC)	Men	19 – 22	B.Sc. (Physics & Maths) or BE

NCC Special Entry Indian Naval Academy, Ezhimala	Men	19 – 24	B.Sc. (Physics & Maths) or BE with Naval Wing Senior Div NCC 'C' Certificate
PC Naval Armament Inspection Centre	Men	19½ – 25	B.E./B.Tech degree in Electronics/ Elect/Mech Engg or Post Graduate Degree in Electronics or Physics
PC Law Cadre	Men	22 – 27	A degree in Law qualifying for enrolment as an Advocate under the Advocates Act 1961 with minimum 55% marks
PC Logistics cadre	Men	19½ – 25	A First Class Degree in B.Com/M Com/ MA (Economics)/ BA (Economics)/ MBA/BBA/BBM/ MCA/BCA/ BSC(IT)/B.Tech/ BE (any discipline including civil Engineering)/B. Architecture/ ICWA/Chartered Accountancy/A graduate degree with Post graduate/ Degree in Materials Management with minimum 60% aggregate marks from a recognized university.

SSC Executive General Service	Men	19½ – 25	BE/B.Tech (Any Discipline) with 60% marks
SSC Hydrography	Men	19½ – 25	BSc/MSc with Physics & Maths with min 55% marks. BE/BTech in any discipline with min 55% marks. B.Sc. (Physics & Maths) holding NCC Naval Wing 'C' Certificate. Graduate/Post Graduate in Op Research/Quantitative Methods with min 75% marks. Graduate/Post Graduate in Maths with Stats or Probability with min 75% marks.
SSC -ATC	Men & Women	19½ – 25	Ist Class Science Graduate with Physics/Maths/Electronics or MSc with Physics/Maths/Electronics with min 55% marks.
SSC Law Cadre	Men & Women	22 – 27	A Degree in Law qualifying for enrolment as an Advocate under the Advocates Act 1961 with min 55% marks

SSC Logistics Cadre	Men & Women	19½ – 25	1st Class Degree in BA (Economics), BCom, BSc (IT), CA/ICWA, Catering Technology or BCA/MCA, or BE/B.Tech in Mechanical, Marine, Electrical, Electronics, Civil, Computers, IT, Architecture or Graduate with PG Diploma in Material Management.
SSC Pilot	Men	19 – 23	BE/ B.Tech in any discipline with minimum 60% marks from a recognized University/Institution with Maths & Physics at 10+2 level.
SSC Observer	Men & Women	19 – 23	BE/ B.Tech in any discipline with minimum 60% marks from a recognized University/Institution with Maths & Physics at 10+2 level.
SSC Naval Armament Inspection cadre	Men	19½ – 25	A degree in Electronics/Elect/Mech Engg or Post Graduate degree in Electronics or Physics

SSC Information Technology	Men	19½ - 25	BE/B.Tech in Computer Science/Computer Engineering/ IT or BSc (IT), BCA, MCA, MSc (Computer), M.Tech (Computer Science) with minimum 50% marks

B. Engineering

a. Engineering General Service Officer

Modern ships, submarines and aircraft are fitted with advanced technology machinery and propulsion systems. As an Engineer Officer, the candidate will be responsible for keeping all these Hi-tech systems serviceable. Opportunities exist to work in gigantic naval dockyards and indigenous production units. In no other career is an engineer exposed to such a wide spectrum of opportunities and to keep abreast of modern developments. An Engineer Officer's career is interspersed with technical courses up to post graduation level in India/abroad.

b. Submarine Engineer Officer

The submarines are hi-tech war machines having awesome firepower, state of the art weapon control system, computer controlled machinery and high standard of habitability. Modern submarines have hi tech engineering equipment as well as the propulsion system. As submarine Engineer officer, you will be responsible for keeping these systems serviceable. Submarine Engineer officer could also get opportunities to work in Naval Dockyards and submarine building units. On successful of the rigorous training conducted at different training establishments, Submarine Engineering officer will be proud processor of "Dolphin Badge" and become a member of a very elite arm of the Navy.

c. Naval Construction Officer

One can also join in the Naval Architecture Cadre of the Engineering Branch. The Indian Navy today employs the largest pool of trained Naval Architects in India. A Naval Architect is involved in design, construction, quality control, repair and new construction work of naval vessels. With the Navy going for more and more sophisticated warship production within the country, the Corps of Naval Architects offer excellent opportunities to keep abreast of the advancement in ship building technology.

Type of Entry	Unmarried Men/ Women	Age Limit	Educational Qualification
Cadet Entry (NDA)	Men	16½ – 19	10+2 or equivalent with Physics & Maths
10+2 (B.Tech) Cadet Entry	Men	16½ – 19	10+2 or equivalent with Physics, Chemistry & Maths (minimum 70% marks in aggregate of PCM, minimum 50% marks in English either in 10th or 12th class
University Entry Scheme (SSC)	Men	19.5 – 25 (Pre-Final year) 19 – 24 (Final year)	Final Year and Pre-final year students of Mechanical, Marine, Aeronautical/Aerospace, B. Architecture, Automobile, Civil engineering, Naval Architecture, Industrial & Production, Metallurgy, Electrical, Instrumentation & Communication, Telecommunication, Power Electronics, Instrumentation, Mechatronics, Control Engg with minimum 60% up to VIth Semester and IVth Semester.

Short Service Commission (GS)	Men	19 – 25	BE/B.Tech in any discipline with minimum 60%.
Short Service Commission (Submarine-Engineering)	Men	19.5½ – 25	BE/B.Tech in Mechanical with minimum 60% marks.
ENGINEERING BRANCH (NAVAL ARCHITECTS)			
10+2 (B.Tech) Cadet Entry	Men	16½ – 19	10+2 or equivalent with Physics, Chemistry & Maths (minimum 70% marks in aggregate of PCM, minimum 50% marks in English either in 10th or 12th class)
Short Service Commission Entry	Men & Women*	21 – 25	BE/B.Tech in Naval Architecture/Mech/Civil/ Aeronautics/Metallurgical/ Aerospace Engg with 60% marks.
University Entry Scheme (SSC)	Men & Women*	19 – 24	BE/B.Tech in Naval Architecture/Mech/ Civil/ Aeronautical/ Metallurgical/Aerospace Engg/B.Arch with 60% marks
Special Naval Architect Entry Scheme (SNAES)	Men & Women*	21 – 25	BE/B.Tech in Naval Architecture with 60% marks (campus recruitment).

C. Electrical

a. General Service

A warship is a mini floating city with an integral power generation and distribution system. In addition, complex missile systems, underwater weapons, radar and radio communication equipment form major part of a warship's equipment. A majority of these are either computer-based or computer aided and incorporate the latest trends in electronics engineering. For a ship to be able to fight effectively, all these equipment must be kept working at peak efficiency. Electrical Officers have this responsibility and other challenging tasks. To sharpen their skills, the Navy offers excellent opportunities for post-graduate courses in India/abroad to deserving candidates. Officers of the Engineering and Electrical Branches can also volunteer for the Aviation/Submarine Arm.

b. Submarine Electrical Officer

The submarines are hi-tech war machines have awesome fire power, state of the art weapon control system, computer controlled machinery and high standard of habitability. Submarine Electrical Officer will deal with computer based or computer aided weapon systems, missile system, underwater weapons, radars and radio communication equipment and ensure that all these sensitive and complex equipment are kept operational at peak efficiency. On successful completion of the rigorous training conducted at different training establishments, Submarine Electrical Officer will be proud processor of "Dolphin Badge" and become member of a very elite arm of the Navy.

Type of Entry	Unmarried Men/ Women	Age Limit	Educational Qualification
Cadet Entry (NDA)	Men	16½ – 19	10+2 or equivalent with Physics & Maths
10+2 (B.Tech) Cadet Entry	Men	16½ – 19	10+2 or equivalent with Physics, Chemistry and Maths (minimum 70% marks in aggregate of PCM, minimum 50% marks in English either in 10th or 12th class)

University Entry Scheme (SSC)	Men	19.5 – 25(Pre-Final year) 19 – 24(Final year)	Final Year and Pre-final year students of Electrical, Electronics, Power Engg, Instrumentation and Control, Electronics & Instrumentation, Electronics & Communication, Instrumentation and Control, Control System, Power Electronics, Computer Science Engg, Instrumentation, with minimum 60% up to VIth Semester.
Short Service Commission (GS)	Men	19.5½ – 25	BE/B.Tech in any discipline with minimum 60%.
Short Service Commission (Submarine)	Men	19½ – 25	BE/BTech in Electrical/Electronics/ Control Engg/ Telecommunication Engg with 60% marks.

For the details of recruitment for various posts in Indian Navy, candidates are advised to visit www.nausenabharti.nic.in.

3. **Indian Air Force (www.careerairforce.nic.in)**

Rank Insignia

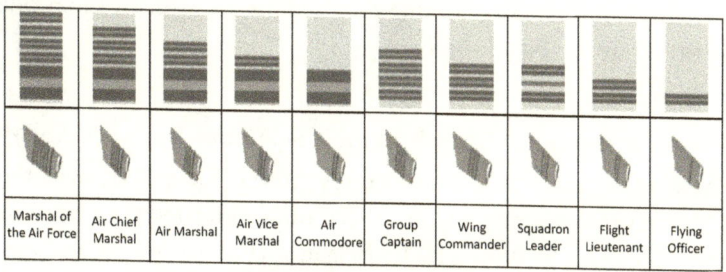

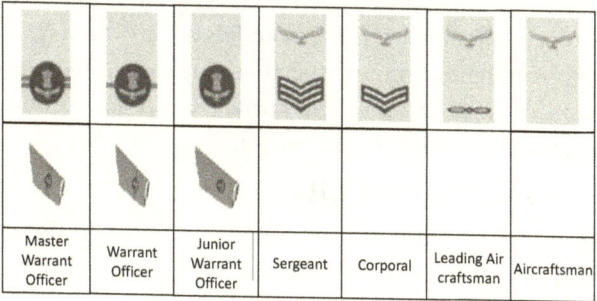

There are two types of selection:

A. Type I In this category the candidates are selected in the following three ways:

1. NDA and CDSE exam conducted by the UPSC

2. AFCAT – Air Force Common Admission Test conducted by the Indian Air Force twice a year for all entries other than the exam conducted by UPSC

Candidates who have successfully cleared Step 1, will receive a Call letter to report to any one of the Air Force Selection Boards located at Dehradun, Varanasi, Gandhinagar and Mysore. At the Air Force Selection Board (AFSB), tests are conducted to ascertain the suitability as an Officer in the Indian Air Force.

After recommendation by the Selection Board, the candidates are sent for the medical examination either at Air Force Central Medical Establishment (AFCME), New Delhi or Institute of Aviation Medicine, Bengaluru.

An All India Merit List is compiled on the basis of the performance in the written test and AFSB interview, subject to being medically fit. Based on the vacancies available in various branches/sub branches, joining instructions are issued to join one of the Training establishments.

B. Type II

Selection through Central Airmen Selection Board (CASB)

There are Airmen Selection Centres (ASCs) located all over the country. On enrolment at the ASCs, the candidates are routed to Basic Training Institute (BTI), Belgaum (Karnataka) to undergo Joint Basic Phase Training (JBPT) for a period of 12 weeks. On successful completion of JBPT, candidates are allocated trades and sent for trade training of specified duration. After successful completion of trade training, the airmen are deployed on ground based jobs as per their allotted trades.

SELECTION PROCEDURE

The selection as an Airman in the IAF is conducted through All India Selection Tests and Recruitment Rallies. All India Selection Tests are conducted at the Airmen Selection Centres (ASCs) located all over India as per schedule, whereas the Recruitment Rallies are conducted from time to time in selected areas/regions of particular States/Union Territories of the country.

(a) All India Selection Tests (STs): Advertisements are published in *Employment News/Rozgar Samachar* inviting the applications for All India Selection Tests (STs). In response to the advertisement, eligible male Indian citizens (including the citizens of Nepal) are to forward application to the President, Central Airmen Selection Board, Post Box No. 11807, New Delhi 110 010. The Board sends admit cards to eligible and short-listed candidates to appear in the Selection Tests.

(b) Recruitment Rallies: Advertisements for Rallies are published with the details of eligibility conditions, selection programme and rally venue in popular local/regional newspapers circulated in the region/area of the rally. For rally recruitment, eligible candidates are to report to the rally venue with the requisite documents. These documents will be scrutinized and verified by the Testing Team.

AIRMEN SELECTION CENTRES

1. Airmen Selection Centre 48, Mansfield Road, Ambala Cantt - 133 001 Tele: 0171-2630048 Email: coascamb@dataone.in	8. Airmen Selection Centre, Air Force Station, Tambaram Chennai - 600 046 Tele: 044-22396565 (Extn No. 7833) 044-22390561 (Direct), 09445299128 (Mobile) Email: ascafstam@dataone.in
2. Airmen Selection Centre Race Course Camp New Delhi - 110 003 Tele: 011-23010231 Extn. 7652 Email: 2asc@bol.net.in	9. Airmen Selection Centre, Near Rajadhani College Baramunda, Bhubaneswar - 751003 Tele: 0674-2561336 Email: no9asc@yahoo.co.in
3. Airmen Selection centre Air Force Station, Chakeri, Kanpur - 208 008 Tele: 0512-2451730 Extn. 4603 Email: co3asc@yahoo.com	10. Airmen Selection Centre, Air Force Station Bihta, Patna Bihar - 801 103 Tele: 06115-250002, 03, 04, 05, 06 & 07 Extn. 4340 Email: co10asc@gmail.in
4. Airmen Selection Centre (Near Palta Gate) Air Force Station Barrackpore, West Bengal - 743 122 Tele: 033-25450895 (Direct) 033-25921251 Extn. 6391 Email: co4asc@yahoo.co.in	11. Airmen Selection Centre Borjhar Guwahati - 781 015 Tele: 0361-2842720 Extn. 333 0361-2843385 Email: elevenasc@rediffmail.com
5. Airmen Selection Centre Old Pali Road Jodhpur - 342 011 Tele: 0291-2511516 Extn. 2110 Email: co5asc@yahoo.co.in	12. Airmen Selection Centre Air Force Station, Bowenpally Secunderabad - 500 011 Tele: 040-27753500 Extn: 467 Email: co12asc@yahoo.com
6. Airmen Selection Centre Air Force Station, Cotton Green, Mumbai - 400 033 Tele: 022-23714982 Extn. 251 Email: co6asc@rediffmail.com	13. Airmen Selection Centre VII/302-B, Vayu Sena Road, Kakkanad, Kochi - 682 030 Tele: 0484-2427010 Email: co14asc@rediffmail.com

7. Airmen Selection Centre No. 1 Cubbon Road, Bangalore - 560 001 Tele: 080-25592199 Email: co7asc@dataone.in	14. Airmen Selection Centre IInd Floor, Phase-II, Rajiv Gandhi Parisar, 35 Shyamala Hills, Bhopal - 462 002 Tele: 0755 - 2661955 Email: 15ascbhopal@gmail.com

SELECTION PROCEDURE

The selection as an Airman in the IAF is conducted through All India Selection Tests and Recruitment Rallies. All India Selection Tests are conducted at the Airmen Selection Centres (ASCs) located all over India as per schedule, whereas the Recruitment Rallies are conducted from time to time in selected areas/regions of particular States/Union Territories of the country.

(a) **All India Selection Tests (STs):** Advertisements are published in Employment News/Rozgar Samachar inviting the applications for All India Selection Tests (STs). In response to the advertisement, eligible male Indian Citizens (including the citizens of Nepal) are to forward application to the President, Central Airmen Selection Board, Post Box No. 11807, New Delhi, 110 010. The Board sends admit cards to eligible and short-listed candidates to appear in the Selection Tests.

(b) **Recruitment Rallies:** Advertisements for Rallies are published with the details of eligibility conditions, selection programme and rally venue in popular local/regional newspapers circulated in the region/area of the rally. For rally recruitment, eligible candidates are to report to the rally venue with the requisite documents. These documents will be scrutinized and verified by the Testing Team.

CHAPTER 4

JOBS IN PUBLIC SECTOR BANKS

Sector Banking Sector is one of the prominent domains of highly paid job opportunities in the government. Reserve Bank of India acts as the Central Bank dealing with monetary policy in the country. It recruits officers and staff through Reserve Bank of India Service Board. The State Bank of India and its five Associate Banks recruit officers and staff through Probationary Officers Examination and Clerk Examination. Besides, there are 26 Public Sector Banks in India, National Bank of Agriculture and Rural Development (NABARD), Cooperative Banks, Land Development Banks etc. This chapter provides information about the different recruitment procedures in Reserve Bank of India, State Bank of India, other Public sector banks, NABARD, Co-operative banks etc. along with the eligibility conditions and exam patter. It also provides a brief of the agencies which does recruitment for specified banks or group of banks. Most importantly strategy for preparation of the Competitive Examinations is provided for general guidance of the job seekers.

There are two types of banks in any country. One is the Central Bank which implements the monetary policy of the Government and acts as the "Bankers Bank". The others are commercial banks which provide banking services to its customers. The Reserve Bank of India (RBI) is the central bank of the country. The Reserve Bank of India (RBI) was set up on the basis of the recommendations of the Hilton Young Commission. The Reserve Bank of India Act, 1934 (II of 1934) provides the statutory basis of the functioning of the Bank, which commenced operations on April 1, 1935. Unlike other banks, RBI does not provide banking services to the customers. But, it regulates the monetary policy of the country. It also provides banking services to the bank.

Seniority levels of RBI Officers are divided into Groups (A to F). Group 'A' is junior-most while Group 'F' is the senior-most level like Deputy-Governor, Governor. All these officers collectively are called as Class-I employees. Apart from these employees RBI also has a large number of Class-III and Class-IV employees who work as service staff and other subordinate levels. There is no Class-II level in RBI. Every year, direct recruitment of Officers is carried out at Group 'A' & 'B' levels and at Group 'C' & 'D' levels for experienced people. While Group 'A', 'C' & 'D' recruitment is nominal, there are frequent recruitments of college graduates and postgraduates for Group 'B' level through examinations conducted by Reserve Bank of India Services Board (RBISB).

A. RESERVE BANK OF INDIA SERVICES BOARD (WWW.RBI.GOV.IN)

The RBISB issues notifications from time to time for the recruitment of following ten posts:

1. Research Officer in Grade B for Department of Economic and Policy Research
2. Research Officer in Grade B for the Department of Statistics and Information Management
3. Officer in Grade B DR General

4. Manager (Technical-Civil) in Grade B
5. Manager (Technical-Electrical) in Grade B
6. Assistant Manager (Technical-Electrical) in Grade A
7. Assistant Manager (Technical-Civil) in Grade A
8. Assistant Manager (Security) in Grade A
9. Assistant Manager (Rajbhasha) in Grade A
10. Assistants (Clerk)

The most common of them is the recruitment for Grade B Officers. Graduates between the age of 21 to 30 years are eligible to apply.

Scheme of Selection for Grade B Officers:

- Selection is done through Examinations and Interview.
- Examinations are held in two phases :

(I) Phase-I ON-LINE Examination (Objective Type): This paper approximately of 3 hours duration for 200 marks. The paper consists of following tests:

(i) General Awareness

(ii) English Language

(iii) Quantitative Aptitude and

(iv) Reasoning

(II) Phase-II Written Examination (Descriptive Type): The Phase-II Written examination (WE) is conducted only for those candidates who are shortlisted for the same. The Examination consists of three Descriptive Type papers –

(i) Paper I – English

(ii) Paper II – Economic and Social Issues and

(iii) Paper III – Finance and Management

Each of these papers is for 3 hours duration carrying 100 marks.

For the details of pattern of examination of other posts recruited in the RBI, it is advised to refer the notification published on the website **www.rbi.org**.

B. STATE BANK OF INDIA AND ITS ASSOCIATE BANKS

State Bank of India (SBI) is the largest commercial bank in India in terms of assets, deposits, profits, branches, customers and employees. The Government of India is the single largest shareholder of this Fortune 500 entity with 61.58% ownership.

The origins of State Bank of India date back to 1806 when the Bank of Calcutta (later called the Bank of Bengal) was established. In 1921, the Bank of Bengal and two other banks (Bank of Madras and Bank of Bombay) were amalgamated to form the Imperial Bank of India. In 1955, the Reserve Bank of India acquired the controlling interests of the Imperial Bank of India and SBI was created by an act of Parliament to succeed the Imperial Bank of India.

Recruitment for SBI as well as the five Associate banks of SBI is done by the Central Recruitment and Promotion Department of the SBI located at Mumbai. The five Associate Banks of SBI are:-

(1) SBBJ : State Bank of Bikaner and Jaipur

(2) SBH : State Bank of Hyderabad

(3) SBM : State Bank of Mysore

(4) SBP : State Bank of Patiala

(5) SBT : State Bank of Travancore

From time to time State Bank of India issues notification for the recruitment of Probationary Officers and Clerks.

1. Syllabus for Probationary Officers Exam

Objective type paper-I - 200 Marks

(A) English Language

(B) Reasoning

(C) General Awareness

(D) Data analysis and interpretation

Paper II- DESCRIPTIVE SECTION – 50 Marks

Letter Writing, Paragraph Writing, Essay Writing, Precis Writing, Reading Comprehension

Interview

2. SBI Clerk Examination

10 + 2 passed candidates from 18 to 26 years can apply for the post.

Each section contains 40 questions for 40 marks. So the total marks for Clerk exam is 200. There is negative marking for each wrong answer. It is always better to prepare intensively and attempt limited questions with correct answer to get a call for next round i.e. Interview.

1. General awareness
2. Quantitative Aptitude
3. Reasoning Ability
4. General English language
5. Computer knowledge/marketing aptitude

Recruitment for other Public Sector Banks

Public sector banks are banks where the majority stakes are held by the Government and the shares are listed on the stock exchange. There are about 79 scheduled commercial banks out of which 26 are public sector banks. RBI is expected to issue more banking licenses to private sector players by 2015. The following are the list of public sector banks:

1. Allahabad Bank (www.allahabadbank.in)
2. Andhra Bank (www.andhrabank.in)
3. Bank of Baroda (www.bankofbaroda.com)
4. Bank of India (www.bankofindia.com)
5. Bank of Maharashtra (www.bankofmaharashtra.in)
6. Canara Bank (www.canarabank.com)
7. Central Bank of India (www.centralbankofindia.co.in)
8. Corporation Bank (www.corpbank.com)
9. Dena Bank (www.denabank.com)
10. IDBI Bank Limited (www.idbi.com)
11. Indian Bank (www.indianbank.in)
12. Indian Overseas Bank (www.iob.in)
13. Oriental Bank of Commerce (www.obcindia.co.in)

14. Punjab & Sind Bank (www.psbindia.com)
15. Punjab National Bank (www.pnbindia.com)
16. State Bank of India (www.statebankofindia.com)
17. Syndicate Bank (www.syndicatebank.in)
18. UCO Bank (www.ucobank.com)
19. Union Bank of India (www.unionbankofindia.co.in)
20. United Bank of India (www.unitedbankofindia.com)
21. Vijaya Bank (www.vijayabank.com)
22. State Bank of Bikaner & Jaipur (www.sbbjbank.com)
23. State Bank of Hyderabad (www.sbhyd.com)
24. State Bank of Mysore (www.statebankofmysore.co.in)
25. State Bank of Patiala (www.sbp.co.in)
26. State Bank of Travancore (www.statebankoftravancore.com)

Public sector banks in India recruit at entry level through a selection process. The advertisements for recruitment are published in the newspapers as well as *Employment News*. The details of the notification can also be accessed on the website of the respective recruiting agency. The recruitment to Reserve Bank of India is done by Reserve Bank of India Services Board.

State Bank of India and its associates conduct written test and interview separately for their recruitment of the clerical cadre and PO posts through the Central Recruitment and promotion department of SBI. Regional rural banks (RRBs) also conduct their recruitment through a test conducted by IBPS.

Recruitment for NABARD is being done by their respective services boards.

A total of 19 public sector banks have come together to participate in the Common Written Exam (CWE) conducted by Institute of Banking Personnel Selection (IBPS). Banks use CWE scores to shortlist candidates for Clerical cadre, Probationary officers (PO) and Specialist officers. Shortlisted candidates are called for group discussion and personal interviews and the final selection is done on the basis of the combined scores of both the stages.

Graduate in any stream can appear for these tests. The test is objective type with questions on reasoning, English language, numerical ability, general awareness and computer knowledge.

Private sector banks have their own aptitude tests and interview process to recruit at the entry level. Most of the banks have their in-house training programs to up-skill the employees. These trainings can be supplemented with exams like JAIIB and CAIIB conducted by Indian Institute of Banking and Finance (IIBF). These objective type exams also help in career advancement from the officer level to the management level.

C. INSTITUTE OF BANKING PERSONNEL SELECTION (WWW.IBPS.IN)

Institute of Banking Personnel Selection (IBPS) is an autonomous agency in India, which started its operation in 1975 as Personnel Selection Services (PSS). In 1984, IBPS became an independent entity at the behest of Reserve Bank of India (RBI) and Public Sector Banks. IBPS is envisioned as a self-governed academic and research oriented institute, with a mission of enhancing human-resource development through personnel assessment. In 2011, IBPS announced a common written examination (CWE) for the selection Officers and Clerks in Indian banks. IBPS CWE is now mandatory for anyone who seeks an employment in 20 public sector and Regional Rural banks except State Bank of India and its Associate Banks. IBPS periodically accepts the exam applications from the candidates at their website www.ibps.in, and the exams are organized at various locations in the country either in online or offline mode.

The Governing Board consists of nominees from Reserve Bank of India, Ministry of Finance Government of India, National Institute of Bank Management, representatives of Public Sector Banks, Insurance sector and academics. The matters related to policy and affairs of the Institute are vested in the Governing Board. The other representatives are from Allahabad Bank, Andhra Bank, Bank of Baroda, Bank of India, Bank of Maharashtra, Bharatiya Mahila Bank, Canara Bank, Central Bank of India, Corporation Bank, Dena Bank, Indian Bank, Indian Overseas Bank, Oriental Bank of Commerce, Punjab National Bank, Punjab & Sind Bank, Syndicate Bank, Union Bank of India, United Bank of India, UCO Bank, Vijaya Bank, IDBI Bank and Export Credit Guarantee Corporation of India Bank. IBPS also does recruitment for the Regional Rural Banks through a separate exam.

IBPS conducts the following examination:

1. **Common Written Exam (CWE) for Probationary Officers/Management Trainee** This is a common exam for the recruitment for the post of Probationary Officers/Management Trainees in the participant member Banks. The successful candidates are initially posted as Probationary Officer or Management Trainee and can reach to higher management ranks on the basis of their performance.
2. **Common Written Exam (CWE) for Specialist Officers** There are several posts like IT Officer, Agricultural Field Officer, Rajbhasha Adhikari, Law Officer, Human Resource/Personnel Officer etc in banks. The recruitment to these posts is done through a separate exam conducted by IBPS for the participant banks.
3. **Common Written Exam (CWE) for Clerks** The clerical posts in banks are filled through a separate exam conducted by IBPS for its participant banks

Exam pattern and marks distribution for IBPS exams are listed below:

Name of the Subject	No. of Questions			Maximum Marks		
	PO	Clerk	Specialist Officer	PO	Clerk	Specialist Officer
Reasoning	50	40	50	50	40	50
English Language	50	40	40	50	40	40
Quantitative Aptitude	50	-	40	50	-	50
General Awareness (Mostly about Banking)	50	40	50	50	40	50

Computer Knowledge	50	40	40		50	40	20
Numerical Ability	-	40	40		-	40	40
Hindi (optional for Specialist Officer)	-	-	40		-	-	40
Total	250	200	200		250	200	200

D. NATIONAL BANK FOR AGRICULTURE AND RURAL DEVELOPMENT (NABARD)

NABARD was set up in 1982 as an apex development bank to focus on facilitating credit flow for the promotion of agriculture, small scale industries, cottage & village industries, handicrafts and other rural crafts. The recruitment for the NABARD is done by NABARD Services Board through special recruitment notification as per the vacancy available. It conducts entrance tests for the post of:

1. Manager Grade B
2. Assistant Manager Grade A
3. Clerk

E. CO-OPERATIVE BANKS

Co-operative banks have been formed to provide financial services to the members of the bank itself who are owners as well as customers. The aim is not to maximize profits but to provide banking services, loans etc. to the members. The co-operative banking structure in India is divided into following main categories:

1. **Primary Urban Co-op Banks/Primary Agricultural Credit Societies:**

   The Primary Co-operative Credit Society is an association of borrowers and non-borrowers residing in a particular locality. The funds of the society are derived from the share capital and deposits of members and loans from central co-operative banks. The borrowing powers of the members as well as of the society are fixed. The loans are given to members for the purchase of cattle, fodder, fertilizers, pesticides, implements, etc.

2. **District Central Co-op Banks**

   These are the federations of primary credit societies in a district and are of two types – those having a membership of primary societies only and those having a membership of societies as well as individuals. The funds of the bank consist of share capital, deposits, loans and overdrafts from state co-operative banks and joint stocks. These banks finance member societies within the limits of the borrowing capacity of societies. They also conduct all the business of a joint stock bank.

3. **State Co-operative Banks**

   The state co-operative bank is a federation of central co-operative bank and acts as a watchdog of the co-operative banking structure in the state. Its funds are obtained from share capital, deposits, loans and overdrafts from the Reserve Bank of India. The state co-operative banks lend money to central co-operative banks and primary societies and not directly to farmers.

4. **Land Development Banks**

   The land development banks are organized in three tiers viz. state, central and primary level and they meet the long term credit requirements of the farmers for developmental purposes. The state land development bank oversees the primary land development banks situated in the districts and tehsils in the state. They are governed both by the state government and Reserve Bank of India. Recently, the supervision of land development banks has been assumed by National Bank for Agriculture and Rural Development (NABARD). The sources of funds for these banks are the debentures subscribed by both central and state government. These banks do not accept deposits from the general public.

Co-operative banks also issue vacancy notifications for the recruitment under various cadres like Manager, Assistant Manager,

Clerks etc. There is no centralized procedure for recruitment and different banks conduct their own examination. Some co-operative banks also conduct recruitment through IBPS.

Note:

Candidates are advised to visit the website of the respective recruiting organizations to access the details of the eligibility and the pattern of examinations.

F. STRATEGY FOR PREPARATION

Note: Please do follow WWW: Win-Win-Win Core Strategy given for UPSC Indian Civil Services Examination for important tips and guidance with necessary modification in approach and methodology, depending on the specificity of a particular competitive examination.

Most of the examinations conducted for recruitment in banks have objective type multiple choice questions. This type of examinations have a common pattern of question papers and a distinct area of testing viz. Maths, Reasoning, English and General Awareness. The main focus of the candidates should be to get the maximum score within the stipulated time. It is a better strategy to avoid questions where the candidates are not certain if there is negative marking for wrong answers. This can be achieved with exhaustive coverage of syllabus with focused preparation and consistent practice of test papers in a strict examination environment. Developing shortcuts and formula for numerical testing and reasoning can be very handy for this type of exam as more questions can be solved in less time. Correctness of answers and time management to complete the paper become crucial factor for good score. The strategy can be framed stage-wise:

Initial Strategy

At the beginning of preparation of bank exam focus should be on the basics. One has to understand the basic concepts as ignoring the fundamentals may adversely affect the preparation at later stage. It is better to understand the basic concepts of Mathematics, Logical Reasoning, Grammar etc. For maths go through the basics of percentage, profit and loss, interest rates averages, mensurations, Geometry, Number System, Ratio Proportion and the other mathematical domains. But the most important part is that it should be frequently revised at proper intervals using latest sample papers. For reasoning, think about the puzzles and develop an interest in solving the same. Start playing Sudoku, solve classic puzzles found in different books like relationship puzzles, number arrangement etc. This will develop and sharpen the analytical skills and train the mind in the right perspective.

For English section go through the grammar books and make a habit of reading English newspapers, magazines and practice writing and solving earlier papers. Continue practicing with standard text books for the purpose till one achieves competency. Try to find out the common grammatical errors people commit during writing or speaking. This will help to solve the common error questions asked in the English section of exam. Also read as much English as possible to improve the vocabulary by collecting word meanings, their antonyms, synonyms and also try to understand the sentence pattern used in the modern English. All these exercise will help in the final preparation.

Intermediate Strategy

Understand the type of questions asked in the bank recruitment exams. List the subjects that study to solve the questions. Prepare a list of topics that has to be covered, divide the list on the basis of number of questions asked from that topic in the previous years, make a time schedule and follow this schedule strictly to complete the topics. Solve old question papers regularly to track the progress and gain confidence.

Final Strategy

Focus on consistent and continuous practice to boost up speed with accuracy. Practice as much as possible by solving sample question papers or old question papers asked in the various bank examinations to manage time. Learn from old mistakes and refine the strategy. Remember main hurdle for success in bank exam is not the difficulty level of question but the time available to solve these questions.

G. SOURCES OF STUDY MATERIAL

There are number of books available for practicing likely questions and solved earlier papers for gaining familiarity and experience in solving problems. Books like *Quantitative Aptitude* by R.S. Agarwal, *Modern Approach to Reasoning* by R.S. Agarwal are handy in understanding the basics. For English, any grammar book would solve the purpose. There are several books available in the market for specialized bank exams and candidates can select the books on the basis of their own preference. Apart from the books there are several websites which offer free study material and practice tests. Candidates can enroll on such websites to avail the various updates on recruitment notification as well. There are certain websites like www.bankexamguide.com, www.bankexampreparation.com, www.bankexam.com etc. which host several study material for preparation and test papers. They also give updated information about latest notifications and results of exams conducted.

CHAPTER 5

JOB OPPORTUNITIES IN THE STATES

India has 29 States and 7 Union Territories after carving out 2 states Telangana and Seemandhra from existing Andhra Pradesh in 2014. There are large numbers of recruitments for filling up vacancies in top, medium and lowest level of the bureaucracy in the States too. As the volume of information is huge of all the states, this section cites a few important websites and details in respect of most of the states. Candidates are advised to visit websites for periodical updates on different examinations conducted by the respective Public Service Commission of the states.

The Chapter covers most essential aspects of job opportunities in all the 29 states, but not in detail more as illustration to guide the candidates. There is no substitute for visiting the websites of the states the job seeker is interested on the lines suggested there in the chapter. The recruitment procedures in the States of Kerala, Maharashtra, Rajasthan and Delhi are discussed more in detail as these states have certain additional features which may help the job seekers with relevant background, general understanding and tips for focused preparation for state services competitive examinations. WWW: Win-Win-Win Core Strategy and tips given for UPSC Indian Civil Services, Staff Selection Examination and Banks Clerical and Probationary Officers' Examination may be understood to formulate state' examination specific customized preparation strategy as most of the tips are applicable with required modifications and a few additions depending on the examination.

India has 29 states and 7 Union Territories. Each State has its own recruitment procedure to fill the various vacancies of the State cadre. Similar to UPSC there are State Public Service Commissions. The Public Service Commission is a body created by the Constitution of India. The provisions relating to the Union Public Service Commission at the Centre and other State Public Service Commissions have been laid down in Chapter II of part XIV of the Constitution. The provisions in the Constitution from Article 315 to 323 ensure the competence of the Commission to deal with the matters relating to the services and enable them to discharge their duties in a fair and impartial manner, free from influence from any quarter. Mostly recruitment to the State cadre is done through the Public Commission of the state. Some of the states have Group A services corresponding to that of the central Group A services. Some of the states have their own State Staff Selection Commission for the recruitment to Group B, C and Group D staff. Some recruitment is also done by the authorized departments in some states.

The recruitment notifications for the state cadres are published in the local newspapers of the respective states, *Employment News* and the websites of the respective State Public Service Commission.

The exam pattern for the State Civil Services is more or less similar to Civil Service Exam conducted by the UPSC except that more emphasis is given on regional topics and language.

The recruitment procedures are discussed to give an insight about recruitments in the various states:

1. KERALA

The recruitment for the various departments of Kerala Government is done by Kerala Public Service Commission (KPSC). The commission advises the government on all matters relating to civil services. KPSC publishes notifications inviting applications for selection to various posts as per the requisitions of the appointing authorities and conduct written tests, practical tests, interviews etc.

KPSC introduced a new feature in 2012 and is available on its website. As per the new feature those who are regularly applying for the examinations can do a "one time registration" with KPSC. This feature simplifies the application process. Those who are registered by uploading their photo and signature need not upload the same for every examination. The candidates can download the admit card directly from the website after the registration for every examination in which they want to appear.

The other specialty of examinations conducted by Kerala PSC is that the question papers for almost all the examinations have a similar pattern. The question papers are of objective type (OMR sheet) with 100 questions and the time allotted is 75 minutes. Only the syllabus varies for different examinations. KPSC publishes the exam schedule for every month for various posts on the basis of the vacancy available. Some of the posts are filled through direct recruitment and some filled through promotion of the existing staff. The final selection is done on the basis of the performance of the candidate in the interview.

KPSC issues the monthly time table along with the syllabus for the recruitment examinations for different posts based on the available vacancy. Candidates can refer to the website **www.keralapsc.gov.in** and **www.keralagov.in** to access the various details.

A list of some of the posts recruited by Kerala PSC is as follows:-

1. Public Relations Officer

Syllabus: An Objective Type Test (OMR Valuation) based on the qualification prescribed for the post.

Main Topics:-

Part I Questions based on Qualification prescribed for the post.

Part II General Knowledge, Current Affairs & Renaissance in Kerala

(Maximum Marks: 100)

(Duration: 1 hour 15 minutes)

(Medium of Questions: English)

2. Demonstrator in Tool and Die Engineering Technical Education

Syllabus: An Objective Type Test (OMR Valuation) based on the qualification prescribed for the post.

Main Topics:-

Part I General Knowledge, Current Affairs & Renaissance in Kerala

Part II (a) Physics (b) Chemistry

Part III Questions based on Diploma in Tool and Die Engineering or Technology.

(Maximum Marks: 100)

(Duration: 1 hour 15 minutes)

(Medium of Questions: English)

3. Junior Assistant Foam Mattings (India) Limited

Syllabus: An Objective Type Test (OMR Valuation) based on the qualification prescribed for the post.

Main Topics:-

Part I General Knowledge, Current Affairs & Renaissance in Kerala

Part II General English

Part III Questions based on Certificate course in MS Office and DTP (English & Malayalam)

(Maximum Marks: 100)

(Duration: 1 hour 15 minutes)

(Medium of Questions: English)

4. Village Extension Officer Grade II Rural Development

Syllabus: An Objective Type Test (OMR Valuation) based on the qualification prescribed for the post.

Main Topics:-

Part I Simple Arithmetic & Mental Ability

Part II General Knowledge and Current Affairs

Part III General English

Part IV Regional Language

(Malayalam/Tamil/Kannada)
(Maximum Marks: 100)
(Duration: 1 hour 15 minutes)
(Medium of Questions: Malayalam/Tamil/Kannada)

5. Technician Grade-II (Electronics)
Kerala Co-Operative Milk Marketing Federation Ltd.
Syllabus: An Objective Type Test (OMR Valuation) based on the qualification prescribed for the post.
(Maximum Marks: 100)
(Duration: 1 hour 15 minutes)
(Medium of Questions: English)

6. Junior Instructor Mechanic Industrial Electronics Industrial Training
Syllabus: An Objective Type Test (OMR Valuation) based on the qualification prescribed for the post
Main Topics:-
Part I Questions based on the Technical qualification
Part II General Knowledge, Current Affairs & Renaissance in Kerala
(Maximum Marks: 100)
(Duration: 1 hour 15 minutes)
(Medium of Questions: English)

Pharma Chemist Animal Husbandry
Syllabus: An Objective Type Test (OMR Valuation) based on the qualification prescribed for the post.
Main Topics:-
Part I Questions based on the qualification i.e., B.Pharm.
Part II General Knowledge, Current Affairs & Renaissance in Kerala
(Maximum Marks: 100)
(Duration: 1 hour 15 minutes)
(Medium of Questions: English)

8. Junior Instructor Front Office Assistant Industrial Training

Syllabus: An Objective Type Test (OMR Valuation) based on the qualification prescribed for the post.

Main Topics:-

Part I Questions based on the technical qualification

Part II General Knowledge, Current Affairs & Renaissance in Kerala

(Maximum Marks: 100)

(Duration: 1 hour 15 minutes)

(Medium of Questions: English)

9. Kerala Khadi Development Officer And Village Industries Board

Syllabus: An Objective Type Test (OMR Valuation) based on Diploma in Textile Technology.

(Maximum Marks: 100)

(Duration: 1 hour 15 minutes)

(Medium of Questions: English)

10. Process Server/Duffedar/Court Keeper Judicial

An Objective Type Test (OMR Valuation) based on the qualification prescribed for the post

Main Topics:-

Part I General Knowledge, Current Affairs, Facts about India & Facts about Kerala

Part II (a) Physical Science (b) Natural Science

Part III Simple Arithmetic

(Maximum Marks: 100)

(Duration: 1 hour 15 minutes)

(Medium of Questions: (Malayalam/Tamil/Kannada)

11. III-Grade Overseer/Tracer Public Works/Irrigation

Syllabus: An Objective Type Test (OMR Valuation) based on the qualification prescribed for the post

(Maximum Marks: 100)
(Duration: 1 hour 15 minutes)
(Medium of Questions: English)

12. Stenographer Grade IV Steel And Industrial Forgings Limited

Syllabus: An Objective Type Test (OMR Valuation) based on the qualification prescribed for the post.

Main Topics:-

Part I General Knowledge, Current Affairs & Renaissance in Kerala

Part II Computer Word Processing, Typing and Document formatting.

(Maximum Marks: 100)
(Duration: 1 hour 15 minutes)
(Medium of Questions: English)

13. Overseer/Draftsman (Mechanical) Grade I (Part I – Direct Recruitment) Irrigation & (Part II – Departmental Quota) Irrigation

Syllabus: An Objective Type Test (OMR Valuation) based on the qualification prescribed for the post.

Main Topics:-

Part I Questions based on Diploma in Mechanical Engineering

Part II Questions based on Engineering Mathematics

Part III Questions based on Basic Science (Physics & Chemistry)

Part IV General Knowledge, Current Affairs, India-National Movements & Renaissance in Kerala and its Leaders

(Maximum Marks: 100)
(Duration: 1 hour 15 minutes)
(Medium of Questions: English)

14. Painter Kerala Agro Machinery Corporation Limited

Syllabus: An Objective Type Test (OMR Valuation) based on the qualification prescribed for the post.

Main Topics:-

Part I General Knowledge, Current Affairs & Renaissance in Kerala

Part II Questions based on NTC painting.

(Maximum Marks: 100)
(Duration: 1 hour 15 minutes)
(Medium of Questions: English)

15. Divisional Accountant Kerala Water Authority

Syllabus: An Objective Type Test (OMR Valuation) based on the qualification prescribed for the post.

Main Topics:-

Part I General Knowledge

Part II General English

Part III Elementary Book Keeping

Part IV Arithmetic and Mensuration

(Maximum Marks: 100)
(Duration: 1 hour 15 minutes)
(Medium of Questions: English)

16. Engineering Assistant Grade II Kerala State Construction Corporation Limited

Syllabus: An Objective Type Test (OMR Valuation) based on the qualification prescribed for the post.

Main Topics:-

Part I Questions based on Diploma in Civil Engg.

Part II Questions based on Engineering Mathematics

Part III Questions based on Basic Science (Physics & Chemistry)

Part IV General Knowledge, Current Affairs and Renaissance in Kerala

(Maximum Marks: 100)
(Duration: 1 hour 15 minutes)
(Medium of Questions: English)

17. Treatment Organiser Grade II Health Services

Syllabus: An Objective Type Test (OMR Valuation) based on the qualification prescribed for the post.

Main Topics:-

Part I (a) - Human Anatomy (Basic Facts) (b) Human Physiology (Basic Facts)

Part II First Aid, Nursing, General Hygiene, Nutrition, Social Welfare, Health Education etc.

Part III TB and Chest Diseases (General)

Part IV (a) - Zoology (b) Botany

Part V General Knowledge, Current Affairs and Renaissance in Kerala.

(Maximum Marks: 100)

(Duration: 1 hour 15 minutes)

(Medium of Questions: English)

18. Peon-cum-Watcher in Kerala State Textile Corporation Ltd.

Syllabus: An Objective Type Test (OMR Valuation) based on the qualification prescribed for the post.

Main Topics:-

Part I General Knowledge, Current Affairs and Renaissance in Kerala

Part II General English

Part III Regional Language (Malayalam/Tamil/Kannada)

Part IV Simple Arithmetic & Mental Ability

(Maximum Marks: 100)

(Duration: 1 hour 15 minutes)

(Medium of Questions: Malayalam/Tamil/Kannada)

19. Senior Superintendent General Education

Syllabus: An Objective Type Test (OMR Valuation) based on the qualification prescribed for the post.

Main Topics:-

Part I Quantitative Aptitude

Part II Mental Ability & Test of reasoning
Part III General Science
Part IV Current Affairs
Part V Facts about Kerala
Part VI Facts about India
Part VII Constitution of India
Part VIII General English
Part IX Social Welfare Schemes and Measures
Part X IT & Cyber Laws
(Maximum Marks: 100)
(Duration: 1 hour 15 minutes)
(Medium of Questions: English)

20. Analyst (Chemical Testing Laboratory) Industries And Commerce

Syllabus: An Objective Type Test (OMR Valuation) based on the qualification prescribed for the post.

Main Topics:-

Part I Questions Based on Technical Qualification

Part II Questions Based on Degree in Chemistry

Part III General Knowledge, Current Affairs and Renaissance in Kerala

(Maximum Marks: 100)
(Duration: 1 hour 15 minutes)
(Medium of Questions: English)

21. Supervisor Foam Mattings (India) Limited

Syllabus: An Objective Type Test (OMR Valuation) based on the qualification prescribed for the post.

Main Topics:-

Part I General Knowledge, Current Affairs, Indian National Movement and Renaissance in Kerala

Part II Questions Based on the experience in the manufacturing of coir products.

(Maximum Marks: 100)

(Duration: 1 hour 15 minutes)
(Medium of Questions: English)

22. Junior Public Health Nurse Grade II Health Services And Municipal Common Services

Syllabus: An Objective Type Test (OMR Valuation) based on the qualification prescribed for the post.

Main Topics:-

Part I Questions based on Auxiliary Nurse Midwifery course.

Part II General Knowledge, Current Affairs & Renaissance in Kerala

(Maximum Marks: 100)
(Duration: 1 hour 15 minutes)
(Medium of Questions: English)

23. Lower Division Clerk in Kerala Water Authority

Syllabus: An Objective Type Test (OMR Valuation) based on the qualification prescribed for the post.

Main Topics:-

Part I General Knowledge, Current Affairs & Renaissance in Kerala

Part II Questions based on Certificate in Data Entry and Office Automation

(Maximum Marks: 100)
(Duration: 1 hour 15 minutes)
(Medium of Questions: English)

24. Assistant Marine Surveyor

Syllabus: An Objective Type Test (OMR Valuation) based on the qualification prescribed for the post.

Main Topics:-

Part I Questions based on the technical qualification prescribed

Part II General Knowledge, Current Affairs & Renaissance in Kerala

(Maximum Marks: 100)
(Duration: 1 hour 15 minutes)

(Medium of Questions: English)

25. Village Extension Officer Grade II Rural Development

Syllabus: An Objective Type Test (OMR Valuation) based on the qualification prescribed for the post.

Main Topics:-
Part I Simple Arithmetic & Mental Ability
Part II General Knowledge and Current Affairs
Part III General English
Part IV Regional Language (Malayalam/Tamil/Kannada)
(Maximum Marks: 100)
(Duration: 1 hour 15 minutes)
(Medium of Questions: Malayalam/Tamil/Kannada)

26. Senior Mechanic Harbour Engineering

Syllabus: An Objective Type Test (OMR Valuation) based on the qualification prescribed for the post.

Main Topics:-
Part I Questions based on Diploma in Mechanical Engineering
Part II Questions based on Engineering Mathematics
Part III Questions based on Basic Science (Physics & Chemistry)
Part IV General Knowledge, Current Affairs, India-National Movements & Renaissance in Kerala and its Leaders
(Maximum Marks: 100)
(Duration: 1 hour 15 minutes)
(Medium of Questions: English)

27. Junior Instructor Health Sanitary Inspector Industrial Training

Syllabus: An Objective Type Test (OMR Valuation) based on the qualification prescribed for the post

Main Topics:-
Part I Questions based on Diploma in Health Sanitary Inspector Trade
Part II General Knowledge, Current Affairs &

Renaissance in Kerala
(Maximum Marks: 100)
(Duration: 1 hour 15 minutes)
(Medium of Questions: English)

28. Draftsman Grade-I Port (Hydrographic Survey Wing)

Syllabus: An Objective Type Test (OMR Valuation) based on the qualification prescribed for the post.

Main Topics:-

Part I Questions based on the technical Qualification prescribed.

Part II General Knowledge, Current Affairs & Renaissance in Kerala

(Maximum Marks : 100)
(Duration: 1 hour 15 minutes)
(Medium of Questions: English)

29. Vocational Instructor Catering & Restaurant Management

Syllabus: An Objective Type Test (OMR Valuation) based on the qualification prescribed for the post.

Main Topics:-
1. Nutrition and Food Science
2. Food Production
3. Food and Beverage Services
4. Hygiene and Food Sanitation
5. Maintenance and Services
6. Catering Management and accounting
7. Law

(Maximum Marks: 100)
(Duration: 1 hour 15 minutes)
(Medium of Questions: English)

30. Hospitality Assistant (NCA Notification) Tourism

Syllabus: An Objective Type Test (OMR Valuation) based on the qualification prescribed for the post.

Main Topics:-

Part I Questions based on craft certificate in Food and Beverage service

Part II General Knowledge, Current Affairs & Renaissance in Kerala

(Maximum Marks: 100)

(Duration: 1 hour 15 minutes)

(Medium of Questions: English)

31. Tide Watcher Hydrographic Survey Wing

Syllabus: An Objective Type Test (OMR Valuation) based on the qualification prescribed for the post

Main Topics:-

Part I General Knowledge, Current Affairs & Renaissance in Kerala

Part II Simple Arithmetic

Part III Questions based on Tide Watching

(Maximum Marks: 100)

(Duration: 1 hour 15 minutes)

(Medium of Questions: (Malayalam/Tamil/Kannada)

32. Junior Instructor Driver-cum-Mechanic Industrial Training

Syllabus: An Objective Type Test (OMR Valuation) based on the qualification prescribed for the post

Main Topics:-

Part I Questions based on Diploma in Driver cum Mechanic Trade

Part II General Knowledge, Current Affairs & Renaissance in Kerala

(Maximum Marks: 100)

(Duration: 1 hour 15 minutes)

(Medium of Questions: English)

33. Technician Grade-II (General Mechanic) (Direct Recruitment)
Kerala State Milk Marketing Federation Limited

Syllabus: An Objective Type Test (OMR Valuation) based on the qualification prescribed for the post

(Maximum Marks: 100)

(Duration: 1 hour 15 minutes)

(Medium of Questions: English)

34. Village Extension Officer Grade II Rural Development

Syllabus: An Objective Type Test (OMR Valuation) based on the qualification prescribed for the post.

Main Topics:-

Part I Simple Arithmetic & Mental Ability

Part II General Knowledge & Current Affairs

Part III General English

Part IV Regional Language (Malayalam/Tamil/Kannada)

(Maximum Marks: 100)

(Duration: 1 hour 15 minutes)

(Medium of Questions: Malayalam/Tamil/Kannada)

35. Draftsman Grade I (Civil) Kerala State Housing Board

Syllabus: An Objective Type Test (OMR Valuation) based on the qualification prescribed for the post

Main Topics:-

Part I Questions based on Diploma in Civil Engg.

Part II General Knowledge, Current Affairs & Renaissance in Kerala

(Maximum Marks: 100)

(Duration: 1 hour 15 minutes)

(Medium of Questions: English)

36. Junior Instructor Mechanic Consumer Electronics Industrial Training

Syllabus: An Objective Type Test (OMR Valuation) based on the qualification prescribed for the post

Main Topics:-
Part I Questions based on Diploma in Mechanic Consumer Electronics
Part II General Knowledge, Current Affairs & Renaissance in Kerala
(Maximum Marks: 100)
(Duration: 1 hour 15 minutes)
(Medium of Questions: English)

37. Various Attenders
Travancore Cochin Chemicals Ltd.
Syllabus: An Objective Type Test (OMR Valuation) based on the qualification prescribed for the post.
Main Topics:-
Part I General Knowledge, Current Affairs & Renaissance in Kerala
Part II General Science
Part III Simple Arithmetic
(Maximum Marks: 100)
(Duration: 1 hour 15 minutes)
(Medium of Questions: Malayalam/Tamil/Kannada)

38. Vocational Teacher Reception, Book-Keeping And Communication Vocational Higher Secondary Education
Syllabus: An Objective Type Test (OMR Valuation) based on the qualification prescribed for the post.
Main Topics:-
Part I Questions based on M.Com
Part II Questions based on DCA
Part III General Knowledge, Current Affairs and Renaissance in Kerala
(Maximum Marks: 100)
(Duration: 1 hour 15 minutes)
(Medium of Questions: English)

39. Lift Operator, Assistant Time Keeper, Printing (Government Press)

Syllabus: An Objective Type Test (OMR Valuation) based on the qualification prescribed for the post.

Main Topics:-

Part I General Knowledge, Current Affairs & Renaissance in Kerala

Part II Simple Arithmetic

Part III General English

(Maximum Marks: 100)

(Duration: 1 hour 15 minutes)

(Medium of Questions: Malayalam/Tamil/Kannada)

40. Lower Division Clerk Various (Direct Recruitment)

Syllabus: An Objective Type Test (OMR Valuation) based on the qualification prescribed for the post.

Main Topics:-

Part I Simple Arithmetic and Mental Ability

Part II General Knowledge & Current Affairs

Part III General English

Part IV Regional Language (Malayalam/Tamil/Kannada)

(Maximum Marks: 100)

(Duration: 1 hour 15 minutes)

(Medium of Questions: Malayalam/Tamil/Kannada)

41. Lecturer in Mechanical Engineering (Polytechnics) Technical Education

Syllabus: An Objective Type Test (OMR Valuation) based on the qualification prescribed for the post.

(Maximum Marks: 100)

(Duration: 1 hour 15 minutes)

(Medium of Questions: English)

42. Driver Grade II – Kerala State Handloom Weaver's Co-Operative Society Ltd.

Syllabus: An Objective Type Test (OMR Valuation) based on the qualification prescribed for the post.

Main Topics:-
Part I General Knowledge & Renaissance in Kerala
Part II Questions based on Driving (HDV)
(Maximum Marks: 100)
(Duration: 1 hour 15 minutes)
(Medium of Questions: Malayalam/Tamil/Kannada)

43. Night Watchman Port Peon/Watchman
District Co-Operative Bank Security Guard Gr-II
Kerala Electrical And Allied Engineering Company Limited

Syllabus: An Objective Type Test (OMR Valuation) based on the qualification prescribed for the post.

Main Topics:-
Part I General Knowledge, Current Affairs & Renaissance in Kerala
Part II General Science
Part III Simple Arithmetic
(Maximum Marks: 100)
(Duration: 1 hour 15 minutes)
(Medium of Questions: Malayalam/Tamil/Kannada)

44. Lower Division Clerk Various (Direct Recruitment)
Syllabus: An Objective Type Test (OMR Valuation) based on the qualification prescribed for the post.

Main Topics:-
Part I Simple Arithmetic and Mental Ability
Part II General Knowledge & Current Affairs
Part III General English
Part IV Regional Language (Malayalam/Tamil/Kannada)
(Maximum Marks: 100)
(Duration: 1 hour 15 minutes)
(Medium of Questions: Malayalam/Tamil/Kannada)

45. Confidential Assistant Grade II
Syllabus: Dictation Test

A passage in English consisting of 400 words will be read in 5 minutes (80 words/minute) and the candidates have to take down the passage in Short Hand and then write the passage in Long Hand using ink within one hour.

(Maximum Marks: 100)

(Duration: 1 hour 05 minutes)

(Medium of Questions: English)

46. Attender (Photography Section) Information And Public Relations

Syllabus: An Objective Type Test (OMR Valuation) based on the qualification prescribed for the post.

Main Topics:-

Part I General Knowledge & Current Affairs

Part II Questions based on knowledge in printing, developing, washing, glacing, mixing of chemicals etc.

(Maximum Marks: 100)

(Duration: 1 hour 15 minutes)

(Medium of Questions: Malayalam/Tamil/Kannada)

47. Full Time Junior Language Teacher Arabic – LPS Education

Syllabus: A Written (Descriptive) Test based on the qualification prescribed for the post.

(Maximum Marks: 100)

(Duration: 2.00 Hours)

(Medium of Questions: Arabic)

48. Radiographer Grade II – Indian Systems of Medicine

Syllabus: An Objective Type Test (OMR Valuation) based on the technical qualification prescribed for the post.

Main Topics:-

Part I General and Radiation Physics

Part II Basic Subjects

Part III Physics of Medical imaging and Radiotherapy (Radio diagnosis)

(Maximum Marks: 100)
(Duration: 1 hour 15 minutes)
(Medium of Questions: English)

49. Vocational Teacher In Computer Application (Direct Recruitment)

Vocational Higher Secondary Education

Syllabus: An Objective Type Test (OMR Valuation) based on the qualification prescribed for the post.

Main Topics:-

Part I Questions based on technical Qualification

Part II General Knowledge & Current Affairs

Part III Facts about India

(Maximum Marks: 100)
(Duration: 1 hour 15 minutes)
(Medium of Questions: English)

50. Lift Operator – District Co-Operative Bank

Syllabus: An Objective Type Test (OMR Valuation) based on the qualification prescribed for the post.

Main Topics:-

Part I General Knowledge, Current Affairs & Renaissance in Kerala

Part II General Science

Part III Simple Arithmetic

(Maximum Marks: 100)
(Duration: 1 hour 15 minutes)
(Medium of Questions: Malayalam/Tamil/Kannada)

51. Tutor Technician Medical Education

Syllabus: An Objective Type Test (OMR Valuation) based on the qualification prescribed for the post.

Main Topics:-

Part I Questions based on B.Sc.(MLT)

Part II General Knowledge, Current Affairs & Renaissance in Kerala

(Maximum Marks: 100)
(Duration: 1 hour 15 minutes)
(Medium of Questions: English)

52. Estimator cum Draftsman – Forest Industries (Travancore) Ltd.

Syllabus: An Objective Type Test (OMR Valuation) based on the qualification prescribed for the post

Main Topics:-

Part I General Knowledge, Current Affairs & Renaissance in Kerala

Part II Questions based on Diploma in Mechanical Engineering

(Maximum Marks: 100)
(Duration: 1 hour 15 minutes)
(Medium of Questions: English)

53. Accountant – Kerala State Industrial Enterprises Limited

Syllabus: An Objective Type Test (OMR Valuation) based on the qualification prescribed for the post

Main Topics:-

Part I General Knowledge, Current Affairs & Renaissance in Kerala

Part II Questions based on M.Com with Financial Management as Optional Subject.

Part III Questions based on Certificate in Computer Application

(Maximum Marks: 100)
(Duration: 1 hour 15 minutes)
(Medium of Questions: English)

54. Lower Division Typist
Various Govt. Owned Companies/Corporations/Boards

Syllabus: An Objective Type Test (OMR Valuation) based on the qualification prescribed for the post

Main Topics:-

Part I General Knowledge, Current Affairs & Renaissance in Kerala

Part II (a) Computer Word Processing

(b) Typing & Document formatting

(Maximum Marks: 100)

(Duration: 1 hour 15 minutes)

(Medium of Questions: English)

55. Junior Instructor Arithmetic cum Drawing Industrial Training

Syllabus: An Objective Type Test (OMR Valuation) based on the qualification prescribed for the post.

Main Topics:-

Part I Questions based on NTC in Arithmetic cum Drawing trade

Part II General Knowledge, Current Affairs & Renaissance in Kerala

(Maximum Marks: 100)

(Duration: 1 hour 15 minutes)

(Medium of Questions: English)

56. Pharmacist Grade II (Ayurveda)

Ayurveda Colleges/Indian Systems of Medicine/Insurance Medical Services

Syllabus: An Objective Type Test (OMR Valuation) based on the qualification prescribed for the post.

Main Topics:-

Part I General Knowledge, Current Affairs & Renaissance in Kerala

Part II General Science (Physics, Chemistry, Botany, Zoology)

Part III Questions based on Ayurveda Pharmacist Certificate Course

(Maximum Marks: 100)

(Duration: 1 hour 15 minutes)

(Medium of Questions: English)

57. Field Officer – Kerala Forest Development Corporation Ltd.

Syllabus: An Objective Type Test (OMR Valuation) based on the qualification prescribed for the post

Main Topics:-

Part I General Knowledge, Current Affairs & Renaissance in Kerala

Part II General Questions on Agriculture, Plantation Crops, Environmental Science and Forestry.

(Maximum Marks: 100)

(Duration: 1 hour 15 minutes)

(Medium of Questions: English)

58. Boat Lascar – Kerala State Water Transport

Syllabus: An Objective Type Test (OMR Valuation) based on the qualification prescribed for the post

Main Topics:-

Part I General Knowledge, Current Affairs & Renaissance in Kerala

Part II Questions based on Lascar Certificate

(Maximum Marks: 100)

(Duration: 1 hour 15 minutes)

(Medium of Questions: Malayalam/Tamil/Kannada)

59. Telephone Operator-cum-Receptionist Gr-II Kerala State Industrial Development Corporation Ltd.

Syllabus: An Objective Type Test (OMR Valuation) based on the qualification prescribed for the post.

Main Topics:-

Part I General Knowledge, Current Affairs & Renaissance in Kerala

Part II General English

Part III Questions based on Technical Experience in Switch Board operation as Telephone Operator

(Maximum Marks: 100)

(Duration: 1 hour 15 minutes)
(Medium of Questions: English)

60. Vocational Instructor - Catering And Restaurant Management Vocational Higher Secondary Education

Syllabus: An Objective Type Test (OMR Valuation) based on the qualification prescribed for the post.

Main Topics:-
1. Nutrition and Food Science
2. Food Production
3. Food and Beverage Services
4. Hygiene and Food Sanitation
5. Maintenance and Services
6. Catering
7. Management and accounting
8. Law

(Maximum Marks: 100)
(Duration: 1 hour 15 minutes)
(Medium of Questions: English)

61. Excise Guard/Women Excise Guard

Syllabus: An Objective Type Test (OMR Valuation) based on the qualification prescribed for the post.

Main Topics:-

Part I General Knowledge, Current Affairs & Renaissance in Kerala

Part II General English

Part III Simple Arithmetic & Mental Ability

(Maximum Marks: 100)
(Duration: 1 hour 15 minutes)
(Medium of Questions: English)

62. Lower Division Clerk Various (Direct Recruitment)

Syllabus: An Objective Type Test (OMR Valuation) based on the qualification prescribed for the post.

Main Topics:-
Part I Simple Arithmetic and Mental Ability
Part II General Knowledge & Current Affairs
Part III General English
Part IV Regional Language (Malayalam/Tamil/Kannada)
(Maximum Marks: 100)
(Duration: 1 hour 15 minutes)
(Medium of Questions: Malayalam/Tamil/Kannada)

63. Assistant Information Officer
Information And Public Relations (Preliminary Test)
Assistant/Auditor
Govt. Secretariat/Kerala P.S.C./Advocate Generals Office (EKM)/LFAD etc.
Syllabus: An Objective Type Test (OMR Valuation) based on the qualification prescribed for the post
Main Topics:-
Part I Quantitative Aptitude
Part II Mental Ability & Test of Reasoning
Part III General Science
Part IV Current affairs
Part V Facts about Kerala
Part VI Facts about India
Part VII Constitution of India
Part VIII General English
Part IX Social Welfare Schemes & Measures
Part X IT & Cyber Laws
(Maximum Marks: 100)
(Duration: 1 hour 15 minutes)

2. MAHARASHTRA

Maharashtra Public Service Commission (MPSC) conducts examinations for appointments to the service of Government

of Maharashtra and its allied organizations. MPSC conducts the following examinations are conducted for direct recruitment:
1. Maharashtra State Services Examination
2. Maharashtra Forest Services
3. Maharashtra Engineering Services, Gr-A Examination
4. Police Sub Inspector Examination
5. Sales Tax Inspector Examination
6. Maharashtra Engineering Services, Gr-B
7. Clerk Typist [Marathi and English] Examination
8. Maharashtra Agricultural Services
9. Civil Judge (Junior Division) Judicial Magistrate (First Class) Competitive Examination
10. Assistant Motor Vehicle Inspector
11. Assistant Engineer(Electrical),Grade-2, Maharashtra Electrical Engineering Services, Group B
12. Assistant Examination

Though the details of the various examinations can be accessed from the website of MPSC i.e. **www.mpsc.gov.in**, the details of some of the examinations have been discussed below to give a general overview.

1. Maharashtra State Service Examination

This Examination is conducted for the recruitment of 19 posts like Deputy Collector, Deputy Superintendent of Police, Sales Tax Officer and other Class I and II Officers of the state.

Educational Qualification: Bachelor's degree in any faculty of a recognized university.

Age limit: 19 to 33 years for general candidates and relaxation to some specified candidates

Stages of Examination - Three

Preliminary Examination Objective type papers in two sessions of two hours each.

Paper I - (200 marks)
- Current events of state, national and international importance

- History of India (with special reference to Maharashtra) and Indian National Movement
- Maharashtra, India and World Geography - Physical, Social, Economic Geography of Maharashtra, India and the World
- Maharashtra and India - Polity and Governance - Constitution, Political System, Panchayati Raj, Urban Governance, Public Policy, Rights issues, etc.
- Economic and Social Development - Sustainable Development, Poverty, Inclusion, Demographics, Social Sector initiatives, etc.
- General issues on Environmental Ecology, Bio-diversity and Climate Change - that do not require subject specialisation.
- General Science.

Paper II - (200 marks)
- Comprehension;
- Interpersonal skills including communication skills;
- Logical reasoning and analytical ability;
- Decision-making and problem-solving;
- General mental ability;
- Basic numeracy (numbers and their relations, orders of magnitude, etc.) (Class X level),
- Data interpretation (Charts, graphs, tables, data sufficiency etc. Class X level);
- Marathi and English Language Comprehension skills (Class X/XII level).

Main Examination - There are six papers.

Two papers are in Languages - English and Marathi, 100 Marks Each, Descriptive type questions

Four papers are of General Studies, 150 Marks Each, Multiple Choice Questions

Paper I History & Geography (in reference to Maharashtra)

Paper II Indian constitution & Law, Politics (with reference to Maharashtra)

Paper III Human Resource Development and Human Rights
Paper IV Economy & Planning, Economics of development & Agriculture, Science & technology development
Interview: Total Marks-100.

2. Police Sub Inspector

There are four stages of PSI -
    a. Preliminary Exam - April
    b. Main Exam - July
    c. Physical Test - Dec/Jan
    d. Interview

Preliminary Exam: It consists of 150 questions of 300 marks. The duration of the exam is of 90 minutes. It has negative marking of 0.25 percent.

Mains Exam:

Paper I 200 Marks, Duration - 2 hours
    English - 70 Marks, Marathi - 130 Marks

Paper II 200 Marks, Duration - 2 hours
    Current Events - 30 Marks; IQ - 40 Marks; Mumbai Police Act - 10 Marks; Human Rights and Responsibilities - 40 Marks; Geography of Maharashtra- 40 Marks; History of Maharashtra) - 25 Marks; Indian Polity) - 15 Marks

Physical Test 200 Marks

Interview 75 Marks

3. Sales Tax Inspector

There are three stages of the exam -
    Preliminary Exam - May
    Main Exam - August
    Interview

Preliminary Exam: It consists of 150 questions of 300 marks for a duration of 90 minutes. There is a negative marking of 0.25 percent.

Main Exam:

Paper I It consists of 200 marks of two hours duration
English - 70 Marks, Marathi - 130 Marks

Paper II It consists of 200 Marks of two hours duration
Current Events - 30 Marks; IQ - 40 Marks; Geography of Maharashtra - 40 Marks; Planning - 15 Marks; Basic Fundamental Development of Urban & Rural - 10 Marks; Economical Development) - 10 Marks; International Trade & International Capital Movements - 15 Marks; Public Financial System) - 25 Marks; Computer & Information Technology) - 25 Marks

Interview 50 Marks

4. Assistant

There are three stages of Assistant examination-

Preliminary Exam- June

Main Exam- September

Interview

Preliminary Exam: It consists of 150 questions of 300 marks of 90 minutes duration

Main Exam:

Paper I It consists of 200 marks of two hours duration
English - 70 Marks, Marathi - 130 Marks

Paper II It consists of 200 marks of two hours duration
Current Events - 30 Marks; IQ- 40 Marks; Right to Information - 15 Marks; History of 15 Marks; Indian Polity - 20 Marks; Computer & Information Technology - 50 Marks; Geography of Maharashtra - 40 Marks

Interview 50 Marks

5. Maharashtra Forest Service Exam

Recruitment for the post of Assistant Forest Conservator (Gr A) and Forest Officer (Gr B) is done through this exam. It has three stages:

Preliminary Exam General Studies objective type 100 questions of 200 marks.

Mains Exam

a. **Paper I** General Studies objective type 100 questions of 200 marks.

b. **Paper II** Nature Conservation objective type 100 questions of 200 marks.

Interview 50 Marks

6. Clerk-Typist Examination

Recruitment for the post of clerk-typist in Gr C across the state in various departments is done through this examination.

Examination Single paper of objective type 200 questions of 400 marks covering Marathi, English, General Knowledge, IQ and Maths.

7. Motor Vehicle Inspector

Recruitment for the post of Motor Vehicle Inspector (Gr B) across the various Regional Transport Offices in the state is done through this exam. It has three stages:

Preliminary Exam Objective type 100 questions. Questions on General Studies, IQ and Automobile Engineering

Mains Exam Objective type 150 questions of 300 marks. Questions on Mechanical Engineering and Automobile Engineering

Interview 50 Marks

3. RAJASTHAN

The recruitment to the various services in the Rajasthan State Government is done by Rajasthan Public Service Commission (RPSC) formed under the statutory provisions of the Constitution. Though the details of the various examinations can be accessed from the website of RPSC i.e. **http://www.rpsc.rajasthan.gov.in** or **http://www.rpsconline.rajasthan.gov.in** the details of some of the examinations have been discussed below to give a general overview.

1. Rajasthan State & Subordinate Services: This exam is conducted for about 16 state services and about 11 subordinate services of Rajasthan Govt. like Rajasthan administration services, Rajasthan police service, Rajasthan account service, Rajasthan co-operative service etc in various pay scale.

Age: 21 to 35 yrs (Non-Gazetted state employee 25 to 45 yrs)

Educational Qualification: Graduation

Name of the Post in Rajasthan Administrative Services (RAS) and Allied Services (RTS) combined competitive examination.

1. Rajasthan Administrative Service (RAS):
- Rajasthan Administrative Service
- Rajasthan Police Service
- Rajasthan Accounts Service
- Rajasthan Cooperative Service
- Rajasthan Employment Office Service
- Rajasthan Jail Service
- Rajasthan Industry Service
- Rajasthan State Insurance Service
- Rajasthan Commercial Tax Service
- Rajasthan Tourism Service
- Rajasthan Transport Service
- Rajasthan Women and Child Development Service
- Rajasthan Devasthan Service
- Rajasthan Rural Development State Service

  Allied Services:
- Rajasthan Subordinate Devasthan Service
- Rajasthan Subordinate Cooperative Service
- Rajasthan Tehsildar Service
- Rajasthan Excise Subordinate Service
- Rajasthan Subordinate Service (Jr. Employment Officer)
- Rajasthan Industry Subordinate Service

- Rajasthan Commercial (Sales) Tax Subordinate Service
- Rajasthan Food Public Distribution Service
- Rajasthan Women and Child Development Service Subordinate Service

Scheme of examination: The Combined Competitive Examination will be held in two successive stages-

(i) Preliminary Examination, and

(ii) Main Examination

(i) Preliminary examination The Preliminary Examination will consist of one paper on the subject specified below, which will be of objective type and carry a maximum of 200 marks. The examination is meant to serve as a screening test only. The Standard of the paper will be that of a Bachelor's Degree Level. The marks obtained in the Preliminary Examination by the candidates who are declared qualified for admission to Main Examination will not be counted for determining their final order of merit.

Subject	Maximum Marks	Duration
General Knowledge & General Science	200	Three hours

Note: Pattern of Question Paper (For Preliminary examination)

1. There will be 150 Questions in the Question Paper.
2. All questions will carry equal marks.
3. There will be Negative Marking − 1/3 part of mark(s) of each question will be deducted for each wrong answer.

(ii) Main examination:

(a) The number of candidates to be admitted for the Main Examination is about 15 times the total number of vacancies to be filled in the year in the various Services and posts.

(b) The written examination consists of the following four papers which will be descriptive/analytical. A candidate must take all the papers listed below which will also consist of question paper of brief, medium long answer and descriptive type questions. The standard of General

Hindi and General English will be that of Sr. Secondary level. The time allowed for each paper shall be 3 hours.

	Papers	Maximum Marks
Paper-I	General Studies-I	200
Paper-II	General Studies-II	200
Paper-III	General Studies-III	200
Paper-IV	General Hindi and General English	200

Personality and viva-voce Examination:-
   (i) Candidates who obtain such minimum qualifying marks in the written test of the Main Examination as may be fixed by the Commission at their discretion shall be summoned by them for an interview for a personality test which carries 100 marks.
   (ii) The Commission shall award marks to each candidate interviewed by them. In interviewing the candidates besides awarding marks in respect of character, personality, address, physique, marks shall also be awarded for the candidate's knowledge of Rajasthani culture. However for selection to the Rajasthan Police Service, candidates having 'C' Certificate of N.C.C. shall be given preference. The marks so awarded shall be added to the marks obtained in the written test by each such candidate.

2. Professor & Associate Professor (Ayurved)
Age Limit
- **Professor:** 55 Years
- **Associate Professor:** 50 Years

Educational Qualification
Professor
- A degree in Ayurved from a University established by law in India or its equivalent as recognized under Indian Medicine Central Council Act, 1970
- A Postgraduate Qualification in the subject/specialty concerned included in the Schedule to Indian Medicine Central Council Act, 1970

- Total 10 years of teaching experience in concerned subject

Associate Professor
- A degree in Ayurved from a University established by law in India or its equivalent as recognized under Indian Medicine Central Council Act, 1970
- A Postgraduate Qualification in the subject/specialty
- At least 05 years of Teaching experience in concerned subject

Selection:- Through screening test of MCQs type.

Syllabus and more Details can be found on RPSC website **http:// www.rpsc.rajasthan.gov.in** or **http://www.rpsconline.rajasthan.gov.in**.

3. Junior law Officer

(Pay Scale-9300-34800, pay band-3600)

Age Limit 21 to 35 yrs

Educational Qualification:
- Must be Law Graduate from a University established by Law in India or its equivalent with three years course of proficiency (Professional) degree.
- Working knowledge of Hindi written in Devnagiri Script and knowledge of Rajasthani Culture

Paper	Subject	Marks	Questions
I	Constitution of India with special emphasis on Fundamental Rights, Directive Principles and enforcement of rights through writs, Functioning of High Court and Supreme Court and attorney General.	50	150
II	Civil Procedure Code and Criminal, Procedure Code. Provisions required to be referred generally in Government Office will be given importance.	50	150

III	Evidence Act, Limitation Act, Interpretation of Statutes, drafting and conveyancing.		50	150
IV	Language	Part-A General Hindi	25	75
		Part-B General English	25	75

NOTE:
   (i) Each Paper shall be of 3 hours duration and the standard of the language paper will be that of senior secondary level.
   (ii) Pass marks shall be 40% in each paper. The Commission may in its discretion award grace marks up to 1 in each paper and up to 3 in the aggregate. The Commission may fix minimum qualifying marks in the written examination for the scheduled caste and the scheduled tribe candidates lower than what is prescribed for other candidates. The marks so awarded shall be added to the marks obtained in the written test by each candidate.

Viva-Voce: Candidates who obtain such minimum qualifying marks in the written examination as may be fixed by the Commission in their discretion shall be summoned by them for an interview for a personality test, which shall carry 25 marks.

Syllabus and more Details can be found on RPSC website http://www.rpsc.rajasthan.gov.in or http://www.rpsconline.rajasthan.gov.in.

4. Junior Accountant & Tehsil Revenue Accountant:
(Pay Scale-9300-34800, pay band-3600)
Age Limit 21 to 35 yrs
Educational Qualification:
- For the Post of Junior Accountant:- A candidate for direct recruitment must hold a degree in Arts, Science or Commerce of University established by Law in India or a Foreign University declared by the Government in consultation with the Commission to be equivalent with a degree of a University established by Law in India.
- For the Post of Tehsil Revenue Accountant:- A candidate for direct recruitment must hold a degree in Arts, Science,

Commerce or Agriculture of a University established by Law in India or of a Foreign University declared by the Government in consultation with the Commission to be equivalent of a degree of a University established by Law in India.

And (for both posts)
- -"O" or Higher Level Certificate Course conducted by DOEACC under control of the Department of Electronics, Government of India. Or Computer Operator & Programming Assistant (COPA)/Data Preparation and Computer Software (DPCS) certificate organized under National/State Council of Vocational Training Scheme. Or Diploma in Computer Science/Computer Applications of a University established by Law in India or of an institution recognized by the Government. Or Diploma in Computer Science & Engineering from a polytechnic institution recognized by the Government. Or Rajasthan State Certificate Course in Information Technology (RS-CIT) conducted by Vardhaman Mahaveer Open University, Kota under control of Rajasthan Knowledge Corporation Limited.
- Working Knowledge of Hindi written in Devnagri Script and Knowledge of Rajasthani culture

Selection: Through screening test of MCQs type.

Syllabus and more Details can be found on RPSC website http://www.rpsc.rajasthan.gov.in or http://www.rpsconline.rajasthan.gov.in.

5. Physical Training Instructor Gr-II & Gr-III (Department of Secondary Education)

Age 18 to 35 Yrs

Essential Qualification Working Knowledge of Hindi written in Devnagari Script and knowledge of Rajasthani Culture.

Educational Qualification:-
- For Physical Training Instructor Gr-II:- Pay Scale-9300-34800, pay band-4200

- Bachelor of Physical Education (B.P.Ed.) recognised by the National Council for Teacher Education.
- For Physical Training Instructor Gr-III:- Pay Scale-9300-34800, pay band-3600
- Bachelor of Physical Education (B.P.Ed.) or Certificate in Physical Education (C.P.Ed.) or Diploma in Physical Education (D.P.Ed.) recognised by the National Council for Teacher Education.

Selection: Through screening test of MCQs type.

Syllabus and more Details can be found on RPSC website http:// www.rpsc.rajasthan.gov.in or http://www.rpsconline.rajasthan.gov.in.

6. Motor Vehicle sub-inspector (Transport Department)

(Pay Scale-9300-34800, pay band-3600)

Age 18-37 yrs

Educational Qualification:-

- Must have passed Secondary Examination of a recognised Board
- A Diploma in Automobile Engineering. (3 years' course) or a diploma in Mechanical Engineering awarded by the State Board of Technical Education (3 years' course)

Or

- Any qualification in either of the above disciplines declared equivalent by the Central Government or State Government
- Working experience of at least one year in a reputed Automobile Workshop which undertakes repairs of both light motor vehicles, heavy goods vehicles and heavy passenger motor vehicles fitted with petrol and diesel engines.
- Working experience of at least one year in a reputed Automobile Workshop which undertakes repairs of both light motor vehicles, heavy goods vehicles and heavy passenger motor vehicles fitted with petrol and diesel engines

Essential Qualification:- Working Knowledge of Hindi written in Devnagri Script and Knowledge of Rajasthani culture.

Physical Fitness:-
- Height 168 cms(M), 152 cms(F)
- Chest 81cms(exhaled) – 86(inspired)

Scheme of Examination & Syllabus for the post of Motor Vehicle Sub Inspector

1. A Candidate must appear in all the papers. There will be three papers of Objective Type unless otherwise stated and a personality and viva-voce test. The name and the total marks and the time allowed for each paper will be as follows:-

Paper I	Knowledge and Everyday Science
	100 Marks 2 Hrs.
Paper II	Language Test
	100 Marks 2 Hrs.
Paper III	Automobile and Mechanical Engineering
	200 Marks 3 Hrs.

2. Personality and Viva-Voce Examination:-
- Candidates who obtain such minimum qualifying marks in the written test as may be fixed by the Commission in their discretion shall be summoned by them for interview, which carries 50 Marks.
- The standard of the papers will be that of a secondary/ Polytechnic Diploma.
- All papers unless specifically required, shall be answered either in English or in Hindi, but no candidate shall be permitted to answer any one paper partly in Hindi or partly in English unless specifically allowed to do so.
- If a candidate's hand-writing is not easily legible a deduction will be made on this account from the total marks otherwise accruing to him.
- Credit will be given for orderly, effective and exact expression combined with due economy of words in all descriptive papers of the examination

Syllabus and more Details can be found on RPSC website http://www.rpsc.rajasthan.gov.in or http://www.rpsconline.rajasthan.gov.in.

7. Assistant Public Prosecutor Gr.-II

(Pay Scale-9300-34800, pay band-4200)

Age 21 to 25 Yrs

Educational Qualifications:-

- Degree in Law (two years course under the old Scheme or three years, course under the New Scheme) or Degree in Law (Professional) from a University established by law in India or qualification recognised by the Govt. as equivalent there to.
- Two years experience at the Bar or if worked as Prosecuting Sub-Inspector experience for 2 years as such.
- Working knowledge of Hindi written as Devnagari Script and Knowledge of Rajasthan Culture.

Selection: Through screening test of MCQs type.

Syllabus and more Details can be found on RPSC website http://www.rpsc.rajasthan.gov.in or http://www.rpsconline.rajasthan.gov.in.

8. LDC Grade-II

(Pay Scale-5200-20200, pay band-2400)

Age 18 to 35 yrs.

Essential Qualification:- Working Knowledge of Hindi written in Devnagri Script and Knowledge of Rajasthani culture.

Educational Qualifications:-

- Senior Secondary from a recognized Board or its equivalent examination
- "O" or Higher Level Certificate Course conducted by DOEACC under control of the Department of Electronics, Government of India.

Or

- Computer operator & Programming Assistant (COPA)/Data Preparation and Computer Software (DPCS) certificate organized under National/ State Council of Vocational Training Scheme.

Or

- Diploma in Computer Science/Computer Applications from a University established by law in India or from an institution recognised by the Government.

Or

- Diploma in Computer Science & Engineering from a polytechnic institution recognised by the Government.

Or

- Rajasthan State Certificate Course in Information Technology (RS-CIT) conducted by Verdhaman Mahaveer Open University, Kota under control of Rajasthan Knowledge Corporation Limited.

Scheme of Exam:-

The Competitive Examination shall include the following papers and each paper shall carry the number of marks as shown against it:-

PAPERS   DURATION   MARKS

PHASE-I

1. General Knowledge, Everyday Science and Mathematics
   3 Hours   100
2. General Hindi and English
   3 Hours   100

PHASE-II

I - For candidates other than persons with disabilities

1. Type – writing in Hindi on Computer
   (a) Speed Test   10 Minutes   25
   (b) Efficiency Test   10 Minutes   25
2. Type-writing in English on Computer
   (a) Speed Test   10 Minutes   25
   (b) Efficiency Test   10 Minutes   25

II - Person with disabilities will be given the average marks obtained by them in Phase-I

Syllabus and more details can be found on RPSC website http://www.rpsc.rajasthan.gov.in or http://www.rpsconline.rajasthan.gov.in.

4. DELHI

The recruitment for the National Capital Territory of Delhi is done by Delhi Subordinate Services Selection Board. The selection for the different post is conducted through separate exams.

The details can be accessed from **http://delhi.gov.in/wps/wcm/connect/doit_dsssb/Delhi+Subordinate+Services+Selection+BoaBo/Home/.**

The details of recruitment to various posts are as indicated below:

A. Posts recruited - Asstt. Director, Asstt. Engineer, Asstt. Law Officer, Manager (DSIIDC), Deputy Manager (DFC), Manager Mech. (DTC), Asstt. Architect and equivalent posts.

Examination – Two Tier

Tier I – 200 Marks of 2 Hrs duration

(A) 1. General Awareness. 2. General Intelligence & Reasoning ability. 3. Arithmetical & Numerical Ability. 4. Test of Hindi Language &Comprehension. 5. Test of English Language & Comprehension. (20 Marks each): 100 Marks

(B) Subject / Qualification Related Paper: 100 Marks

Tier II-275 Marks (including 25 for interview) of 3 Hrs duration

Part I (MCQ): Subject / Qualification related Paper: 200 Marks (80% weightage)

Part II (Descriptive) (50 Marks)

Essay (In English): 30 Marks

Letter writing/ : 20 Marks

Expansion of idea (In English) (20% weightage)

Posts recruited: Asstt. Assessor & Collector/Administrative Officer, Zonal Revenue Officer and equivalent posts.

Examination – Two Tier

Tier I   200 Marks of 2 Hrs duration

1. General Awareness. 2. General Intelligence & Reasoning ability. 3. Arithmetical & Numerical Ability. 4. Test of Hindi Language & Comprehension. 5. Test of English Language & Comprehension. (40 Marks each)

Tier II   300 Marks of 3 Hrs duration

Part I (MCQ): 1. General Intelligence & Reasoning. 2. Quantitative Abilities. 3. General awareness with special emphasis on the History, Culture, Demography, Geography & Economy of Delhi, Administrative set up and Governance in NCT of Delhi. 4. English Language and comprehension. (50 Marks each)

Part II (Descriptive) (75 Marks)

Essay (In English): 50 Marks

Letter writing/ Expansion of ideas (In English): 25 Marks

C. Posts recruited: Post Graduate Teacher, Junior Law Officer, Welfare Officer Gr. II, Publicity Officer and District Staff Officer.

Examination: Two Tier

Tier I   200 Marks of 2 Hrs duration

(A) 1. General Awareness. 2. General Intelligence & Reasoning ability. 3. Arithmetical & Numerical Ability. 4. Test of Hindi Language &Comprehension. 5. Test of English Language & Comprehension. (20 Marks each): 100 Marks

(B) Subject/Qualification Related Paper: 100 Marks

Tier II   250 Marks of 3 Hrs duration

Part I (MCQ): Subject/Qualification Related Paper: 200 Marks (80% weightage)

Part II (Descriptive) (50 Marks)

Essay (In English): 30 Marks

Letter writing/: 20 Marks

Expansion of idea (In English) (20% weightage)

D. Posts recruited: Junior Engineer, Sub Officer, Motor Vehicle Inspector, Food Inspector, Wild Life Inspector, Section Officer (Horticulture), Junior Manager (DFC) and equivalent posts

Examination: Two tier

Tier I 200 Marks of 2 Hrs duration

(A) 1. General Awareness. 2. General Intelligence & Reasoning ability. 3. Arithmetical & Numerical Ability. 4. Test of Hindi Language & Comprehension. 5. Test of English Language & Comprehension. (20 Marks each): 100 Marks

(B) Subject / Qualification Related Paper: 100 Marks

Tier II 200 Marks of 2 Hrs duration

(A) Subject / Qualification Related Paper 150 Marks (150 Question)

(75% weightage)

(B) English Language & Comprehension 50 Marks (50 Question)

(25% weightage)

E. Posts recruited: Gr. II-DASS / Head Clerk, Assistants and equivalent posts.

Examination: Two tier

Tier I 200 Marks of 2 Hrs duration

1. General Awareness. 2. General Intelligence & Reasoning ability. 3. Arithmetical & Numerical Ability. 4. Test of Hindi Language & Comprehension. 5. Test of English Language & Comprehension. (40 Marks each)

Tier II 275 Marks of 2 Hrs duration

Part I (MCQ): 1. General Intelligence & Reasoning. 2. Quantitative Abilities. 3. General awareness with special emphasis on the History, Culture, Demography, Geography & Economy of Delhi, Administrative set up and Governance in NCT of Delhi. 4. English Language and comprehension. (50 Marks each)

Part II (Descriptive) (75 Marks)

Essay (In English): 50 Marks

Letter writing / Expansion of ideas (In English): 25 Marks

F. PB 2 Posts recruited Trained Graduate Teacher, Nurse, Sound Technician, Primary Teacher, Nursery Teacher, Lab. Technician, Technical Asstt. and equivalent posts.

PB 1 Posts recruited Security Supervisor, DEO, Librarian, Asstt. Sanitary Inspector, ANM, Veterinary and Livestock Inspector, etc.

Examination: 200 Marks of 2 Hrs duration

(A) 1. General Awareness. 2. General Intelligence & Reasoning ability. 3. Arithmetical & Numerical Ability. 4. Test of Hindi Language & Comprehension. 5. Test of English Language & Comprehension. (20 Marks each)

(B) Objective type multiple choice questions on the subject concerned as per the qualification prescribed for the post. (100 Marks)

G. Posts recruited: LDC, Steno, Steno-typist, Warder, Patwari, C.W., Driver and equivalent posts.

Examination: 200 Marks of 2 Hrs duration

1. General Awareness. 2. General Intelligence & Reasoning ability. 3. Arithmetical & Numerical Ability. 4. Test of Hindi Language & Comprehension. 5. Test of English Language & Comprehension. (40 Marks each)

5. ARUNACHAL PRADESH

The recruitment for the various services in the state is done by Arunachal Pradesh Public Service Commission. The Arunachal Pradesh Public Service Commission was established on 4th April 1988. The details of various examinations can be accessed from the website **www.appsc.gov.in**.

List of Important Examinations Conducted By Arunachal Pradesh Public Service Commission:
- Arunachal Pradesh Civil Services
- Deputy Superintendent of Police
- Finance and Account Officer/Treasury Officer
- Assistant Registrar of Cooperative Society

- Sub-Treasury Office
- Child Development Project Officer
- Assistant Director (Industries)
- Assistant Employment Officer
- Station Superintendent
- Recruitment for the post of Assistant Engineer
- Recruitment for the post of Range Forest Officer
- Recruitment for the post of Veterinary Officer
- Recruitment for the post of Assistant Engineer
- Recruitment for the post of Range Forest Officer
- Recruitment for the post of Assistant Professor

The scheme of examination, syllabus and minimum qualifying marks varies for the above mentioned examinations. For further details about the same, candidates can visit: **www.appsc.gov.in**

6. ASSAM

The recruitment to the various services in the state of Assam is done by Assam State Public Service Commission. The details of the various examinations can be accessed from the website of APSC i.e. **www.apsc.nic.in** some of the examinations have been discussed below to give a general overview.

The following Examinations are conducted by the APSC:
  i. Combined Competitive Examination
  ii. Departmental Examinations

Combined Competitive Examination

As per requisition of the Govt. of Assam for recruitment in various posts to the Civil Services, advertisement is generally published through print media inviting applications in prescribed form. The written examination consists of two stages:
  a. The Preliminary
  b. The Main Examination

Preliminary Examination

The examination consists of two papers of two hours duration each. The questions are of multiple choice objective types:

Paper	Subject	Marks	Duration
Paper-I	General Studies	200	2 hours
Paper-II	One optional subject to be selected from the list of optional subjects	200	2 hours

List of optional subjects - Combined Competitive Exam. (Pre)-(Total-28)

1. Agriculture
2. Anthropology
3. Animal Husbandry & Veterinary Science
4. Botany
5. Chemical Engineering
6. Civil Engineering
7. Chemistry
8. Commerce
9. Computer Science
10. Economics
11. Education
12. Electrical Engineering
13. Electronics
14. Fisheries
15. Geography
16. Geology
17. Indian History
18. Law
19. Mathematics
20. Mechanical Engineering
21. Medical Science
22. Philosophy
23. Physics
24. Political Science
25. Psychology
26. Sociology
27. Statistics
28. Zoology

Main Examination and Interview

The Main Examination consists of a written Examination and a viva-voce test as below: Candidates who are declared qualified in the Main Examination shall be summoned for a viva-voce test. The viva-voce test carries 200 marks with no qualifying marks.

The questions of the Main Examination will be conventional essay type:

Paper	Subject	Marks	Duration
Paper-I	General English	300	3 hours
Paper-II	General Studies	300	3 hours

Paper-III (a & b)	Any two optional subjects to be selected from the list of optional subject (two papers each)	200	3 hours
		200	3 hours
Paper-IV (a & b)	Any two optional subjects to be selected from the list of optional subject (two papers each)	200	3 hours
		200	3 hours

List of optional subjects-Combined Competitive Exam (Main)-(Total-29)

1. Agriculture
2. Anthropology
3. Animal Husbandry & Veterinary Science
4. Botany
5. Chemical Engineering
6. Civil Engineering
7. Chemistry
8. Commerce
9. Computer Science
10. Economics
11. Education
12. Electrical Engineering
13. Electronics
14. Fisheries
15. Geography
16. Geology
17. History
18. Law
19. Modern Languages and Literature & Classical Language (any one only)
    (a) Assamese
    (b) Bengali
    (c) English
    (d) Hindi
    (e) Arabic
    (f) Persian
    (g) Sanskrit
    (h) Bodo
20. Mathematics
21. Mechanical Engineering
22. Medical Science
23. Philosophy
24. Physics
25. Political Science
26. Psychology
27. Sociology
28. Statistics
29. Zoology

Candidates are not allowed the following combinations of subjects

1. Anthropology & Sociology
2. Mathematics & Statistics
3. Philosophy & Psychology

4. Agriculture & Animal Husbandry & Vety. Science

5. Of the Engineering subjects not more than one subject

The Commission has discretion to fix qualifying marks in any or all the subjects of the Examination.

Interview Test: Marks 200. The candidates are interviewed by a Board which takes into account their academic career.

7. ANDHRA PRADESH

Though the details of the various examinations can be accessed from the website of APPSC i.e. *www.apspsc.gov.in* some of the examinations have been discussed below to give a general overview.

Name of Posts: Deputy Collectors, Commercial Tax, Deputy Superintendent of Police (Civil), Deputy Superintendent of Jails (MEN) in A.P. Jail, Divisional Fire Officers in Fire &Emergency Services, District Registrar in A.P. Registration and Stamps Service, District Tribal Welfare Officer etc

Eligibility:

Candidates have to download and read carefully the different eligibility criteria www.apspsc.gov.in.

Age Limit: Candidates should complete graduation from recognized University. To appear in exam the age of candidate is not below 18 years and above 34 years. Concession in age for ST, SC, and BC candidate is allow

APPSC Group – 1 Exam Pattern Details: Andhra Pradesh Public Service Commission (APPSC)'s Group I exam pattern details given below...

APPSC Group – 1 Exam is Conducted in 3 Stages:

(1) Preliminary Examination (Objective paper)

(2) Main's Examination (Conventional Type)

(3) Interview/Oral Test

(1) Preliminary Examination: The exam consists of one objective type paper. Minimum qualifying marks will be given for reservation candidates as per the rules.

Preliminary Examination Subjects, Maximum marks, Time duration is as follows:

Subject	No. of Questions	Maximum Marks	Time Duration
General Studies & Mental Ability (Objective Type)	150	150	2½ Hours
	Total	150	

(2) **Main Examination:** Candidate's who qualified in preliminary examination will go to second stage i.e. Main examination which contains five papers in conventional type & is of degree standard syllabus . The General English paper is of qualifying one and its marks are not counted for final ranking. All the question papers except General English may be answered either in English or Telugu or Urdu chosen by the candidate. Minimum qualifying marks will be given for reservation candidates as per the rules.

Main Examination Subjects, Maximum marks, Time duration details given below:

	Subject	Maximum Marks	Time Duration
	General English (Conventional Type)	150	3 Hours Time Duration for all conventional type Papers
Paper-I	General Essay	150	
Paper-II	(i) History & Cultural heritage of India with emphasis on 20th century history of India. (ii) Social history of Andhra Pradesh i.e., the history of various social and cultural movements in Andhra Pradesh (iii) General overview of the Indian Constitution	150	

Paper-III	(i) Planning in India & Indian Economy (ii) Land Reforms and social changes in Andhra Pradesh after independence (iii) Andhra Pradesh's Economy, present status	150	
Paper-IV	(i) The role and impact of Science &Technology in the development of India with emphasis on the applied aspects (ii) General awareness with the modern trends in life sciences. (iii) Development and environmental problems	150	
Paper-V	(i) Data appreciation and interpretation. (ii) The candidates will be asked to draw their own conclusion from the data presented in the tabular form in graphical or otherwise (iii) Problem solving – duly structured situation will be presented to the candidates and they will be asked to suggest their own solutions to the problem arising out of situation. Alternatively, they may be called upon to prove the understanding of the situation by answering certain searching questions based on the situation	150	
	Total	750	

(3) Interview/Oral Test: Candidate's who appeared and found eligible in Main exam will be called for Interview which carries 75 marks. In this Interview, the board will test the candidate's attitude and decision making skills.

8. BIHAR

The Bihar Public Service Commission (BPSC) is a statutory body created under the provisions of the Constitution of India to select applicants for the various services of Bihar. The details of the various examinations can be accessed from the websites of BPSC i.e. www.bpsc.bih.nic.in, www.bssc.bih.nic.in, www.bihartet.co.in and biharpolice.bih.nic.in. The details of some of the examinations have been discussed below to give a general overview.

1. Bihar Public Service Commission Exam

(i) BPSC PT (Preliminary Test): This is an objective type questions based test of 200 marks.

Syllabus: Current events of national and international importance, History of India and Indian National Movement, Indian and World Geography, Indian Polity and Economy, General Mental Ability Questions.

(ii) BPSC Main Test: Consists of three papers

Compulsory paper (Common for all)

Paper-1 Samanya Hindi (Hindi language) 100 marks

Paper-2 (General Studies-I) 200 Marks

Paper-3 (General Studies-II) 200 Marks

(iii) BPSC Interview Test: Subjects for Bihar Public Service Commission (BPSC) Exam

Out of the following, any two can be chosen as optional subjects for BPSC mains examination – Geology, Mathematics, Physics, Mechanical Engineering, Civil Engineering, Statistics, Economics, Agriculture, Botany, Chemical Engineering, Chemistry, Zoology

2. Bihar Staff Selection Commission Graduate Level Exam

Age Limit: Candidates age limit should be between 21-37 years for male candidates and between 21-40 years for female candidates.

Educational Qualification: Candidates should possess minimum Graduation Degree in any discipline from recognized university.

Selection Process: Candidates would be selected based on their performance in preliminary examination and main examination.

(i) Preliminary Exam (Objective type): 150 questions

Syllabus: General studies, General science and Maths, Mental ability.

(ii) Mains Examination:

Paper I General Knowledge 150 marks

Paper II Hindi Grammar 100 marks

(iii) Personality Test

3. Bihar Staff Selection Commission Inter Level Exam

Age Limit: Candidates age limit should be between 18-37 years for male candidates and between 18-40 years for female candidates.

Educational Qualification: Candidates should possess minimum Graduation Degree in any discipline from recognized university.

Selection Process: Candidates would be selected based on their performance in preliminary examination and main examination.

(i) Preliminary Exam (Objective type): 150 questions

Syllabus: General studies, General science and Maths, Mental ability.

(ii) Mains Examination:

Paper I General Knowledge 150 marks

Paper II Hindi Grammar 100 marks

(iii) Personality Test

4. Bihar Teachers Eligibility Test (BTET)

BTET Eligibility:-

Minimum Qualifications for Classes I-V:

Senior Secondary (or its equivalent) with at least 50% marks and passed or appearing in final 2–year Diploma in Elementary Education (or its equivalent)

(i) Relaxation of 5% in minimum qualifying marks at BA/B. Sc./Senior Secondary level is admissible for SC/ST/ Differently abled Candidates.

(ii) For this year only, a candidate with BA/B.Sc. with at least 50% marks and B.Ed qualification shall also be eligible for test for classes I to V, provided he/she undergoes, after appointment, an NCTE recognized 6–month special program in Elementary Education.

Minimum Qualifications for Classes VI-VIII:

B.A./B.Sc and passed or appearing in final 2–year Diploma in Elementary Education* (or its equivalent)

A person who intends to be a teacher both for classes I to V and for classes VI to VIII will have to appear in both papers (Paper I and Paper II).

Bihar TET (BETET) Paper I (for classes I to V):

No. of Multiple Choice Questions (MCQ) – 150

Duration of Examination: One-and-a-half hours

(i) Child Development and Pedagogy- 30 Marks

(ii) Language I – Assamese, Bangla, Bodo, Hindi, Nepali, Garo, Manipuri and Hmar 30 Marks

(iii) Language II – English – 30 Marks

(iv) Mathematics – 30 Marks

(v) Environmental Studies – 30 Marks

Paper II (for classes VI to VIII):

No. of Multiple Choice Questions (MCQ) – 150

(i) Child Development & Pedagogy (compulsory) – 30 Marks

(ii) Language I – Assamese, Bangla, Bodo, Hindi, Nepali, Garo, Manipuri and Hmar 30 Marks

(iii) Language II – English (compulsory)- 30 Marks

(iv) (a) For Mathematics and Science teacher : Mathematics and Science- 60 Marks

(iv) (b) For Social studiesteacher : Social Studies – 60 Marks

(iv) (c) For any other teacher – either iv (a) OR iv (b)

5. Bihar police recruitment (Police Constable)

Eligibility: 10 + 2 or equivalent

Age Limit: 18 – 23 yrs.

Scheme of examination:

Written exam: Objective

Total Questions: 100 Total Marks: 300 Marks (3 marks for each question) Candidates scoring 30% of total marks are eligible for Physical examination

Physical Examination

Height 165cm for males and 155cm for females, Chest 86 cm Running for 1 mile in 6 mins for males and 1 km in 6 mins for females.

9. CHHATTISGARH

Chhattisgarh Public Service Commission was formed under the provisions of the Constitution of India on 23rd May 2001 for the recruitment of State Service Officers. The official website for the Chhattisgarh Public Service Commission is **http://psc.cg.gov.in/**

List of important examinations conducted by Chhattisgarh Public Service Commission:

- Chhattisgarh Civil Service
- Chhattisgarh Forest Service
- Recruitment to the post of Drug/Food Inspector & Drug Analyst
- Recruitment to the post of Medical Officer in different disciplines
- Recruitment to the post of Lecturers & Asst. Professors in different disciplines
- Recruitment to the post of Mining Officer & Mining Inspector
- Recruitment to the post of Civil Judge
- Recruitment for various posts under Health and Family Welfare Department regarding Medical Education.

- Recruitment to the post of Asst. Block Education Officer
- Recruitment to the post of Asst. Surgeons in different disciplines
- Recruitment to the post of Jail Superintendent
- Recruitment to the post of Chief Municipal Officer
- Recruitment to the post of Scientific Officer

Candidates are advised to visit the website for the updates on recruitment for various services. The eligibility criteria, method of recruitment, syllabi and other details can be obtained by visiting the Commission's website.

10. GOA

Public Service Commission Recruitment

The recruitment to various services in Goa is done by Goa Public Service Commission. The details of the various examinations can be accessed from the website of GPSC i.e. **www.nicgoa.nic.in** the details of some of the examinations have been discussed below to give a general overview.

Name of Posts: Civil Registrar, Software engineer, Assistant director of civil supplies, Legal assistant etc.

Eligibility:

Candidates have to download and read carefully the different notifications on www.nicgoa.nic.in / before applying.

Age Limit: Candidates should complete graduation from recognized University. To appear in exam the age of candidate is not below 21 years and above 30 years. Concession in age for ST, SC, and BC candidate is allow

Examination: Examination held in to two stages first stage is preliminary examination question are objective type second stage is main examination question are conventional type and personality test.

11. GUJARAT

The recruitment to various services in Gujarat is done by Gujarat Public Service Commission (GPSC). It was formed on 1st May

1960. The details of the various examinations can be accessed from the website of GPSC i.e. **www.gpsc.gujarat.gov.in** some of the examinations have been discussed below to give a general overview.

1. Gujarat Administrative Service

1. Class-I (Pay Scale: Rs.15600-39100+Rs.5400 Grade-pay and other allowances)

- Gujarat Administrative Service
- Deputy Superintendent of police
- District Registrar, Cooperative Societies

2. Class-II (Pay Scale : Rs. 9,300-34,800 + Rs. 4,600 Grade-pay and other allowences)

- Mamlatdar
- Section Officer (Sachivalay)
- Taluka Development Officer
- Govt. Labour Officer
- Assistant District Registrar, Cooperative Societies
- District Land Record Inspector
- Superintendent Prohibition & Excise
- Assistant Director

Educational qualification:-

A candidate shall hold a Bachelor's degree of any University incorporated by an Act of the Parliament or State Legislature in India or other educational institution established by an Act of Parliament or declared to be deemed as a University under section 3 of the University Grants Commission Act, 1956 or possess an equivalent qualification recognized by Government. Provided that a candidate who has appeared at a degree examination, the passing of which would render him educationally qualified for the examination but the result is not declared, shall also be eligible for admission to the Preliminary Examination.

Age:

A candidate shall not be less than 20 years of age and not be more than 35 years. Age will be calculated as on the last date of receipt of application. Upper age limit shall be relaxed as per rules.

Examination pattern
Preliminary exam:-

1.	Verbal Skill Gujarati + Verbal Skill English	150 Marks	90 Minutes
2.	Quantitative Skill + Test of Reasoning (Non quantitative)	150 Marks	90 Minutes
3.	General Studies	200 Marks	2 hours
	TOTAL	500 Marks	

Main exam:-

1.	Gujarati (descriptive)	200 Marks	3 hours
2.	English (descriptive)	100 Marks	3 hours
3.	Optional Paper (descriptive)	200 Marks	3 hours
4.	General Studies-1 (Objective type, multiple choice questions)	200 Marks	100 Minutes
5.	General Studies-2 (Objective type, multiple choice questions)	200 Marks	100 Minutes
	TOTAL		900 Marks

Note:- optional subject can be chosen from the 28 different subjects

Oral interview:- 100 Marks

2. Assistant Public Prosecutor, in the General State Service, Class-II

Educational Qualification: A candidate shall possess (i) a degree in law of the University incorporated by an Act of the Central or State Legislature in India or other educational institution established by an Act of parliament or deemed to be a University under section 3 of the University Grants Commission Act, 1956 or possess an equivalent qualification recognized as such by the Government, (ii) three years continuous and regular practice and experience on the criminal side of the Bar, (iii) adequate knowledge of Gujarati language and be thoroughly conversant with and be able to read and write in Gujarati, (iv) the basic knowledge of Computer application as prescribed in the Gujarat Civil services Classification and Recruitment (General) Rules, 1967; and (v) adequate knowledge of Gujarati and Hindi or both.

Pay Scale: 9300 − 34800 + 5400 Grade-pay

Age: A candidate shall not be less than 25 years of age and not be more than 35 years of age

Upper age limit shall be relaxed as per rules

3. Assistant Inspector of Motor Vehicles, Class-III

Educational Qualification:-

(A) Possess a Diploma in Mechanical Engineering (3 yrs course) or Diploma in Automobile Engineering (3 yrs course) or (2) a Degree in Mechanical engineering or Automobile Engineering of a recognized University or deemed university.

(B) The candidate shall possess a motor driving licence of motor cycle and light motor vehicles at the time of appointment.

(C) The Candidate shall obtain a driving licence of heavy goods vehicles or heavy passenger motor vehicles during the stipulated period of service on contractual basis.

(D) The candidate shall possess the basic knowledge of Computer Application as prescribed in the Gujarat Civil Service Classification and Recruitment (General) Rules, 1967

(E) The candidate shall possess the following minimum physical standards:

(i) For Male candidate height 162 centimetres (155 centimetres for Scheduled Tribes of Gujarat origin) and chest measurement 79 centimetres and weight 50 Kg.

(ii) For Female candidate height 158 centimetres (151 centimetres for Scheduled Tribes of Gujarat origin) and weight 45 Kg.

(iii) A candidate shall not be colour blind and have clear vision with or without glasses.

Age:- Not less than 19 years and not more than 30 years

Pay:- Rs. 10000 (Ten thousand only) per month for first five years. The candidate appointed shall be given, at the end of contractual period, the prescribed pay scale of the post of assistant inspector of motor vehicles, class-III

Examination pattern:-

There will be a written test for selection. There will be two question paper in written test and both papers are compulsory and multiple choice type.

Question paper-1 will be of either Mechanical Engineering or Automobile engineering of 200 marks with 155 minutes duration. In which Part-I will consist of 100 Questions each of one mark and Part-II will consist of 200 Questions each of one half mark. Question paper-2 will be of Gujarati language of 50 marks with 25 minutes duration, consist of 50 Questions each of one mark. Candidates have to give an option in the application form for Mechanical Engineering or Automobile Engineering.

Entry in written examination is provisional and without any scrutiny of the application.

Result of Question paper-1 will be prepared by using suitable scaling formula.

4. Assistant Engineer (Civil), Class-2

Educational Qualification:-

(1) Possess a degree of a B.E. in Civil Engineering of a recognized University or its equivalent qualification recognized by the Government of Gujarat.

(2) Possess the basic knowledge of Computer Application as prescribed in the Gujarat Civil Service Classification and Recruitment (General) Rules, 1967.

(3) Adequate knowledge of Gujarati and Hindi

Pay:- Rs. 9300 – 34800 (Grade pay – Rs. 4,600)

Age:- Not more than 30 years.

Selection Pattern:-

(1) The number of candidate to be called for Interview test shall be about three times of the number of vacancies.

(2) If the number of candidates available for Interview test is more than three times then Preliminary Test will be held.

(3) If the Commission decides to conduct the Preliminary Test considering the number of post and application received, the marks obtained by the candidate in the Preliminary Test shall be considered for short-listing the candidates to be called for Interview and such marks shall not be considered for final selection.

5. Horticulture Officer, Class-II

Educational Qualification:-

(i) A post graduate degree or a second class bachelor degree in any branch of Horticulture obtained from any of the Universities established or incorporated by or under the Central or State Act in India, or any other educational institution recognized as such or declared to be deemed as University under section 3 of the University Grants Commission Act, 1956, or possess on equivalent qualification recognized by the Government.

(ii) Basic knowledge of computer application as prescribed in the Gujarat Civil Services Classifications and Recruitment (General) Rules, 1967, as amended from time to time.

(iii) Adequate knowledge of Gujarati or Hindi or both.

Pay:- Rs. 9300 – 34800 (Grade pay – Rs. 4400)

Age:- Not more than 30 years.

Selection Pattern:-

(1) The number of candidate to be called for Interview test shall be about three times of the number of vacancies.

(2) If the number of candidates available for Interview test is more than three times then Preliminary Test will be held.

(3) If the Commission decides to conduct the Preliminary Test considering the number of post and application received, the marks obtained by the candidate in the Preliminary Test shall be considered for short-listing the candidates to be called for Interview and such marks shall not be considered for final selection.

6. Gujarat Educational Service class-II
Educational Qualification:-

(1) A bachelor's degree in Arts, Science, Commerce, Agriculture, or Law obtained from Indian or Foreign University recognized by the Government.

(2) Have passed B.T./B.Ed. or an equivalent degree or diploma of recognized University.

(3) About five years' teaching, inspecting or administrative experience after obtaining the B.T./B.Ed. or equivalent qualifications

(4) Adequate knowledge of Gujarati. Possess the basic knowledge of Computer Application as prescribed in the Gujarat Civil Services Classification and Recruitment (General) Rules, 1967.

Pay: Rs. 9300 – 34800 + Grade Pay Rs. 4600/-

Age: Not more than 36 years.

7. Dowry Prohibition Officer cum Protection Officer, General State Service, Class-II
(A) Educational Qualification:-

(1) A Post Graduate Degree in Social Work or Sociology or Psychology obtained from any of the Universities established or incorporated by or under the Central or State Act in India or any other educational institution recognized as such or declared to be a deemed University under Section-3 of the University Grants Commission Act, 1956; or possess an equivalent qualification recognized by the Government;

And

(2) (i) At least three years' experience of Social Work or Social Administration in Government or Local Bodies or Government Undertaking Board or Corporation on the post which can be considered equivalent to the post not below the rank of a Senior Clerk, Class- III in the Subordinate Service of the Directorate of Social Defence, or

(ii) At least three years' experience of Social Work or Social Administration or in the field related to Social Service of the Registered Non Government Organisation, or

(iii) At least three years' experience on the post connected with Social Services in the Private or Public Sector Organisation which can be considered equivalent to the post not below the rank of Senior Clerk, Class- III in the Subordinate Service of the Directorate of Social Defence;

And

(3) The basic knowledge of computer application as prescribed in the Gujarat Civil Services Classification and Recruitment (General) Rules, 1967

And

(4) Adequate knowledge of Gujarati and/or Hindi.

Note: The preference shall be given in such a way that the candidates selected are as far as possible women. For that purpose, 7% of actual marks obtained by women candidates shall be added in the Primary Test and Interview.

(B) Pay:- Pay Band Rs. 9300-34800/- Plus Grade pay Rs.4600/-

(C) Age:- Not more than 35 years

8. Assistant/Jr. Clerk Recruitment:-

Pay scale: Rs. 5200 – 20200/- plus Grade Pay of Rs. 1900/-.

Educational Qualification:- Candidate should be 12th pass with English Typing 30 w.p.m OR Gujarati Typing 25 w.p.m or equivalent.

Age Limit: 18 to 25 years

(For any query or for detailed information please visit http://gpsc.gujarat.gov.in)

12. HARYANA

Haryana Public Service Commission does the recruitment for the state. Haryana Public Service Commission also came into existence from 1st November, 1966.

Though the details of the various examinations can be accessed from the website of HPSC i.e. www.hpsc.gov.in some of the examinations have been discussed below to give a general overview.

Haryana Civil Services (Ex. Br.) & Other Allied Services

Sr. No	Post	Scale of Pay
1.	HCS (Ex. Br.)	15600 – 39100 + GP 5400/-
2.	E.T.O	9300 – 34800 + GP 5400/-
3.	District Food & Supplies Controller	9300 – 34800 + GP 5400/-
4.	Asstt. Registrar Co-Op. Societies	9300 – 34800 + GP 4600/-
5.	Asstt. Excise & Taxation Officer	9300 – 34800 + GP 4600/-
6.	Block Development & Panchayat Officer	9300 – 34800 + GP 4600/-
7.	Traffic Manager	9300 – 34800 + GP 4600/-
8.	Asstt. Employment Officer	9300 – 34800 + GP 4600/-
9.	District Food & Supplies Officer	9300 – 34800 + GP 4600/-

Essential Qualifications: Candidates must possess Degree of a recognized University of Bachelor of Arts/Science/Commerce or an equivalent degree of a recognized University.

Age: The candidate should not be less than 21 years and not more than 40 years of age.

Scheme of Examination: The examination will be Combined Competitive examination (CCE) comprising of the following stages:

(i) Preliminary Examination (Objective Type/Multiple choice) for screening only (General Studies & Optional paper)

(ii) Main Examination (Conventional/Essay Type)

(iii) Personality Test (Viva-voce)

1. Accounts Officer

Scale of Pay: Rs. 15600 – 39100 + Rs. 5900 with Grade Pay

Age:- A candidate should not be less than 18 years and not more than 40 years

Essential Qualification:
   (a) CA/ICWA with 2 years' post qualification experience (i.e. CA with 2 years experience or ICWA with 2 years experience)
   (b) Hindi/Sanskrit upto Matric standard.

2. Haryana Forest Service (Group 'B')

Pay scale:- 9300 – 34800 + 4600/- Grade Pay.

Age:- A candidate should not be less than 19 years and not more than 40 years

Essential Qualifications:
   (i) At least 2nd class degree of Bachelor or Master of natural science, Mathematics, Geology, Engineering or Agriculture or an equivalent qualification of a recognized University.
   (ii) Knowledge of Hindi up to Matric standard

Selection Procedure

(a) Written Examination

Compulsory papers
   (1) General Knowledge 100 marks
   (2) General English (Grammar, Essay and Precis Writing etc.) 100 marks

Optional papers (two subjects)

(b) Physical Test: Those who qualify the written examination shall have to undergo a physical test consisting of walk 25 kms & 14 kms in 4 hours by the male and female candidates respectively. The candidates must conform to the following minimum standards of physical fitness.

For Male Candidates

Height - 152.5 cms for male candidates belonging to SCs and races like Gorkhas, Napalese, Assamese, Meghalayese, Sikkimese, Bhutanese, Garhwalis etc. and 163 cm for other male candidates.

Chest - 79 cms unexpanded, 84 cms fully expanded

For Female Candidates

Height - 145 cms for female candidates belonging to SCs and races like Gorkhas, Napalese, Assamese, Meghalayese, Sikkimese, Bhutanese, Garhwalis etc. and 150 cm for other female candidates.

Chest - 74 cms unexpanded, 79 cms fully expanded

(c) Interview/viva-voce: Candidates who qualify in the written examination and also in the physical test shall be called for interview/viva-voce. Number of such candidates shall not exceed thrice the number of advertised vacancies. Marks for interview/viva-voce will be 85.

3. Treasury Officer (Group-B) in Finance Department

Scale of Pay: Rs. 9300 – 34800 + Rs. 5400 Grade Pay + Rs. 200 Special Pay

Age:- Candidate should not be below 21 years and not more than 40 years

Essential Qualifications:

(i) Bachelor Degree or its equivalent from a recognized University.

(ii) Knowledge of Hindi/Sanskrit up to Matric

Selection:- Screening test and interview

4. Assistant District Attorneys in Administration of Justice Department

Essential Qualifications:

(i) Degree of Bachelor of Laws (Professional) of a recognized University.

(ii) Should have enrolled as an Advocate with Bar Council.

(iii) Hindi or Sanskrit upto Matric Standard.

Scale of Pay: PB–2 - Rs. 9300 – 34800 + 4600 Grade Pay + 200 Special Pay.

Age: A Candidate should not be below 21 years and not more than 40 years

Selection:- Screening test and interview

5. Editor (Class-II)

Essential Qualifications:

(i) Graduate from a recognized University with Economics or Public Administration or Commerce or Sociology or Law Degree with Labour Laws as one of the subjects.

(ii) Degree or Diploma in Journalism from any recognized University or Institution.

(iii) Adequate knowledge of Hindi/Sanskrit

Scale of Pay: Rs. 9300 – 34800 + 4200/- G.P.

Age: A Candidate should not be below 21 years and not more than 40 years

Selection:- Screening test and interview

6. Curator (Group-B) (Unreserved) in Archaeology & Museums Department

Scale of Pay: Rs. 9300 – 34800 + Rs. 4200/- Grade Pay

Age: Not below 21 years and not more than 40 years

Essential Qualifications:

(1) Second Class M.A. in Ancient Indian History, Culture and Archaeology (with Archaeology Group) from a recognized University.

(2) Post Graduate Diploma in Archaeology.

(3) Hindi/Sanskrit up to Matric standard.

Preferential:-

(a) Research Experience with published research work in the field of Archaeology.

(b) Field experience and practical Training in Numismatic and Epigraphy.

(c) Sanskrit upto B.A. standard.

7. Distt Welfare Officer Class-II (Group-B) and Distt Social Welfare Officer (Group-B)

Scale of Pay: Rs. 9300 – 34800 + Rs. 4600 Grade Pay

Age: A Candidate should not be below 30 years and not more than 45.

Essential Qualifications:-
  (i) Master degree from a recognized University in Social work or Sociology or Economics.
  (ii) Five years field experience in the Development or Welfare Department of the Central or any state Govt.
  (iii) Hindi or Sanskrit up to Matric standard
  (iv) 2 years experience in Planning, Development and implementation of Renewable Energy/ Energy Conservation Projects/programmes in the Government Department/ Public Sector undertaking commercial organization of repute on the post of carrying pay scale not below the PB-2 9300–34800+3300 Grade Pay for equivalency the minimum average gross monthly pay in Private sector shall be Rs. 16000/-.

8. Assistant Statistical Officer

Scale of Pay: Rs. 9300 – 34800 + 4200/- Grade Pay.

Age: A Candidate should not be below 21 years and not more than 40 years.

Essential Qualifications:
  (i) At least 2nd Class Master's Degree in Statistics or Master's Degree in Economics with Statistics or Mathematics with Statistics or Agriculture Economics with Statistics from a recognized University/Institution.
  (ii) Hindi or Sanskrit up to Matric standard.

OR

  10+2/BA/MA with Hindi as one of the subjects.

9. 'A' Class Naib Tehsildar (Apprentices) Gazetted Class-II (Group 'B') in Revenue Department

Scale of Pay: Rs. 9300 – 34800 + Rs. 4600/- Grade Pay

Essential Qualifications:-
  (a) Graduate of a recognized University.
  (b) Knowledge of Hindi/Sanskrit upto Matric standard.

The selected candidates shall undergo revenue training as prescribed in section 10 of Haryana Revenue (Group-B) Rules, 1988 and amended in the year 2007.

Age: 21 to 40 years

Selection:-

a. **Screening test** It will consists General Science, Current Events of National & International importance, History of India & Indian National Movement, Indian & World Geography, Indian Culture, Indian Polity & Indian Economy, General Mental Ability, Haryana-Economy & people, Social, Economic & Cultural institutions and language of Haryana. The screening test will be of two hours duration. The question paper comprising of 100 questions and will be of 100 marks. There will be no negative marking. The Screening test will be of qualifying nature and marks obtained in the screening test will not be given any weightage for final selection.

b. **Interview** For detailed information regarding Haryana state examination candidates are advised to visit the website http://hpsc.gov.in

13. HIMACHAL PRADESH

The recruitment to various services in the state is done by Himachal Pradesh Public Service Commission (HPPSC). There are following types of entrance tests:

Recruitment through examination followed by viva-voce: Through this method of recruitment the candidates are first to appear in the examination and thereafter, the qualified candidates are called for Viva-Voce. Merit list is prepared on the basis of written examination plus viva-voce and thereafter the candidates are selected on the basis of rank. The services for which such examinations are conducted are as under:

- Himachal Pradesh Administrative Services etc. Examination (HPAS)
- Himachal Pradesh Judicial Services (HPJS)
- State Forest Services (HFS)
- Forest Rangers

Recruitment through examination without viva-voce: Through this method of recruitment, the Departmental candidates (in-service candidates) are put into examination for such posts as are received by the Commission from different Departments of State Government. The Examinations as being conducted by the Commission for various categories of posts are as under:
- State Accounts Services (O.B.) – S.A.S.-OB
- State Accounts Services (L.A.D.) – S.A.S.-L.A.D.

The candidates are selected on the basis of merit of written examination

Recruitment through interview preceded by screening test: Wherever there is a large number of candidates for some posts the method of short-listing of candidates by conducting Screening Test is adopted and those who qualify in the screening test are called for interview and candidates thereafter are selected on merit basis only.

Recruitment through interview without conducting screening test: Where the number of candidates is less in comparison to the number of posts available, the candidates are directly called for interview and selected on merit basis.

Though details of the various examinations can be accessed from the website i.e. **www.hp.gov.in** some of the examinations have been discussed below to give a general overview.

1. H.P. Administrative Combined Competitive Examination
The following posts fill up on the basis of H.P.A.S. Combined Competitive Examination
   1. **Himachal Pradesh Administrative Services**
   2. **Himachal Pradesh Police Services**
   3. **Tehsildar**
   4. **Excise & Taxation Officer**
   5. **Block Development Officer**
   6. **District Panchayat Officer**
   7. **Manager, District Industries Centre;**
   8. **District Welfare-cum-Probation Officers**
   9. **Assistant, Registrar Co-operative Societies**

10. **District Employment Officer**
11. **District Treasury Officer**
12. **District Food & Civil Supplies Controller**
13. **Assistant Controller, Weights & Measures**

Eligibility Criteria

1. A candidate must be a citizen of India
2. Minimum Educational Qualifications
(a) A candidate must possess a Bachelor's Degree or its equivalent from a recognized University.
(b) A candidate who has appeared at an examination, the passing of which would render him eligible to appear at this examination but has not been informed of result, may apply for admission to the examination. A candidate, who intends to appear at such a qualifying examination, may also apply provided the qualifying examination is completed before the commencement of this examination. Such candidates will be admitted to the examination, if otherwise eligible, but the admission would be deemed to be provisional and subject to cancellation if they do not produce proof of having passed the examination as soon as possible and in any case not later than two months after the commencement of this examination, failing which their candidature shall automatically stand cancelled.
(c) Candidates who have passed the final professional M.B.B.S. or any other Medical Examination equivalent thereto but have not completed their internship by the time of submission of their application for the HAS etc. examination will be provisionally admitted to the examination provided they submit along with their applications a copy of certificate from the University/Institutions that they had passed the requisite final professional medical examination. In such cases, the candidates will be required to produce, at the time of their interview, original degree or a certificate from the concerned competent authority of the University/ Institutions that they had completed or requirement

(including completion of internship) for the award of degree.

3. **Age Limit:** A candidate must have attained the age of 21 years and must not have attained the age of 35 years.

SCHEME OF EXAMINATION:

1. **Preliminary Examination**

   (A) Initially, Preliminary examination consisting of 02 papers based on objective type (multiple choices) questions on the following pattern will be held.

   Paper-I General Studies (Code No. 01). This paper shall be of 200 marks and there shall be 100 objective type (Multiple choice) questions.

   Paper-II Aptitude Test (Code No. 02). This paper shall be of 200 marks and in this paper there shall be 100 objective type (multiple choice) questions.

   The duration of Papers I and II (General Studies and Aptitude Test) will be two hours each.

   (B) This preliminary examination will consist of two objective type papers (multiple choice questions) and carry a maximum of 400 marks.

2. **Main Written Examination**

3. **Viva-Voce**

NOTE: Marks obtained by the candidates in the (Preliminary) examination will not be counted for the purpose of final order of merit. However, marks obtained in the Main written examination as well as in the viva-voce test would determine their final merit for selection.

2. Himachal Pradesh Forest Service (HPFS) (Assistant Conservator of Forests) Class-I, Gazetted

Pay Scale:- Rs. 10300 – 34800 + 5000 G.P.

Age: 21 to 34 years

Eligibility Criteria

1 A candidate must be a citizen of India.

2 Minimum Educational Qualifications

(a) A candidate must possess a Bachelor's Degree or its equivalent in Science or Engineering from a recognized University with at least one of the following subjects:-

Agriculture, Botany, Chemistry, Computer Application/Science, Engineering (Agriculture/Chemical/Civil/Computer/ Electrical/ Electronics/Mechanical), Environmental Science, Forestry, Geology, Horticulture, Mathematics, Physics, Statistics, Veterinary Science, Zoology.

3 Desirable Qualification:-

The knowledge of customs, manners and dialects of Himachal Pradesh and suitability for appointment in the peculiar conditions prevailing in the State of Himachal Pradesh.

Physical Standard:-

For Male	For Female
• Height: 163 cms.	• Height: 150 cms.
• Chest: 79 cms without expansion & 84 cms with expansion.	• Chest: 74 cms without expansion & 79 cms with expansion.
• Capacity to walk: 25 kms in 04 hours.	• Capacity to walk: 16 kms in 04 hours.

Scheme of Examination: The written examination shall include three compulsory and two optional papers. All papers shall be of three hours duration.

Sr. No.	Papers	Marks
COMPULSORY PAPERS		
	General Knowledge	100
	General English	100
	Hindi	100
OPTIONAL SUBJECTS		
	Optional Paper - I	200
	Optional Paper - II	200
VIVA-VOCE		
	Interview	100

The candidates who qualify in the Written Examination will be called for Physical Standard Test and then for Interview.

3. Child Development Project Officer, Class-II (Gazetted)

Pay band:- Rs. 10300 – 34800/- + 4400/- (Grade Pay)

Tehsil Welfare Officer, Class-II (Non-Gazetted)

Pay band:- Rs. 10300 – 34800/- + 4200/- (Grade Pay)

Essential Qualification:-

Bachelor's Degree in any discipline from a recognized University.

Desirable Qualification:- Knowledge of customs, manners and dialects of Himachal Pradesh & suitability for appointment in the peculiar conditions prevailing in the Pradesh.

Age: Between 18 & 45 years.

SCHEME OF EXAMINATION

Screening Test:- Paper of 02 hours duration consisting of 120 marks (General Knowledge) (Objective type). The marks obtained by the candidates in the screening test will not be counted for determining their final order of merit.

Main written examination:-

Paper No.	Paper	Max. Marks	Duration of paper
I	General Knowledge & Current Affairs	100 Marks	02 hours
II	General English	50 Marks	1:30 hours
III	English Essay	50 Marks	1:30 hours
IV	Hindi	50 Marks	1:30 hours

Naib Tehsildar ('A' Class), Class-II (Gazetted)

Pay band:- Rs. 10300 – 34800/- + 4800/- (Grade Pay)

Essential Qualification:- Graduate from a recognized University.

Desirable Qualification:- Knowledge of customs, manners and dialects of Himachal Pradesh & suitability for appointment in the peculiar conditions prevailing in the Pradesh.

Age:- A candidate must have attained the age of 21 years and must not have attained the age of 45 years.

SCHEME OF EXAMINATION

Screening Test:- Screening Test of two hours' duration, will be conducted consisting of one paper of General Knowledge of 120 questions of multiple choice answers for short listing the candidates for the Main Examination. The marks obtained by the candidates in the screening test will not be counted for determining their final order of merit.

Main Examination:-

Paper No.	Paper	Max. Marks	Duration of paper
I	General Knowledge & Current Affairs	100 Marks	02 hours
II	General English	50 Marks	1:30 hours
III	English Essay	50 Marks	1:30 hours
IV	Hindi	50 Marks	1:30 hours

4. Civil Judge (Jr. Div.)

(Pay scale Rs. 27,700-44,770)

Essential Qualifications:

(a) Candidate must be a holder of degree in Law as recognized by the Bar Council of India.

(b) A candidate must be a citizen of India.

Desirable Qualification:

Knowledge of customs, manners and dialects, and suitability for appointment in the peculiar conditions prevailing in the State of Himachal Pradesh.

Age Limit: A candidate must have attained the age of 22 years but must not be more than 30 years of age.

SCHEME OF EXAMINATION:

Preliminary Examination:

The preliminary examination shall be an objective type examination consisting of the following three papers of 100 marks each:-

- Civil Law-I
- Civil Law-II
- Criminal Law

Each paper shall be of one-hour duration and the examination in all the three papers shall be held on the same day.

Main (Narrative) Examination:

Main Examination will be consisting of 05 papers as follows:-

Paper No.	Paper	Max. Marks	Duration of paper
I	Civil Law-I	200 Marks	03 hours
II	Civil Law-II	200 Marks	03 hours
III	Criminal Law	200 Marks	03 hours
IV	English Composition	200 Marks	03 hours
V	Language (Hindi)	100 Marks	03 hours

Minimum Qualifying Marks:

(i) No candidate shall be credited with any marks in any paper unless he obtains at least 45 per cent marks in that paper, except Hindi language paper (paper-V) in which candidate should obtain at least 33 per cent marks.

(ii) No candidate shall be considered to have qualified the written test unless he obtains 50 percent marks in aggregate in all papers and at least 33 percent marks in language paper i.e. Hindi in Devnagiri script.

Viva-Voce: The maximum marks for the viva-voce shall be 100. The marks obtained in the viva-voce will be added to the marks obtained in the main written examination for purpose of selection of the candidates.

5. Clerk

Pay Scale:- Rs. 7810/- p.m. consolidated fixed contractual amount.

(A) Essential Qualification

(i) Should have passed 10+2 examination or its equivalent from a recognized Board of School Education/University.

(ii) Should possess a minimum speed of 30 words per minute in English typewriting or 25 words per minute in Hindi typewriting on computer.

(iii) Should have the Knowledge of word processing in computer as prescribed by the recruiting authority.

(B) Desirable Qualification

Knowledge of customs, manners and dialects of Himachal Pradesh and suitability for appointment considering the peculiar conditions prevailing in the state.

Age: A candidate must have attained the age of 18 years and must not have attained the age of 45 years.

Selection is done through screening test/interview.

14. JAMMU & KASHMIR

The Jammu and Kashmir Public Service Commission was constituted under section 128 of the Constitution of J&K, on September 2, 1957 for the recruitment of State Service Officers. The functions of the Commission, as defined under section 133 of the Constitution of the State. The official website for the Jammu & Kashmir Public Service Commission is **http://www.jkpsc.nic.in/**

List of important examinations conducted by Jammu and Kashmir Public Service Commission:

- Jammu & Kashmir Civil Services
- Jammu & Kashmir Judicial Services
- Examination for J&K Statistics & Statistical cum Evaluation Service
- Recruitment to the post of Range Officers
- Recruitment to the post of Assistant Director (Statistics)
- Recruitment to the post of Assistant Conservator of Forest
- Recruitment to the post of Medical Officer in different disciplines
- Recruitment to the post of Assistant Surgeons in different disciplines

- Recruitment to the post of Lecturers in different disciplines
- Recruitment to the post of Assistant Engineers in different disciplines
- Recruitment to the post of ITI Superintendent
- Recruitment to the post of Assistant Research Officer
- Recruitment to the post of Horticulture Development Officer
- Recruitment to the post of Fisheries Development Officer
- Recruitment for Various Group B & Group C posts for various departments

Candidates are advised to visit the website for the updates on recruitment for various services. The eligibility criteria, method of recruitment, syllabi and other details can be obtained by visiting the Commission's website.

15. JHARKHAND

The Jharkhand Public Service Commission was constituted under the provisions of the of the Constitution of India for the recruitment of State Service Officers. The official website for the Jharkhand Public Service Commission is http://www.jpsc.gov.in

List of important examinations conducted by Jharkhand Public Service Commission:

- Jharkhand Civil Service Examination
- Recruitment to the post of Civil Judge
- Recruitment to the post of Medical Officer
- Recruitment to the post of Drug Inspector
- Recruitment to the post of Asst. Public Prosecutor
- Recruitment to the post of Engineers & Asst. Engineers in different disciplines
- Recruitment to the post of District Fisheries Officer

Candidates are advised to visit the website for the updates on recruitment for various services. The eligibility criteria, method of recruitment, syllabi and other details can be obtained by visiting the Commission's website.

16. KARNATAKA

The KPSC (Karnataka Public Service Commission) was established in 1951 under the provisions of the Constitution for the recruitment of candidates to the various services across the state of Karnataka.

The details of the various examinations can be accessed from the website of KPSC i.e. **www.kpsc.kar.nic.in, www.ksp.gov.in, www.kset.uni-mysore.ac.in, www.kptcl.com** the details of some of the examinations have been discussed below to give a general overview.

1. Karnataka Administrative Services (Recruitment of Gazetted probationers Examination)

KPSC conducts KAS exam to recruit the various candidates for various posts in Group I and II.

KPSC KAS Exam Pattern: KAS exam is conducted into three parts:

Part A: Preliminary examination

Part B: Main examination

Part C: Personality Test

Age limit: 19 to 35 years for general candidates and relaxation to some specified candidates

Educational Qualification:- Graduation

Part – A Preliminary Examination:

Paper – I:

Part I (National/International/Current Affairs)

Part II (Humanities/Arts/History)

Part I contains 40 questions from National & International current affairs; carries 80 marks in total.

Part II contains 60 questions from Humanities, Arts & History; carries 120 marks in total.

Part – B Main Examination

Compulsory Papers:- Kannada and English

Paper I: Kannada Language paper – 150 Marks

Paper II: English Language Paper – 150 Marks

Paper III: General Studies

Modern History of India and Indian Culture with special reference to the History and Culture of Karnataka, Current events of State, National and International importance, Statistical Analysis, Graphs and Diagrams

Paper IV: General Studies

Indian Polity with special reference to Karnataka State, Indian Economy and Geography of India with Special reference to Karnataka, Economy and Karnataka Geography, The role and impact of Science and Technology in the development of Karnataka and India.

Papers V, VI, VII & VIII

Two subjects to be selected from the list of optional subjects. Each subject will have two papers-300 marks for each paper

Elective Subjects: (Subject Code: Elective Subjects)

Botany, Chemistry, Civil, Engineering, Electrical Engineering, History, Mechanical Engineering, Philosophy, Agriculture, Sericulture, Agricultural, Marketing and Co-operation, Commerce, Accounting, Business Organization Secretarial Practice, Criminology, Economics, Karnataka Zoology, Fisheries Economy, Animal Husbandry, Veterinary Sciences, Urdu Syllabus, Geography, Law, Mathematics, Political Science and Public, Administration, Kannada, English, Management, Geology, Physics, Sociology, Statistics, Rural Development & Cooperation, Hindi, Anthropology, International Relations, Psychology

Part C. Personality Test

2. Karnataka State Police

Eligibility criteria:

Contenders should have possessed PUC, 12th standard, JOC or JLC from any recognized university or institute.

Age Limitation:

Age Limitation of the aspirants should be minimum 19 years old to 25 years old for General Category and the applicants belonging to the reserved category should be minimum 19 years to 27 years old.

Selection Process:

Job seekers will be selected on the basis of:
- Endurance Test
- Physical Standard Test
- Written Examination: It will consist of multiple choice questions of 100 marks - duration of 1 hour.

3. Karnataka State Eligibility Test (KSET) for Lecturer/ Assistant Professors

Eligibility

(1) Candidates who have secured at least 55% of marks (without rounding off) for general category and 50% for Schedule Category (SC), Scheduled Tribe (ST), Persons With Disability (PWD-VH/PH), Category I, IIA, IIB, IIIA, IIIB candidates, in master's degree OR equivalent examination from universities/institutions recognized by UGC New Delhi, in subjects like Science, Humanities (including languages), Social science, Computer Science & Applications, Electronic science etc., are eligible to appear for this test.

(2) Candidates who have appeared OR will be appearing at the qualifying Master's degree (final year) examination and whose result is still awaited OR candidates whose qualifying examinations have been delayed may also appear for this Test. However, such candidates will be admitted provisionally and for those who clear the KSET examination, eligibility certificate will be issued only on production of proof for having passed the Master's degree or equivalent examination securing at least 55% marks (50% in case of SC, ST, PWD (VH/PH), Category I, IIA,

IIB, IIIA, IIIB candidates) within two years from the date of KSET examination, failing which they will be treated as disqualified.

(3) The Ph.D. Degree holders whose Master's level examination had been completed on or before 19th September 1991 (irrespective of declaration of result) shall be eligible for a relaxation of 5% marks for appearing in KSET examination.

(4) Candidates shall appear for KSET examination in their relevant subject of their post-graduation only, in case the candidate did not find the subject of his post-graduation in the list of KSET subjects, the candidate may appear in UGC-NET/UGC-CSIR NET which is held twice a year.

Age limit:

(1) There is no upper age limit to apply for KSET examination.

Exemption:

(1) KSET shall remain the minimum eligibility condition for recruitment of Lecturers/Assistant Professors in Universities/ Colleges/Institutions of Higher education (Government/ Aided/ Private) in Karnataka State.

(a) However, as per UGC guidelines, candidates, who have awarded Ph.D. Degree in compliance with the UGC Regulation 2009 (minimum standards and procedures for award of Ph.D. Degree), shall be exempted from KSET eligibility as the minimum requirement for recruitment of Lecturers/Assistant Professors in Universities/Colleges/Institutions of Higher education.

(b) The candidates who have passed the UGC-NET/CSIR JRF examination prior to 1989 are also exempted from KSET examination.

Scheme and date of examination:

The test will be consisting of three papers. The test for all the three papers will consist of only Multiple-choice Questions (MCQ).

Session	Paper	Max. Marks	Number of Question
I	100	60 out of which 50 questions to be attempted	1 ¼ Hours
II	100	50 questions all are compulsory	1 ¼ Hours
III	150	75 questions all are compulsory	2 ½ Hours

Paper I: General Paper is on Teaching and Aptitude: This Paper shall be of general nature, intended to assess the teaching/research aptitude of the candidate. It will primarily be designed to test reasoning ability, comprehension, divergent thinking and general awareness of the candidate.

Paper II: Subject Paper: This Paper shall consist of questions based on the subject selected by the candidate. Each paper will consist of a Test Booklet containing 50 compulsory Multiple-choice questions (MCQ) of two marks each and maximum marks will be 100.

Paper III: Subject paper (in depth questions): This Paper will consist of 75 Multiple-choice (MCQ) compulsory questions from the subject selected by the candidates. Each question will carry two marks and maximum marks will be 150.

Syllabus

Syllabus for KSET exam will be same as that for UGC/CSIR-NET.Syllabi for all the KSET subjects can be downloaded from the KSET website http://kset.uni-mysore.ac.in.

4. Karnataka Power Transmission Corporation Limited (KPTCL) Assistant Lineman

Eligibility:

ITI candidates - Should have a pass certificate of 18/24 months course in "Electrician/Electronics/Electronic Mechanic" trade from Industrial Training Institutes (ITI) recognized by Government of Karnataka.

ITC Candidates - Should have passed 10th Std Examination and pass certificate of three years "Lineman trade/Electrician trade" (ITC) imparted by the Industrial Training Institutes of KEB/KPTCL.

Age Limit: 35 years for General; 38 years for Category candidates; 40 years for SC/ST candidates.

Selection Process: Endurance Test.

5. Karnataka Post Office Recruitment

Postal Assistant, Sorting Assistant, Multi-Tasking Staff (MTS), Postman

Age Limit: Between 18-27 years as on 28/07/2014 with permissible relaxation in upper age limit as per rules for SC/ST/OBC.

Educational Qualification: Matriculation/SSLC from a recognized Board or University.

Selection Process: Aptitude Test of the level of 10th Class/ Matriculation.

6. Panchayat Development Officer

Age limit: 18-40 years

Eligibility: Graduation

Selection:

Paper I: Computer Literacy (Qualifying examination only)

Paper II:
1. General Knowledge – 30 marks
2. Kannada Language – 30 marks
3. Rural development and Panchayati Raj – 30 marks
4. General English – 30 marks

17. MADHYA PRADESH

Madhya Pradesh Public Service Commission (MPPSC) was formed on 1st November 1956 under the provisions of the constitution for recruitment to various services in the state.

The details of the various examinations can be accessed from the website of MPPSC i.e. **www.mppsc.nic.in** some of the examinations have been discussed below to give a general overview.

MPPSC State Service Examination
Details of Post

1. **General Administration Department – Deputy Chairman**
   (Pay scale 15600 – 39100 + 5400 grade pay)

2. **Home (Police) Department - Deputy Superintendent of Police**
   (Pay scale 15600 – 39100 + 5400 grade pay)

3. **Jail Department – Superintendent, District Jail**
   (Pay scale 15600 – 39100+5400 grade pay)

4. **Commercial Tax Department – Commercial Tax Officer**
   (Pay scale 15600 – 39100 + 5400 grade pay)

5. **Commercial Tax Department – District Registrar**
   (Pay scale 15600 – 39100 + 5400 grade pay)

6. **Urban Administration and Development Department - Chief Municipal Officer**
   (Pay scale 15600 – 39100 + 5400 grade pay)

7. **Public Relations Department – Assistant Director**
   (Pay scale 15600 – 39100 + 5400 grade pay)

8. **Food, Civil Supplies and Consumer Protection Department - Assistant Director, District Supply Officer**
   (Pay scale 15600 – 39100 + 5400 grade pay)

9. **Women and Child Development Department - Assistant Director**
   (Pay scale 15600 – 39100 + 5400 grade pay)

10. **Women and Child Development Department - Child Development Project Officer**
    (Pay scale 9300 – 34800 + 3600 grade pay)

11. **Transport Department - Assistant Regional Transport Officer**
    (Pay scale 9300 – 34800 + 3600 grade pay)

12. **Jail Department – Assistant Jail Superintendent**
    (Pay scale 5200 – 20200 + 2800 grade pay)
13. **Revenue Department – Nayab Tehsildar**
    (Pay scale 5200 – 20200 + 2800 grade pay)
14. **Municipal Admin and Dev. Dept – Chief Municipality Officer (Class-C)**
    (Pay scale 5200 – 20200 + 2800 grade pay)
15. **Commercial Tax Dept – Excise Sub-Inspector**
    (Pay scale 9300 – 34800 + 3600 grade pay)
16. **Commercial Tax Dept – Deputy Registrar**
    (Pay scale 9300 – 34800 + 3600 grade pay)

Educational Qualification: Graduate or equivalent.

Age: 21 yrs to 40 yrs.

For Home (Police) Department - Deputy Superintendent of Police: 20-25yrs.

Jail Department – Superintendent, District Jail: 21-30 yrs.

Jail Department – Assistant Jail Superintendent: 18-30 yrs

Commercial Tax Dept – Excise Sub-Inspector: 20-30 yrs

PLAN OF EXAMINATION

1. The combined competitive examination comprises two successive stages:

(1) **Preliminary Examination** (Objective types) having two papers

Paper	Subject	Time	Marks
Paper I	General Studies	2 hrs	200
Paper II	General Aptitude	2 hrs	200

(2) **Main Examination** (written and interview)

Main Examination will consist of a written examination and an interview test.

(1) Written Examination – The written examination will consist of seven papers of conventional essay type questions as given below:-

(a) Compulsory Papers

Paper I	General Studies 3 hrs.	300 Marks
Paper II	General Studies 3 hrs.	300 Marks
Paper III	General Hindi 3 hrs.	300 Marks

(b) Optional Papers:- Any two subjects are to be selected. Each subject will have two papers of 3 hours duration and 300 marks for each paper.

(2) Interview Test – The interview test will carry 250 marks.

(For details please visit http://www.mppsc.nic.in/)

I. Assistant Professor
Name of Discipline

Commerce	Economics	Hindi	Home Science	Law
Botany	Mathematics	Music	Philosophy	Political Science
Physics	Sociology	Zoology		Urdu

Eligibility Criteria
Educational Qualification:

(a) Graduate level there should be at least 55% marks provided that for the Scheduled Castes and Scheduled Tribes candidates the percentage of marks shall be 50%.

(b) Passed National Eligibility Test (NET) or Madhya Pradesh State Level Eligibility Test (SLET) or Ph.D. Degree Holder.

(c) National Eligibility Test (NET) shall be compulsory qualification for appointment as Assistant Professor for those who are having only Post Graduate Degree. However, the candidates having Ph.D. Degree in the concerned subject are exempted from National Eligibility Test (NET) Examination for postgraduate level and undergraduate level teaching. The candidates having M. Phil. Degree in the concerned subject are exempted from National Eligibility Test (NET) for undergraduate level teaching only.

Age Limit: Between 21 – 40 years

Selection: Final selection will be made on the total marks obtained in written competitive exam, interview and bonus marks obtained by experience gained as guest faculty in the govt. college of Madhya Pradesh.

II. **Assistant Research Officer**

Pay Scale: Rs. 15600 – 39100 Grade Pay 5400/-

Educational Qualification: The candidates must have attained a post graduation degree with a minimum of second division marks.

Age Limit as on 01 January: The age of candidate must be between 21 to 40 years.

Selection: Through written exam and interview.

III. **Legal Assistant/Law Clerk cum Research Assistant**

Eligibility: Candidate's minimum educational qualification must be graduate degree in law or equivalent from a recognized college/university/institute

IV. **City Program Manager**

Minimum Qualification: Post-graduate degree in Economics/Sociology/History/Political Science/Ancient Indian History Culture and Archeology/Social Work/Geography/Psychology or equivalent

Salary offered: 60000/pm.

V. **Consultant Community Officer**

Minimum Qualification: Post-graduate in Economics/Sociology/History/Political Science/Ancient Indian History Culture and Archeology/Social Work/Geography/Psychology.

Salary offered: Rs. 50000/pm.

VI. **Data Assistant (LDC Support for MIS)**

Minimum Qualification: Post-graduate degree or equivalent.

Salary offered: Rs. 30000/pm

VII. **Scientific Officer (Physics/Chemistry/Biology)**

(Pay scale 15600 – 39100 + 5400 grade pay)

Minimum Qualification: Post Graduation Degree in the concerned subject.

Age: 21 - 40 yrs

Selection: Written exam and interview

18. MANIPUR

The Manipur Public Service Commission is the Constitutional body constituted for recommending candidates for recruitment to various posts of the Government of Manipur (gazetted posts). It also gives concurrence on the recommendation of Departmental Promotion Committee for appointment to various posts. The Commission also gives concurrence on the framing/ amendment of Recruitment Rules. It also tenders advice to the Government Departments on service matters including disciplinary cases.

List of important examinations conducted by Manipur Public Service Commission:
- Manipur Civil Services
- Manipur Police Services
- Manipur Educational Services
- Manipur Engineering Services
- Manipur Health Services
- Recruitment for the post of Election Officer
- Recruitment for the post of Assistant Conservator of Forests
- Recruitment for the post of Section Officer Grade I & II

The scheme of examination, syllabi and minimum qualifying marks varies for the above mentioned examinations. Candidates are advised to visit the following website for further details: **www.mpscmanipur.gov.in**

19. MEGHALAYA

Meghalaya Public Service Commission (MPSC) has been formed under the provisions of constitution for recruitment to various services in the state. It came into existence on 14th September 1972.

List of important examinations conducted by Meghalaya Public Service Commission:
- Meghalaya Civil Services Examination
- Meghalaya Police Services Examination
- Recruitment for the post of Treasury Officer and Finance and Accounts Officer
- Recruitment for the post Judicial Magistrate Grade – III
- Recruitment for the post Junior Engineer Grade – I
- Recruitment for the post Assistant System Engineer
- Recruitment for the post Orchidologist
- Recruitment for the post District Sports Officer
- Recruitment for the post Health Education Instructor
- Recruitment for the post Motor Vehicle Inspector
- Recruitment for the post Enforcement Inspector
- Recruitment for the post Food Safety Officer
- Recruitment for the post Junior Divisional Accountant
- Recruitment for the post Tourist Officer
- Recruitment for the post Nutritionist under Social Welfare Department
- Recruitment for the post Health Instructor under Social Welfare Department
- Recruitment for the post Animal Husbandry & Veterinary Officers

The scheme of examination, syllabi and minimum qualifying marks varies for the above mentioned examinations. Candidates are advised to visit the following website for further details: **www.mpsc.nic.in**

20. MIZORAM

It has become a constitutional necessity under the provisions of the Constitution of India to have a Public Service Commission to be consulted by the State Government on the matters of appointment to Civil Services and posts under the Government of Mizoram. The very first action of the State Government towards constituting its own Public Service Commission was to create various posts under envisaged Public Service Commission like Secretaries, Clerical Staff, drivers and peon which were a necessity for an establishment.

List of important examinations conducted by Mizoram Public Service Commission:

Mizoram Civil Services

Mizoram Educational Services

Mizoram Engineering Services

Recruitment for the post of Law Officer

Recruitment for the post of District Sainik Welfare & Resettlement Officer

The scheme of examination, syllabus and minimum qualifying marks varies for the above mentioned examinations. Candidates are advised to visit the following website for further details: **http://www.mpsc.mizoram.gov.in**

21. NAGALAND

The recruitment to various services in the state is done by Nagaland Public Service Commission. It came into existence in 1965.

Types of Examinations

  (a) **NCS/NPS/NSS & Allied Services Examination:**

    (i) Stage I   -   Preliminary Examination

    (ii) Stage II   -   Main Examination

    (iii) Stage III   -   Interview

  (b) **Technical Services and others not included under (a) above:**

    (i) Stage I   -   Written Examination

    (ii) Stage II   -   Interview

  (c) **Recruitment of LDA-cum-Computer Assistants in the Nagaland Civil Secretariat, Directorates and Districts Offices.**

    (i) Stage I   -   Written Examination only

    (ii) Stage II   -   Practical Examination

(d) Selection by Interview only

List of important examinations conducted by Nagaland Public Service Commission

- NCS, NPS, NSS & Allied Services Examination
- Common Educational Services Examination
- Combined Technical Services Examination
- Recruitment for Post of Extra Assistant Commissioner
- Recruitment for Post Deputy Superintendent of Police
- Recruitment for Post Youth Resources Officer
- Recruitment for Post Station Superintendent
- Recruitment for Post Secretariat Assistant
- Recruitment for Post Research Assistant
- Recruitment for Post Veterinary Assistant Surgeon
- Recruitment for Post Assistant Geologist
- Recruitment for Post District Evaluation Officer
- Recruitment for Post Assistant Soil Survey Officer
- Recruitment for Post Assistant Research Officer

The scheme of examination, syllabi and minimum qualifying marks varies for the above mentioned examinations. For further details about the same, kindly visit: **http://www.npsc.co.in**

22. ODISHA

Odisha Public Service Commission was constituted on 1st April 1949 under the provisions of Constitution for recruitment of State Service Officers. The official website for the Odisha Public Service Commission is **http://www.opsc.gov.in**

List of important examinations conducted by Odisha Public Service Commission:

- Odisha Civil Service Examination
- Odisha Judicial Service Examination
- Recruitment to the post of Lecturers & Professors in different disciplines
- Recruitment to the post of Scientific Officer

- Recruitment to the post of Assistant Agriculture Officer
- Recruitment to the post of Homoeopathic Medical Officer, Ayurvedic Medical Officer etc.
- Recruitment to the post of Drugs Inspector
- Recruitment to the post of Public Prosecutor
- Recruitment to the posts of Radiologist, Geologist, Anaesthetists, Geophysicist etc.
- Recruitment to the post of Surgeons
- Recruitment to the post of Tourist Officer
- Recruitment to the post of Mining Officer
- Recruitment to the post of Engineers & Jr. Engineers in different disciplines

Candidates are advised to visit the website for the updates on recruitment for various services. The eligibility criteria, method of recruitment, syllabi and other details can be obtained by visiting the Commission's website.

23. PUNJAB

The Punjab Public Service Commission was formed in February, 1948 and is placed under the provisions of the Constitution of India for the recruitment of State Service Officers. The official website for the Punjab Public Service Commission is **http://www.ppsc.gov.in/**

List of important examinations conducted by Punjab Public Service Commission:

- Punjab State Civil Services
- Recruitment to the post of Sub Divisional Engineers
- Recruitment to the post of Scientific Officer & Scientific Assistant
- Recruitment to the post of Assistant Geologist
- Recruitment to the post of Mining Officer
- Recruitment to the post of District Sports Officer
- Recruitment to the post of Assistant District Attorney & Deputy District Attorney

- Recruitment to the post of Section Officer
- Recruitment to the post of Medical Officer in different disciplines
- Recruitment to the post of Assistant Town Planner
- Recruitment to the post of Audit Officer
- Recruitment to the post of District Programme Officer
- Recruitment to the post of Drug Inspector
- Recruitment to the post of Assistant Director/Principal
- Recruitment to the post of Child Development Project Officer
- Recruitment to the post of Assistant Architect
- Recruitment to the post of Civil Judge (Junior Division) & Judicial Magistrate
- Recruitment to the posts of System Analyst, Senior Assistant, Accountant, Senior Scale Stenographer, Programmer, Database Administrator, Network Engineer
- Recruitment for Various Group B & Group C posts for various Departments

Candidates are advised to visit the website for the updates on recruitment for various services. The eligibility criteria, method of recruitment, syllabi and other details can be obtained by visiting the Commission's website.

24. SIKKIM

Sikkim Public Service Commission was formed in 1982 for recruitment to various services in the state.

List of important examinations conducted by Sikkim Public Service Commission

- Sikkim Civil Services
- Sikkim Police Services
- Recruitment for the post of Assistant Engineers and Junior Engineers
- Recruitment for the post of Tibetan Teacher at Pemayangtse Monastery

- Recruitment for the post of Junior Mechanical
- Recruitment for the post of Principal and Lecturer
- Recruitment for the post of Account Officer
- Recruitment for the post of Senior Information Assistant
- Recruitment for the post of Post Graduate Teacher
- Recruitment for the post of Assistant Geologist
- Recruitment for Para-Medical Service
- Recruitment for the post of Sub Inspector

The scheme of examination, syllabus and minimum qualifying marks varies for the above mentioned examinations. Candidates are advised to visit the following website for further details: **www.spcskm.gov.in**

25. UTTAR PRADESH

The Uttar Pradesh Public Service Commission (UPPSC) is the state agency authorized to conduct the Civil Services Examination for entry-level appointments to the various Civil Services of Uttar Pradesh.

Though the details of the various examinations can be accessed from the website of UPPSC i.e. www.uppsc.org, www.allahabadhighcourt.in, www.uptet.co.in, details of some of the examinations have been discussed below to give a general overview.

Examination Conducted by the Commission
- Combined State/Upper Subordinate Preliminary and Main Examination
- R.O./A.R.O. Preliminary and Main Examination
- Additional Private Secretary Examination

1. Combined state/upper subordinate services examination

Eligibility: Graduation in any discipline

Age Limit: Between 21 years to 40 years

Plan of Examination: The competitive examination comprises three successive stages viz:-

(1) Objective Type Test (200 marks) (2) Mains test (Written test) (3) Viva-Voce (Personality Test)

UPPCS Syllabus
PAPER – I
General Studies-I (200 marks)

History of India and Indian National Movement, Current events of national and international importance, Indian Polity and governance – Constitution, Political System, Panchayati Raj, Public Policy, Rights Issues etc., Indian and World geography – Physical, Social, Economic Geography of India and the World, Economic and Social Development – Sustainable Development Poverty Inclusion, Demographics, Social Sector Initiatives, etc., General Issues on Environmental ecology, Bio-diversity and Climate Change- that, Do not require subject specialization, General Science.

PAPER-II
General Studies-II (200 marks)

Comprehension, Interpersonal skills including communication skills, Logical reasoning and analytical ability, Decision making and problem solving, General mental ability, Elementary Mathematics up to Class X level - Arithmetic, Algebra, Geometry and Statistics. General English up to Class X level, General Hindi up to Class X level, Current events of national and international importance.

Subjects for the UPPSC Combined State Upper Subordinate Services Main (Written)

The UPPSC Combined State Upper Subordinate Services Written examination will consist of the following compulsory and optional subjects. The candidates have to select any two subjects from the list of optional subjects for UP Public Service Commission Each optional subject will consist of two papers.

Compulsory Subjects:

General Hindi – 150 marks, Essay – 150 marks, General Studies (I – Paper) – 200 marks, General Studies (II – Paper) – 200 marks

UPPSC General Studies Paper – I & Paper – II:

Shall be objective type containing 150 questions and for solving the questions two hours time is allowed. For other compulsory and optional papers three hours time is allowed. Two hundred maximum marks are allotted for each optional question paper.

2. Review Officer/Assistant Review Officer

Eligibility: Graduate in any discipline.

Age limit: 21 – 40 years

Preliminary Examination

Paper 1 General Studies (Objective Type), Time duration: Two hours, Total No. of Questions: 140

Paper 2 General Hindi, Maximum marks 60, Time duration: one hour, Total Questions: 60

Review Officer

Paper 1 Syllabus

General Science, History of India, Indian National Movement, Indian Polity, Economy & Culture, Indian Agriculture, Commerce and Trade. Population, Ecology and Urbanisation (in India Context), World Geography and Geography and Natural Resources of India. Current National and International Important Events. General Intelligentsia, Special Knowledge regarding Education, Culture, Agriculture, Industry Trade, Living & Social Traditions of Uttar Pradesh.

Paper 2 Syllabus

Opposites, Sentence and Correction in framing, One word for several words, Same usage and same nature words, Nouns as Defined by adjectives, Synonymous words.

Mains examination

General Hindi and Drafting

Part – 1 (Conventional) (General Vocabulary and Grammar) (Objective Type)

Time - 2.5 Hours   Maximum Marks: 100

Heading of Given Passage, Precis and explanation of the underlined parts, Precis in Tabular Form of any given Govt. Letter, Correspondence, Definition Vocabulary (Administrative and Commercial)

Computer Knowledge

Part – 2 (General Vocabulary and Grammar) (Objective Type)
Time-One hour   Maximum Marks: 60   Questions – 60
Opposites, Sentence and Correction in framing, One word for several words, Same usage and same nature words, A Noun as Defined by an adjective & an adjectives, Synonymous words.

Part – 3 Hindi Essay
Time - 3 hours   Maximum Marks: 120   Questions – 3
There will be three questions in this paper. Selecting one heading (A/B/C) from each question essays will have to be written (in given words limit).

3. Post Name: Additional Private Secretary (UP Secretariat)
Eligibility
Candidates should have their Bachelor degree from any recognized university established by law in India, or Qualification recognized by the government.

Age Limit: 21 - 40 years

Exam pattern and Syllabus for UPPSC Additional Private Secretary Examination A typing Test will be conducted for the posts of APS. Candidates are required to ensure at least 80 words per minute speed in Hindi shorthand and 25 words per minute in Hindi typewriting. Competitors are expected to transcribe the dictated prose in 5 minutes in the determined speed by type write for which one hour time will be given.

Written Exam Pattern for passing
A test will be conducted for English shorthand and English which is an option for selected candidates to take it in Hindi or English or both, depending on their competence. They will be entitled for bilingual allowance. There will be total 8 question papers for APS posts.

Paper 1: General knowledge, Maximum marks 100, Total Time Duration 2 Hours
Syllabus: abbreviation, famous book and their writer, History (ancient , mid-level, and modern India science, geography, Indian constitution, Important cities, memoirs and building, important events national and international, arithmetic of class 8th level.

Paper 2: General Hindi 100 marks, 3 hours time duration

Paper 3: Hindi shorthand – 135 marks

Paper 4: Hindi typewriting – 15 marks

Paper 5: General English – max 50 marks, 1 hour time duration

Paper 6: English shorthand – 135 marks

Paper 7: English typewriting – 15 marks

Paper 8: Computer knowledge test – 100 marks, 1 hour time duration

4. Food Safety Officer (Food Safety And Drug Administration Deptt., U.P.)

Eligibility:

Essential Qualification: Degree in Medicine from any of the 209 recognized universities or any other equivalent qualification/ recognized qualification notified by the Central Government.

Age Limit: Candidates must have attained the age of 21 years and must not have crossed the age of 40 years.

Plan of Examination: The competitive examination comprises two successive stages viz:- (1) Objective Type Test (2) Viva-Voce (Personality Test).

Subjects for the Objective Type Test:

Paper I General Studies 75 Questions 150 Marks 01 Hour

Paper II Main Subject 125 Questions 250 Marks 02 Hours

(2) Personality Test/Viva-Voce: (i) Personality Test will be of 50 marks. (ii) This test will relate to the matter of General Interest keeping in view of general awareness, intelligence, character, personality, expression power and general suitability for the service.

Syllabus

(1) First Paper – General Studies: This paper will include questions on the following topics:-

    1. General Science

    2. Current Events of National and International Importance

3. History of India
4. Indian National Movement
5. Indian Polity and Economy
6. World Geography and Population

(2) Second Paper – Main Subject: The paper will include questions on the following topics:-

Chemical constituents of foods, Enzymes, General characteristics of microorganism, Fluid Milk

5. Routine Grade Clerk (Allahabad High Court)

Eligibility: The candidates should have Bachelor's degree with CCC certificate Diploma/Degree in Computer Science

Age Limit: 21 - 35 years

Examination:

The High Court will hold written examinations (objective type) and computer knowledge test.

6. Uttar Pradesh Teacher eligibility test (UPTET)

Uttar Pradesh Teacher eligibility test (UPTET) is an eligibility exam for the recruitment of primary and upper primary teachers in the state.

In UPTET, there will be two exams on one day in two shifts:-
- Paper 1 – Exam for eligibility of Primary Teachers (Classes I-V)
- Paper 2 – Exam for eligibility of Upper Primary Teachers (Classes VI-VIII)

Exam pattern for Paper 1
- In this paper, there will be 150 objective type questions, carrying 150 marks
- The time duration for the exam is only 90 minutes

Format of the question paper (Paper 1)

There will be five parts in the question paper:
1. Pedagogy - 30 marks
2. Languages (Hindi & English/Urdu) - 30 marks

3. Mathematics -30 marks
4. EVS - 30 marks
5. Environmental Studies - 30 marks

Exam pattern for Paper 2
- In this paper, there will be 150 objective type (questions), carrying 150 marks
- The time duration for the exam is only 90 minutes

Format of the question paper (Paper 2)
Basically there will be three parts in the question paper:
1. Pedagogy - 30 marks
2. Languages (Hindi & English/Urdu) - 30 marks
3. Mathematics & Science/Social Studies - 30 marks

26. TAMIL NADU

The **Tamil Nadu Public Service Commission (TNPSC)** was formed in 1923 under the provisions of the Constitution for recruitment to various posts in the state.

List of important examinations held by Tamil Nadu Public Service Commission

General
- Tamil Nadu Civil Service
- Tamil Nadu Police Service
- Tamil Nadu Forest Subordinate Service

Industries & Engineering
- Tamil Nadu Engineering Service
- Tamil Nadu Architect Service
- Tamil Nadu Electrical Inspectorate Service
- Tamil Nadu Factory Service
- Tamil Nadu Boiler Service
- Tamil Nadu Engineering Subordinate Service
- Tamil Nadu Industries Subordinate Service
- Tamil Nadu Industries Service

Others

- Tamil Nadu Secretariat Service
- Tamil Nadu General Service
- Tamil Nadu General Subordinate Service
- Tamil Nadu Jail Service
- Tamil Nadu Fire and Rescue Subordinate Service
- Tamil Nadu Registration Service
- Tamil Nadu Commercial Taxes Service
- Tamil Nadu Registration Subordinate Service
- Tamil Nadu Medical Service
- Tamil Nadu Agricultural Service
- Tamil Nadu Municipal Commissioner Subordinate Service

S. No.	Category	Name of the Service Cadre	Name of the Posts	Related Positions
1.	Tamil Nadu Civil Service Group-I Services	Tamil Nadu Civil Service	Deputy Collector	Principal Secretary, Secretary, Additional Secretary, Joint Secretary, Deputy Secretary, Under Secretary, Collector, Assistant Collector, Tehsildar
2.	Tamil Nadu Civil Service Group-I Services	Tamil Nadu Police Service	Deputy Superintendent of Police (Category – I)	Principal Secretary, Secretary, Additional Secretary, Joint Secretary, Deputy Secretary, Under Secretary, Collector, Assistant Collector, Tehsildar

3.	Tamil Nadu Civil Service Group-I Services	Tamil Nadu Commercial Taxes Service	Assistant Commissioner (Commercial Taxes)	Deputy Commissioner (ct), Joint Commissioner (ct), Additional Commissioner (ct)
4.	Tamil Nadu Civil Service Group-I Services	Tamil Nadu Registration Service	District Registrar	
5.	Tamil Nadu Civil Service Group-I Services	Tamil Nadu General Service	District Employment Officer	

The scheme of examination, syllabi and minimum qualifying marks varies for the above mentioned examinations. Candidates are advised to visit the following websites for further details:

http://www.tnpsc.gov.in

http://www.tnpsc.gov.in/new_syllabus.html

27. TRIPURA

Tripura Public Service Commission was established on 30th October, 1972, under the provisions of the Constitution of India for the recruitment of State Service Officers. The official website for the Tripura Public Service Commission is **http://tpsc.nic.in/**

List of important examinations conducted by **Tripura** Public Service Commission:

- Tripura Civil Service
- Tripura Police Service
- Tripura Forest Service
- Tripura Judicial Service
- Tripura Secretariat Service
- Recruitment to the post of Sub-Inspector of Police

- Recruitment to the post of Sub-Jailor
- Recruitment to the post of Personal Assistant, Grade-II
- Recruitment to the post of Lecturers & Professors in different disciplines
- Recruitment to the post of Scientific Officer
- Recruitment to the post of Fisheries Officer
- Recruitment to the post of Jr. Engineers in different disciplines
- Recruitment to the post of Forest Ranger
- Recruitment to the post of Surgeons
- Recruitment to the post of Veterinary Officer
- Recruitment to the post of Agriculture Officer

Candidates are advised to visit the website for the updates on recruitment for various services. The eligibility criteria, method of recruitment, syllabi and other details can be obtained by visiting the Commission's website.

28. UTTARAKHAND

The Uttarakhand Public Service Commission was constituted under the provisions of the Constitution of India on 14th March, 2001 for the recruitment of State Service Officers. The official website for the Chhattisgarh Public Service Commission is **http://ukpsc.gov.in/**

List of important examinations conducted by **Uttarakhand Public Service Commission:**

- Uttarakhand Civil Services (Upper Subordinate)
- Uttarakhand Civil Services (Lower Subordinate)
- Uttarakhand Judicial Service
- Recruitment to the post of Forest Ranger
- Recruitment to the post of Asst. Engineers & Jr. Engineers in different disciplines
- Recruitment to the post of Assistant Registrar
- Recruitment to the post of Assistant Geologist
- Recruitment to the post of Regional Inspector

- Recruitment to the post of Lecturers in different disciplines
- Recruitment to the post of Assistant Prosecuting Officer
- Recruitment to the post of Assistant Radio Officer
- Recruitment to the post of Assistant Review Officer/ Assistant Accountant/Inspector
- Recruitment to the post of Medical Officer
- Recruitment for various Group B & Group C posts for various departments

Candidates are advised to visit the website for the updates on recruitment for various services. The eligibility criteria, method of recruitment, syllabi and other details can be obtained by visiting the Commission's website.

29. WEST BENGAL

West Bengal Public Service Commission came into existence in April 1937. The Commission is responsible for the recruitment to various services in the state.

List of important examinations conducted by West Bengal Public Service Commission:

- West Bengal Civil Service (Exe) Examination
- West Bengal Judicial Service Examination
- West Bengal Forest Service & Subordinate Forest Service Examination
- Junior Law Officers Recruitment Examination
- Combined Competitive Examination for Recruitment to the posts of Sub-Inspector, Sergeant in Kolkata Police & West Bengal Police
- Sub-Assistant Engineers (Civil/Mechanical/Electrical) Recruitment Examination
- Assistant Archivists Recruitment Examination
- Assistant Public Prosecutors Recruitment Examination
- Sub-Inspector in the Subordinate Food & Supplies Service, Grade – III

The scheme of examination, syllabi and minimum qualifying marks varies for the above mentioned examinations. Candidates are advised to visit the following websites for further details:

www.pscwbonline.gov.in

http://www.pscwb.org.in/

CHAPTER 6
Opportunities of Employment in Central and State Government Companies

This chapter introduces those seeking jobs in government companies to the government corporate jobs landscape. It provides essential information about Central and States Public Sector Undertakings in India. The Central PSUs or enterprises are categorized into Maharatna, Navratna, Miniratna companies based on gross turnover, profitability and certain other performance parameters. Some of the Central and States companies are listed in the Mumbai and National Stock Exchanges and some even in international stock exchanges like New York Stock Exchange. The categorization of the corporate giants helps the job seekers to aim at jobs on the basis of importance and career prospects. Most important tip for jobs in companies is to visit the concerned websites of the companies the job seeker is interested to know the authentic information from time to time pertaining to different recruitments for emerging job opportunities. Many of these companies go for campus recruitments for many entry level positions. Core WWW: Win-Win-Win strategy given for preparation for UPSC Indian Civil Services Examination, Staff Selection Commission Examination and Banking Clerical and Probationary Officers Examination by suitable customization depending on the methodology of recruitment may help in formulating appropriate strategy for recruitment in the corporate sector also in addition to specific technical expertise and knowledge expected for the positions advertised.

There are 400 odd Central Public Sector Undertakings (CPSUs) and 1200 odd State Public Sector Undertakings (SPSUs) spread across the States and Union Territories. Some of them are listed on the stock exchange. The Central PSUs have been categorized into Maharatna, Navratna and Miniratna based on certain performance parameters like gross turnover, profitability etc. There are a number of State Public Sector Undertakings in the field of electricity generation, distribution and transmission; state transportation, housing, renewable energy sector and various other activities of the state governments.

The recruitment for the higher level posts in Central PSUs are done by the Public Sector Enterprise Board (PSEB) and the other posts by the PSU themselves. The recruitment for the State PSUs is done by the PSUs themselves.

Classification of Central Public Sector Undertakings

Public Sector Undertakings (PSUs) are also classified as Central Public Sector Enterprises (CPSEs), State Public Sector Enterprises (SPSEs) and Public Sector Banks (PSBs).

The Central Public Sector Enterprises (CPSEs) are also classified into 'strategic' and 'non-strategic'. Areas of strategic CPSEs are:

- Arms & Ammunition and the allied items of defence equipments, defence air-crafts and warships
- Atomic Energy (except in the areas related to the operation of nuclear power and applications of radiation and radio-isotopes to agriculture, medicine and non-strategic industries)
- Railways transport

All other CPSEs are considered as non-strategic.

Maharatna/Navratna/Miniratna status for some Public Sector Undertakings

The status of Maharatna, Navratna, Miniratna to CPSEs is conferred by the Department of Public Enterprises to various Public Sector Undertakings. These are CPSEs of high market capitalization, gross turnover and profitability and have greater autonomy in its functioning.

Maharatna

A company qualifying for the Maharatna status should have an average annual turnover of Rs. 20,000 crore during the last three years against Rs. 25,000 crore prescribed earlier. The average annual net worth of the company should be Rs. 10,000 crore.

The Maharatna status empowers mega CPSEs to expand their operations and emerge as global giants. The coveted status empowers the boards of firms to take investment decisions up to Rs. 5,000 crore as against the present Rs. 1,000 crore limit without seeking government approval. The Maharatna firms would now be free to decide on investments up to 15% of their net worth in a project, limited to an absolute ceiling of Rs. 5,000 crore.

Examples:
1. Bharat Heavy Electricals Limited
2. Coal India Limited
3. GAIL (India) Limited
4. Indian Oil Corporation Limited
5. NTPC Limited
6. Oil & Natural Gas Corporation Limited
7. Steel Authority of India Limited

Navratna

The Central Public Sector Enterprises (CPSEs) fulfilling the following criteria are eligible to be considered for grant of Navratna status:

- Having Schedule 'A' and Miniratna Category-1 status.
- Having at least three 'Excellent' or 'Very Good' Memorandum of Understanding (MoU) ratings during the last five years.

The Navratna status empowers PSEs to invest up to Rs. 1,000 crore or 15% of their net worth on a single project without seeking government approval. In a year, these companies can spend up to 30% of their net worth not exceeding Rs. 1,000 crore. They also enjoy the freedom to enter joint ventures, form alliances and float subsidiaries abroad.

Examples:
1. Bharat Electronics Limited
2. Bharat Petroleum Corporation Limited
3. Engineers India Limited
4. Hindustan Aeronautics Limited
5. Hindustan Petroleum Corporation Limited
6. Mahanagar Telephone Nigam Limited
7. National Aluminium Company Limited
8. National Buildings Construction Corporation Limited
9. NMDC Limited
10. Neyveli Lignite Corporation Limited
11. Oil India Limited
12. Power Finance Corporation Limited
13. Power Grid Corporation of India Limited
14. Rashtriya Ispat Nigam Limited
15. Rural Electrification Corporation Limited
16. Shipping Corporation of India Limited

Miniratna

Category-I

For Miniratna Category I status, the CPSE should have made profit in the last three years continuously, the pre-tax profit should have been Rs. 30 crore or more in at least one of the three years and should have a positive net worth. For category II, the CPSE should have made profit for the last three years continuously and should have a positive net worth.

Miniratnas can enter into joint ventures, set subsidiary companies and overseas offices but with certain conditions. This designation applies to PSEs that have made profits continuously for the last three years or earned a net profit of Rs. 30 crore or more in one of the three years.

Category-II

Category II miniratnas have autonomy to incurring the capital expenditure without government approval up to Rs. 300 crore or up to 50% of their net worth whichever is lower.

Examples:
1. Airports Authority of India
2. Antrix Corporation Limited
3. Balmer Lawrie & Co. Limited
4. Bharat Dynamics Limited
5. BEML Limited
6. Bharat Sanchar Nigam Limited
7. Bridge & Roof Company (India) Limited
8. Central Warehousing Corporation
9. Central Coalfields Limited
10. Chennai Petroleum Corporation Limited
11. Cochin Shipyard Limited

Jobs & Career

The best way to hunt for jobs in the central and states corporate sector is to visit their websites for emerging job opportunities and the methodology of recruitment with details of domain knowledge and technical expertise expected. Most of the Public Sector Undertakings (PSUs) have their own recruitment procedures. This sector provides job opportunities to both technical and non-technical personnel.

There are two ways through which a PSU hires:

1. On-campus Selection

All these PSUs have a list of campuses that they visit every year for recruiting graduates. The list is decided by the recruitment committee of respective PSUs and generally consists of Tier 1 colleges. The company visits the campus, interviews the list of shortlisted candidates (short listing is done on the basis of graduation, SSC and HSC score) and then hires the candidates accordingly.

2. Off-campus Recruitment Drive

The majority of the recruitment is done through the off-campus recruitment process conducted by each of these PSUs. The information is published in all the newspaper dailies and also mentioned on the respective websites.

- Initially the candidates are filtered according to the marks obtained in B.Tech/BE, 12th & 10th. After applying the cut-offs the list of candidates is prepared for the written round.
- The written round consists of multiple-choice questions of the relevant subject discipline of the candidate.
- After clearing the written, the shortlisted candidates are interviewed by a panel.

After clearing the Personal Interview the candidate is finally selected as Graduate Engineer Trainee (GET).

GATE Advantage

Graduate Aptitude Test in Engineering (GATE) is an all-India examination administered and conducted jointly by the Indian Institute of Science (IISc) and seven Indian Institutes of Technology (IIT) for admission into their post-graduate programmes. Some of the PSUs also consider GATE score and give preference to candidates in the written round of their selection securing a decent score. There are also some PSUs (like ISRO, NTPC, IOCL, IOC) which give direct interview calls to the candidates solely on the basis of their GATE score.

The Public Enterprises Selection Board (PSEB) is responsible for selection and placement of personnel in the posts of Chairman, Managing Director or Chairman-cum-Managing Director (Level-I), and Functional Director (Level-II) in PSEs as well as in posts at any other level as may be specified by the Government.

Exam Structure for some of the PSUs

Organization	Post	Exam Pattern	Related links
BSNL	JTO	Written Test - Objective Set A: Engg stream - 50 questions Set B: Engg stream - 50 questions Section C: General Ability Test - 20 questions	www.bsnl.co.in

Opportunities of Employment in Central and State Government Companies 223

NTPC	Executive Trainees	Written Test – GATE Exam Set A: 55 questions (Engg Stream) Set B: 35 questions (Executive Aptitude Test) Negative marking: ¼ marks Group Discussion; Personal Interview	www.ntpccareers.net
BHEL	Engineer Trainees	Written test-objective GATE Exam Personal Interview	www.careers.bhel.in
DRDO	Scientist-B Entry	Written Test-objective – 3 hours Set A: 100 questions Set B: 50 questions Personal Interview	www.drdo.com www.rac.drdo.in
IOCL	Engineers/ Graduate Apprentice Engineers	Written Test – GATE Exam; Group Discussion; Personal Interview	www.iocl.com/Peoplecareers/Recruitment.aspx
DMRC	Junior Engineers	Written test (2 papers), Psycho Test/PI	www.delhimetrorail.com
ONGC	Graduate Trainees	Written test (Objective and Subjective) Psychometric test and PI	www.ongcindia.com
NHPC	Trainee Engineers	Written test Set A: Engg Stream – 140 questions Set B : General Awareness – 30 questions Set C: Reasoning – 30 questions Personal Interview	www.nhpcindia.com

ECIL	Graduate Engineer Trainee	Written test Personal Interview	www.ecil.co.in
SJVNL	Executive Trainees	Written Test – Objective; Group Discussion; Personal Interview	www.sjvn.nic.in/recruitment.asp
BPCL	Management Trainee	Written test Personal Interview	www.bpclcareers.com
HPCL	Officer Trainees	Written test Interview	www.hindustanpetroleum.com
BARC	JRF, SRF, Research Associates	Application Screening/ GATE Score Personal Interview	www.barc.ernet.in
PGCIL	Executive Trainees	GATE Score Basis or Written Test – Objective – 2 hrs Set A: Technical knowledge test - 120 questions Set B: Executive Aptitude test - 50 questions. Group Discussion Personal Interview	www.powergridindia.com
NALCO	Graduate Engineer Trainee	Written Test Interview	www.nalcoindia.com
SAIL	Management Trainee	Written Test – Objective; Group Discussion; Personal Interview	www.sail.co.in
MTNL	JTO	Written Aptitude Test; Skill Test; Personal Interview	www.mtnl.net.in
Bridge & Roof Co. (I) Ltd	Trainee Engineers	Written Test – Objective; Personal Interview	www.bridgeroof.co.in

ISRO	Scientist/ Engineer	Written Test – Objective; Personal Interview	www.shar.gov.in
GAIL	Executive Trainee	Written test Subject Specialization: 100 questions. General Aptitude: 50 questions Duration: 2hrs Personal Interview	www.gailonline.com
VIZAG STEEL	Management Trainee	Written test Set A: Engg Stream Set B: Aptitude & English Personal Interview	www.vizagstel.com
BEL	Probationary Engineer	Written Test – Objective; Personal Interview	www.bel-india.com/index

Selection Procedure in PSUs (Non-GATE)

The usual selection procedure followed by majority of PSUs is through Written Examination of objective type questions followed by Interview and Group Discussion.

STAGE - I Written Examination. Duration: 1–3 hours (Avg. 2 hours)

- Written exam of various PSUs can be divided mainly into 4 sections:-
- Technical
- Aptitude & reasoning
- English & reading comprehension
- General awareness & current affairs

Technical:
- 60 – 120 questions (exact no. varies for different PSUs)
- Average no. of questions - 80

Aptitude & Reasoning:
- Quantitative reasoning (speed-distance, percentage, profit-loss etc), Maths of 10th std level, figure based questions etc.

English & RC
- Reading comprehension, questions based on vocabulary and English grammar etc.

General Awareness & Current Affairs
- Current affairs and questions based on general knowledge
- Some PSUs ask specific questions related to their institutions in this section eg:- DRDO asks about its labs in India (1 or 2 questions).

Stage – II Interview/Group Discussion
Personal Interview:
(1) Maximum stress on testing the technical knowledge of the candidate.

(2) Percentage of HR questions limited to the general introduction, work experience (if any), hobbies etc.

Group Discussion:
- Average duration is 20-30 minutes.
- Usually easy topics are given for discussion and topics on environmental and technical issues can also be given.
- Apart from these, there can be an additional stage in some of the PSUs where only short-listed candidates are allowed to appear for the written exam. All the applicants fulfilling the eligibility criteria are screened again on the basis of their percentage in B.Tech primarily and depending upon the number of vacancies. Only selected candidates are called for the written exam. eg ISRO, BHEL etc.
- Some PSUs don't hold interviewer as a part of their selection procedure e.g. - BSNL (JTO).
- Though it has not ever been declared by any PSU, the general trend seen in according weightage to different stages in the final selection is:-

   Written – 70-85%

   Interview – 15-30%

   GD – 5%

Exam-Date:
- Throughout the year.
- Entrance exam of different PSUs are held at different times during the year.
- Peak duration during which maximum exams occur - May-Sept

CHAPTER

PUBLIC SECTOR INSURANCE COMPANIES

This chapter takes the job seeker to Insurance Sector. It has been decided to liberalize this sector in the budget 2014-15 for foreign investment and adequate resources for this purpose have been provided by the government. This sector provides new opportunities. The Chapter discusses details of Central Public Sector Insurance Companies, their recruitment process and examination pattern for the entrance test. There are six Central Public Sector Insurance Companies in India viz.

1. *Life Insurance Corporation of India (LIC);*
2. *General Insurance Corporation of India (GIC);*
3. *National Insurance Company Ltd;*
4. *Oriental Insurance Company Ltd;*
5. *New India Assurance Company Ltd; and*
6. *United India Insurance Company Ltd.*

Though the Public Sector Insurance Companies are Central PSUs, these companies are dealt separately to give adequate focus to job opportunities available in this promising and emerging sector of the Indian economy. There is no substitute for visiting the relevant websites for detailed specific recruitments advertised by these companies and methodology of recruitments. It is important to go over the WWW: Win-Win-Win Core Strategy for helping the job-seeker to formulate a customized strategy for preparation in addition to job specific technical know-how and expertise expected for the positions advertised.

There are six nationalized insurance companies in India. They are:

1. Life Insurance Corporation of India (LIC) The company was founded in 1956 when the Parliament of India passed the Life Insurance of India Act that nationalized the private insurance industry in India. Over 245 insurance companies and provident societies were merged to create the state owned Life Insurance Corporation. Today, the LIC has eight zonal offices, around 109 divisional offices, 2,048 branches and 992 satellite offices and corporate offices. It also has 54 customer zones and 25 metro-area service hubs located in different cities and towns of India. It also has a network of 1,337,064 individual agents, 242 Corporate Agents, 79 Referral Agents, 98 Brokers and 42 Banks for soliciting life insurance business from the public.

2. General Insurance Corporation of India (GIC) The entire general insurance business in India was nationalized by the Government of India (GOI) through the General Insurance Business (Nationalization) Act (GIBNA) of 1972. 55 Indian insurance companies and 52 general insurance operations of other companies were nationalized through the Act.

The General Insurance Corporation of India (GIC) was formed in pursuance of Section 9(1) of GIBNA. It was incorporated on 22nd November 1972 under the Companies Act, 1956 as a private company limited by shares. GIC was formed to control and operate the business of general insurance in India.

The GOI transferred all the assets and operations of the nationalized general insurance companies to GIC and other public-sector insurance companies. After a process of mergers and consolidation, GIC was re-organized with four fully-owned subsidiary companies: National Insurance Company Limited, New India Assurance Company Limited, Oriental Insurance Company Limited and United India Insurance Company Limited. Now all the subsidiaries have been demerged since 2002 and the main function of GIC is of re-insurance after the enactment of IRDA (Insurance Regulatory Development Authority) Act, 1999.

3. National Insurance Company Limited The company was incorporated on 6th December, 1906 with its registered office in Kolkata. Consequent to passing of the General Insurance Business Nationalization Act in 1972, 21 Foreign and 11 Indian companies were amalgamated with it and National Insurance Company became a subsidiary of General Insurance Corporation of India (GIC) which is fully owned by the Government of India. Since 7th August 2002, after the legislative enactment in the form of Insurance Amendment Act, National Insurance Company has been de-linked from its holding company General Insurance Company and is presently operating as an independent insurance company which is wholly owned by Government of India. National Insurance Company Ltd (NIC) is one of the leading public sector insurance companies of India, carrying out non life insurance business. It is headquartered in Kolkata with a network of about 1000 offices across the country.

4. Oriental Insurance Company Limited A wholly owned subsidiary of the Oriental Government Security Life Assurance Company Ltd, the Oriental Insurance Company Limited was incorporated on 12th September 1947, in Bombay (now Mumbai). The main aim behind its establishment was to venture into the business of General Insurance. It became a subsidiary of Life Insurance Corporation of India in 1956 and continued as such till 1973 till nationalization of General Insurance.

In 2002, after the Insurance Amendment Bill was passed, Oriental Insurance Company was de-linked from General Insurance Corporation (GIC) of India. The following year, all the shares of the company that had been held by GIC were transferred to the Central Government. Oriental Insurance Company Limited has as many as 26 Regional Offices in India with the head office being in New Delhi. Apart from that, there are more than 900 operating offices of this company across the country. It is also involved in overseas operations in Nepal, Kuwait and Dubai.

5. New India Assurance Company Limited The New India Assurance Co. Ltd., based in Mumbai, is one of the five wholly Government of India owned assurance companies of India. It was founded by Sir Dorabji Tata in 1919, and was nationalized in 1973.

Previously it was a subsidiary of the General Insurance Corporation of India (GIC). But when GIC became an re-insurance company as per the IRDA Act 1999, its four primary insurance subsidiaries New India Assurance, United India Insurance, Oriental Insurance and National Insurance got autonomy. The company with its corporate office in Mumbai has about 28 regional offices, 397 divisional offices, 588 branches, 27 direct agent branches and 23 extension counters.

6. United India Insurance Company Limited It was formed by the merger of 22 companies, consequent to the nationalization of General Insurance companies in India. Since 2002 it has become independent. Its headquarters is at Chennai. It has 1340 offices spread across the country.

Recruitment

The Life Insurance Corporation of India conducts its own tests for recruitment in different posts. Recruitment to the other public sector insurance companies is done in a combined entrance test conducted by the GIC for different posts. The summarized details of the recruitment process in public sector insurance companies have been discussed below.

Life Insurance Corporation of India (LIC)
1. LIC Officers' Exam

A competitive examination for the recruitment of the Assistant Administrative Officers, etc., in Life Insurance Corporation (LIC) is held once a year, generally in the month of June. The blank application form and particulars are published in the *Employment News*, generally in the second week of April, and the last date for submission of application forms is usually the second week of May every year.

Educational Qualification:

Bachelor's/Master's Degree from a recognized Indian or foreign university with a minimum of 50% marks (relaxable in the case of SC/ST candidates to 40%) in aggregate in either of the degrees.

Age Limit:

21 to 28 years on 1st April of the year of examination. Upper age limit is relaxable for Scheduled Castes, Scheduled Tribes, confirmed LIC employees, etc.

Initial Pay:

Scale of Rs. 4250-2304940-350-5290-230-8510

Scheme of the Examination:

The examination comprises

- Written Examination
- Interview of such candidates who qualify in the written test.

Examination Papers:

The written examination will consist of the following papers:

Paper I (Objective)

It will consist of

1. Reasoning Ability (Bilingual)
2. General Knowledge and Current Affairs (Bilingual)
3. Numerical Ability (Bilingual)
4. English Language with special emphasis on grammar and vocabulary.

Paper II (Descriptive)

It will consist of

- Test on Essay (can be written in Hindi or English)
- Precis and Comprehension in English

2. LIC Development Officers' Examination

A competitive examination for the recruitment of Assistant Development Officers in the Life Insurance Corporation is held once a year, generally in the month of September. The blank application forms and particulars are published in the *Employment News*, generally in the month of July and the last date for submission of applications is generally the first week of August.

Educational Qualification:

Candidates must hold a Bachelor's Degree in Arts, Science, Commerce, Agriculture or Law of an Indian or Foreign University or an equivalent qualification.

Age Limit:

The applicants should have completed the age of 21 years on 1st July of the year of examination.

Initial Pay:

Scale of Rs. 4250-2304940-350-5290-230-8510.

Scheme of the Examination:

The examination comprises: (i) Written Examination (ii) Interview of such candidates, who qualify in the written test.

Examination Papers:

The written test will consist of (i) Test of Reasoning and Numerical Ability; and (ii) General English/Hindi and General Knowledge. The test papers will be set bilingual and the candidates will have choice to write answers either in English or in Hindi.

General Insurance Corporation of India

1. GIC Officers' Examination

GIC officers' Examination is a combined examination conducted for recruitment of Assistant Administrative Officer (AAO-Generalist) in the establishments of General Insurance Corporation of India that are mentioned hereunder:

- National Insurance Company Ltd, Calcutta
- The New India Assurance Company Ltd, Mumbai
- The Oriental Fire and General Insurance Company Ltd, New Delhi
- United India Insurance Company Ltd, Mumbai.

GIC Assistant Administrative Officer (AAO) Examination is a direct entry to the officer cadre. AAOs are normally appointed as Branch Managers in smaller branches and, as the name of the post indicates, are responsible for overall general administration of the branch.

Even in the bigger branches and higher offices, AAOs are assigned important tasks and assist not only in better administration of the branch/said office but also help in achieving the financial goals.

Important Dates
- The notification for the GIC Officers' examination commences in the month of March/April, generally.
- The examination generally is conducted in the month of May/June.
- The last date for submission of application is generally in the first week of April.

Educational Qualification
Graduate/postgraduate with 50% marks (relaxable in the case of Scheduled Castes/Tribes at 40%)

Age Limit
21-30 years on 1st October of the year previous to the year of examination (relaxable in the case of SC/ST/OBC, ex-servicemen and serving confirmed employees of G.I.C.)

Exam Pattern comprises of two stages:

Stage I: Written Examination

Candidates who have submitted duly filled applications and who fulfill all the eligibility criteria are called for the objective type written examination that comprises of the following:
- Test of Reasoning
- English Language
- General Awareness
- Professional Knowledge

Stage II: Interview

Only those candidates who pass the written examination are called for the Interview.

2. GIC Assistants' Examination

GIC Assistants' Examination is an Exam to get an entry into the General insurance Companies of India to serve in Assistant cadre in any of the following mentioned Establishments of General Insurance Corporation of India:

- National Insurance Company Ltd, Calcutta
- The New India Assurance Company Ltd, Mumbai
- The Oriental Fire and General Insurance Company Ltd, New Delhi
- United India Insurance Company Ltd, Mumbai.

These Assistant cadre positions provide a person with tremendous opportunities to grow further to officer cadre.

Important Dates

This examination is held once a year, generally in the month of August.

Notification of the exam is published in the Employment News, generally in the month of March.

Eligibility

Age Limit

18 to 28 years on the first June of the year of examination.

Educational Qualification

Pass in Higher Secondary (Senior Secondary) with 60% marks or a Graduate of a recognized University.

GIC Assistants Exam Pattern

The pattern of GIC Assistants Exam comprises of two stages:

Stage I: Written Examination

The Exam will have both objective type and descriptive type papers. The Objective Paper will consist of Test of Reasoning, Numerical Ability, Clerical Aptitude, English Language and General Knowledge. Objective tests except English will be bilingual, i.e., both in English and Hindi. The Descriptive Test will be on Essay, Letter Writing and Précis writing in English.

Stage II: Interview

Those who successfully complete the written exam will be called for personal interview.

Note:

Recruitment in the clerical cadre is also conducted by these insurance companies based on the available vacancies. The details can be seen as and when the notification for the same is published.

CHAPTER 8

JOBS IN CENTRAL UNIVERSITIES

Jobs landscape in education sector includes jobs in universities, colleges, schools and other educational establishments both of private and government sector. of various categories of universities in the country like Central Universities, State Universities, Deemed Universities and Private Universities, one of the most important categories for the job seeker is 42 or so Central Universities located in different states and union territories. This Chapter familiarizes the job seeker with the jobs landscape of Central Universities in India. It deals with the examinations like NET, SLET and JRF which opens up a gateway of career progression in Indian Universities. Most important point for the job seekers is Google search and find out the right website of the university to know about the new recruitments, policy and methodology and expected domain of expertise, knowledge, eligibility criteria, educational and professional qualifications, etc.

National Eligibility Test (NET)

The National Educational Testing Bureau of University Grants Commission (UGC) conducts National Eligibility Test (NET) to determine eligibility for lectureship and for award of Junior Research Fellowship (JRF) for Indian nationals in order to ensure minimum standards for the entrants in the teaching profession and research. The test is conducted in Humanities (including languages), Social Sciences, Forensic Science, Environmental Sciences, Computer Science and Applications and Electronic Science.

The Council of Scientific and Industrial Research (CSIR) conducts the UGC-CSIR NET for other Science subjects, namely, Life Sciences, Physical Sciences, Chemical Sciences, Mathematical Sciences and Earth Atmospheric Ocean & Planetary Sciences jointly with the UGC. The tests are conducted twice in a year generally in the months of June and December. For candidates who desire to pursue research, the Junior Research Fellowship (JRF) is available for five years subject to fulfillment of certain conditions. UGC has allocated a number of fellowships to the universities for the candidates who qualify the test for JRF. The JRFs are awarded to the meritorious candidates from among the candidates qualifying for eligibility for lectureship in the NET. JRFs are available only to the candidates who opt for it in their application forms.

The test for Junior Research Fellowship is being conducted since 1984. The Government of India, through its notification dated 22nd July, 1988 entrusted the task of conducting the eligibility test for lectureship to UGC. Consequently, UGC conducted the first National Eligibility Test, common to both eligibility for Lectureship and Junior Research Fellowship in two parts, that is, in December 1989 and in March, 1990.

NET Schedule

UGC conducts NET twice a year, i.e., in the months of June and December. The notifications announcing the June and December examinations are published in the months of March and September respectively in the weekly journal of nation-wide circulation, viz, *Employment News*.

NET Results Declaration Schedule

The result of June, UGC-NET is declared generally in the month of October. Similarly December, UGC-NET result is usually declared in the month of April. The UGC-NET results published in the *Employment News* are also available on UGC website (www.ugc.ac.in).

NET for Science Subjects

The NET in major science subjects, viz., Chemical Sciences; Earth Atmospheric Ocean & Planetary Sciences; Life Sciences; Mathematical Sciences and Physical Sciences is conducted jointly with the Council of Scientific and Industrial Research (CSIR), New Delhi. The concerned notifications are issued separately by CSIR.

Concept and Scope of NET and SET/SLET

It was felt that an eligibility test at the national level may not be completely able to represent the subjects which are regional in their character. Moreover, the demand for enabling the candidates to appear for the test in their own mother tongue was also being made. The state governments and union territories were, therefore, given the option of conducting their own test for eligibility for Lectureship at the state level. Thus was born the concept of SET, i.e., State Eligibility Test for Lectureship Eligibility only. It is conducted both in English and the vernacular.

The Commission at its meeting held on 25th May, 1990 decided to constitute a UGC Committee on Accreditation of Test (U-CAT). The terms of reference of U-CAT are as follows:

- Laying down guidelines for holding the tests
- Accreditation of tests conducted by agencies other than UGC/CSIR
- Monitoring of tests conducted by other agencies and suggesting follow-up measures
- Extend guidance and help to State level agencies in the organization of the tests

Based on the recommendations made by U-CAT, the following guidelines are given to the states regarding test design, course content, organization of the test etc. for conducting State Eligibility Test (SET) for Lectureship only.

Guidelines for conducting SET

In accordance with the mandate given by the Government of India, the University Grants Commission (UGC), on request of State Governments, proposed to have STATE ELIGIBILITY TEST (SET) duly accredited by UGC for a fixed term. This state level Test is based on the pattern of the National Eligibility Test (NET) conducted by UGC and UGC/CSIR for Humanities, Social Sciences and Sciences subjects respectively. The State Governments and Union Territories, which are desirous of conducting their own SET, are required to obtain accreditation from UGC from time to time.

Besides conducting the NET, the role of the NET Bureau is to assess and accredit state identified agencies to conduct SET examination. The SET assessment is done by evaluating the performance of the state agency designated by the state government. The Certification of Accreditation is given to the state for a stipulated period of time.

Identification of State Agency - A State Government may identify an agency, which may be a University, or an examination body of repute or a reputed agency associated with recruitment of teachers for higher education.

States conducting SLET - Presently, SET is being conducted in the following states:

1. Maharashtra & Goa
2. Tamil Nadu
3. Madhya Pradesh
4. Andhra Pradesh
5. Himachal Pradesh
6. Jammu & Kashmir
7. Rajasthan
8. West Bengal
9. NE-SLET (which includes all North Eastern states and Sikkim)

The Commission constitutes an Accreditation Committee from time to time to assess the performance of the states conducting the SET Examination. The Commission takes a final decision about any state on the basis of the Report of the Committee.

Scope of NET & SLET

• Eligibility for Lectureship

Clearing of NET confers eligibility for lectureship upon Indian nationals, i.e. the NET qualified candidates are eligible to apply for the post of lecturer in all Indian universities/institutes/colleges.

It was resolved in the UGC's Commission Meeting held on 1.11.2001 that commencing from the SET examinations scheduled in or after June, 2002, the SET qualified candidates shall be eligible for appointment to the post of lecturer only in the universities/colleges belonging to the state from where they have passed the SET examination. The status of SET shall remain unchanged for SET examinations conducted prior to 1st June, 2002, i.e. the candidates clearing SET were eligible for appointment to the post of lecturer anywhere in India.

• Junior Research Fellowship

The candidates who qualify the Junior Research Fellowship (JRF) Examination of UGC/CSIR NET are also eligible for the post of lectureship. In addition they are also eligible to receive Fellowships (UGC/CSIR) under various schemes subject to the candidates finding their placement in the universities/IITs/other national organizations. The validity of the offer is two years w.e.f. the date of issue of JRF award letter. The validity period of the offer has been raised from one year to two years for JRF Award Letters issued on or after 1st April, 2005. However, in case the candidates have already joined M.Phil/Ph.D., the date of commencement of fellowship will be from the date of declaration of NET examination result or date of their joining, whichever is later.

NET is conducted for determining the eligibility of Indian nationals for the Award of Junior Research Fellowships (JRF) and eligibility for Lectureship in various Indian universities and colleges. National Eligibility Test (NET) is conducted in 78 subjects at 74 selected university centres around the country. The examination is conducted in Humanities (including languages), Social Sciences, Forensic Science, Environmental Sciences, Computer Science and Applications and Electronic Science.

The national level test for determining the eligibility of candidates for the award of Junior Research Fellowship/ Lectureship in Science subjects (Chemical Sciences; Mathematical Sciences and Earth, Atmospheric, Ocean & Planetary Sciences; Life Sciences; Physical Sciences) is conducted jointly with the Council of Scientific and Industrial Research (CSIR), New Delhi. The candidates in science subjects, desirous of availing UGC-JRF or obtaining eligibility for Lectureship in these subjects are advised to appear in the Joint CSIR-UGC Test for Junior Research Fellowship and Eligibility for Lectureship conducted by CSIR.

Candidates who qualify for the award of Junior Research Fellowship are eligible to pursue research in the subject of their post-graduation or in a related subject. The universities, institutions, IITs and other national organizations may select the JRF awardees for whole time research work in accordance with the procedure prescribed by them. The award of JRF will depend on the performance of the candidate in NET. The qualified candidates will also be eligible for Lectureship. However, the candidates qualifying exclusively for Lectureship will not be considered for award of JRF.

Candidates appearing in NET should clearly specify in the prescribed application form whether they are applying for both JRF & eligibility for Lectureship or only for eligibility for Lectureship. Candidates who qualify the test for eligibility for Lectureship will be governed by the rules and regulations for recruitment of Lecturers of the concerned universities/colleges/state governments, as the case may be. Scheduled Caste (SC)/Scheduled Tribe (ST)/Visually Handicapped (VH)/ Physically Handicapped (PH) candidates will be given such special concessions as may be decided by the Commission. Candidates qualifying for the award of Junior Research Fellowship will be eligible to receive fellowship of the UGC under various schemes, subject to finding their placement in universities/IITs/institutions. The validity period of the offer is one year w.e.f. the date of issue of JRF Award Letter. However, in case the candidates have already joined M.Phil/Ph.D., the date of commencement of fellowship shall be from the date of declaration of NET result or date of their joining, whichever is later.

Format of Exam

UGC has included at least 78 subjects in NET. All of them follow a three-paper format.

Paper I: Research Methodology and Aptitude Test:

50 multiple-choice questions, each carrying 2 marks. One can answer any 50 out of the 60 questions presented.

Total time allocated: 75 minutes

Paper II: Objective Test (in chosen subject):

50 multiple-choice questions, each carrying 2 marks in the subject opted for by the candidate.

Total time allocated: 75 minutes.

Paper III: Subjective Test (in chosen subject):

A total of 26 questions spread over five sections, all of which require written answers of varied lengths in the optional subject opted by the candidate.

- Section I: 5 questions with 30-word answers based on a passage, each question carries 5 marks (25 marks).
- Section II: Definitional-specific with fifteen 30-word questions, which test conceptual understanding, 5 marks each (75 marks).
- Section III: Analytical or evaluative with five 200-word questions, 12 marks each (60 marks).
- Section IV: Essay type, one 1000-word question (40 marks).

Total time allocated: 150 minutes.

CHAPTER

OTHER GOVERNMENT JOBS

This Chapter discusses recruitment in other government organizations and Institutions like Autonomous Bodies like IITs, IIMs, Societies registered under the Societies Registration Act, Research Institutions, Regulatory Bodies like SEBI, Completion Commission, Educational Institutions, Research Institutions, various organizations like ICAR, AIIMS, Doordharshan, Air India, Prashar Bharati, states Autonomous Bodies, Societies, Boards, Research and Educational Institutions and other bodies, Urban Local Bodies like City Corporations, Municipal Bodies, Panchayatis Raj Institutors like Zila Parishad, Gram Panchayats and Judiciary. These organizations are numerous and have their individual process of recruitment. The job seeker is advised to search the right website on the Internet for getting update on their recruitments and methodology for selection. The Central Government and State Governments' websites give detailed information about such organizations. The Ministry-wise attached and subordinate offices, Autonomous Bodies, Companies, Boards like Rubber Board, Coir Board, and other organizations like KVIC etc can be searched out both for the Central Government and the State Governments and then the job seeker can visit the concerned websites for detailed information on recruitment and emerging job opportunities along with

eligibility criteria, methodology of recruitment and expected standards in general competitive subjects and additions job specific experience and specialization. For preparation of general awareness and national and international current affairs, English and other general competitive papers are relevant; it is important to go over the WWW: Win-Win-Win Strategy for preparing customized strategy. These jobs are organizations specific and therefore it is expected that candidates to know about the organization and why the job seeker is interested in them. It is therefore important to visit the relevant website and other relevant websites by Google search to gather adequate organization specific updates to score better marks in written examination and interview.

There are several other Government organizations and institutions like Autonomous Bodies, Societies registered under the Society Act 1860, Educational Institutions, Research Institutions, Attached Offices, Subordinate Offices of Ministries and Departments, Urban Local Bodies like Municipalities and Corporations, Panchayati Raj institutions at District and Panchayat levels where recruitment across various cadres is done by general or special process. These organizations are large in numbers and do their own recruitment for different posts depending on the vacancy position. These recruitment notifications are published in the newspapers, *Employment News* and their respective websites. Candidates can get access to these recruitment notifications by visiting the various job-related websites also.

AUTONOMOUS BODIES

There are more than 292 central autonomous bodies and thousands of state autonomous bodies across various states. These autonomous bodies function under different departments of the Central Government. The list of central autonomous bodies can be seen on **http://goidirectory.nic.in/union_organisation.php?ct=E007**.

- Agharkar Research Institute (ARI)
- Aligarh Muslim University (AMU)
- Ali Yavar Jung National Institute for the Hearing Handicapped (AYJNIHH)
- All India Chess Federation
- All India Institute of Medical Sciences (AIIMS)
- All India Institute of Speech and Hearing (AIISH), Mysore
- All India Radio (AIR)
- All India Radio (AIR), Guwahati
- All India Radio (AIR), Panaji
- Archery Association of India (AAI)
- Armed Forces Tribunal

- Aryabhatta Research Institute of Observational Sciences (ARIES)
- Assam University
- Atomic Energy Central School, Narwapahar, Jharkhand
- Atomic Energy Commission (AEC), Department of Atomic Energy (DAE)
- Atomic Energy Education Society (AEES)
- Birbal Sahni Institute of Palaeobotany
- Board of Apprenticeship Training (Southern Region), Chennai
- Board of Practical Training (BOPT), Eastern Region
- Bose Institute, Kolkata
- Building Materials and Technology Promotion Council (BMTPC)
- Central Adoption Resource Authority (CARA), New Delhi
- Central Board for Workers Education (CBWE)
- Central Board of Secondary Education (CBSE)
- Central Council for Research in Yoga & Naturopathy (CCRYN), New Delhi
- Central Footwear Training Institute, Chennai
- Central Government Employees Welfare Housing Organisation (CGEWHO)
- Central Hindi Directorate
- Central Institute of Educational Technology (CIET)
- Central Institute of English and Foreign Languages (CIEFL)
- Central Institute of Indian Languages (CIIL)
- Central Institute of Plastics Engineering and Technology (CIPET)
- Central Institute of Tool Design (CITD)
- Central Power Research Institute (CPRI), Bangalore, Karnataka

- Central Pulp and Paper Research Institute (CPPRI), Saharanpur
- Central Tibetan Schools Administration (CTSA)
- Central Wool Development Board
- Centre for Cultural Resources and Training (CCRT)
- Centre for Development of Advanced Computing (C-DAC)
- Centre for Development of Advanced Computing (C-DAC),Hyderabad
- Centre for Development of Advanced Computing (C-DAC), Kolkata
- Centre for Development of Advanced Computing (C-DAC), Mohali
- Centre for Development of Advanced Computing (C-DAC), Mumbai
- Centre for Development of Advanced Computing (C-DAC), Noida
- Centre for Development of Advanced Computing (C-DAC), Pune
- Centre for Development of Advanced Computing (C-DAC), Thiruvananthapuram
- Centre for DNA Fingerprinting and Diagnostics (CDFD)
- Centre for Liquid Crystal Research (CLCR)
- Centre for Social Studies
- Centre for Wind Energy Technology (CWET)
- Centre for Women's Development Studies (CWDS)
- Chennai Port Trust
- Chief Labour Commissioner (Central)
- Children's Film Society, India
- Coal Mines Provident Fund Organisation (CMPFO)
- Cochin Port Trust
- Commission for Scientific and Technical Terminology (CSTT)
- Consultancy Development Centre (CDC), DSIR

- Controller of Defence Accounts, Chennai
- Council for Advancement of Peoples Action and Rural Technology (CAPART)
- C. P. Ramaswamy Ayar Environmental Education Centre (CPREEC)
- Customs, Excise and Service Tax Appellate Tribunal (CESTAT)
- Delhi Public Library
- Doordarshan - National Television Network, India
- Dr. Ambedkar Foundation
- Dr. B. R. Ambedkar National Institute of Technology, Jalandhar
- Educational Consultants India Limited (EDCIL)
- Education and Research Network (ERNET)
- Electronics and Computer Software Export Promotion Council (ESC)
- Employees State Insurance Corporation (ESIC)
- Federation of Indian Export Organisations (FIEO)
- Film and Television Institute of India (FTII)
- Food Safety and Standards Authority of India (FSSAI)
- Gandhi Smriti and Darshan Samiti (GSDS)
- Gujarat Institute of Development Research (GIDR)
- Haryana Olympic Association (HOA)
- Himalayan Forest Research Institute
- Homoeopathic Pharmacopoeia Laboratory (HPL), Ghaziabad, Uttar Pradesh
- Howrah Bridge (Rabindra Setu), Kolkata
- ICAR Zonal Co-ordinating Unit Zone-III, NEH Region
- India Government Mint, Kolkata
- India Government Mint, Noida
- Indian Academy of Sciences, Bangalore, Karnataka
- Indian Association for the Cultivation of Science (IACS)

- Indian Council of Forestry Research and Education (ICFRE)
- Indian Council of Philosophical Research, ICPR, New Delhi
- Indian Council of Social Science Research (ICSSR)
- Indian Institute of Advanced Study (IIAS)
- Indian Institute of Astrophysics (IIA)
- Indian Institute of Entrepreneurship
- Indian Institute of Forest Management (IIFM), Bhopal, Madhya Pradesh
- Indian Institute of Geomagnetism
- Indian Institute of Information Technology, Allahabad (IIITA)
- Indian Institute of Information Technology and Management (IIITM), Gwalior
- Indian Institute of Management, Bangalore (IIMB)
- Indian Institute of Management, Calcutta (IIMC)
- Indian Institute of Management, Indore (IIMI)
- Indian Institute of Management, Kozhikode (IIMK)
- Indian Institute of Management, Lucknow (IIML)
- Indian Institute of Management, Raipur (IIMR)
- Indian Institute of Management, Ranchi (IIMR)
- Indian Institute of Management, Rohtak (IIMR)
- Indian Institute of Mass Communication (IIMC)
- Indian Institute of Packaging
- Indian Institute of Public Administration (IIPA)
- Indian Institute of Science (IISC), Bangalore
- Indian Institute of Technology, Delhi (IITD)
- Indian Institute of Technology, Guwahati (IITG)
- Indian Institute of Technology (IIT), Kharagpur
- Indian Institute of Technology (IITK), Kanpur
- Indian Institute of Technology (IIT), Madras
- Indian Institute of Technology, Roorkee

- Indian Institute of Tourism and Travel Management (IITTM)
- Indian Military Academy
- Indian Museum, Kolkata
- Indian National Academy of Engineering (INAE)
- Indian National Centre for Ocean Information Services (INCOIS)
- Indian National Science Academy (INSA)
- Indian Nursing Council
- Indian Pharmacopoeia Commission (IPC)
- Indian Plywood Industries Research and Training Institute (IPIRTI)
- Indian Rubber Manufacturers Research Association (IRMRA)
- Indian School of Mines (ISM)
- Indian Science Congress Association
- Indira Gandhi National Centre for the Arts (IGNCA)
- Indira Gandhi National Open University (IGNOU)
- Indira Gandhi Rashtriya Uran Academy (IGRUA)
- Inland Waterways Authority of India (IWAI)
- Institute for Defence Studies and Analyses (IDSA)
- Institute for Plasma Research (IPR)
- Institute for Social and Economic Change (ISEC)
- Institute for Studies in Industrial Development (ISID)
- Institute of Bioresources and Sustainable Development (IBSD)
- Institute of Development Studies (IDS), Jaipur, Rajasthan
- Institute of Life Sciences
- Institute of Physics (IOP)
- Integrated handloom Cluster Development Scheme
- International Advanced Research Centre for Powder Metallurgy and New Materials

- International Centre for Alternative Dispute Resolution (ICADR)
- International Institute for Population Sciences (IIPS)
- Inter University Accelerator Centre (IUAC) New Delhi
- Inter-University Centre for Astronomy and Astrophysics (IUCAA)
- Jamia Millia Islamia
- Jawaharlal Institute of Postgraduate Medical Education and Research (JIPMER)
- Jawaharlal Nehru Aluminium Research Development and Design Centre (JNARDDC)
- Jawaharlal Nehru Centre for Advanced Scientific Research (JNCASR)
- Jawaharlal Nehru Port Trust
- Jawaharlal Nehru University (JNU)
- Jawahar Navodaya Vidyalaya
- Jawahar Navodaya Vidyalaya, Allmatti
- Jawahar Navodaya Vidyalaya Dodballapur, Bangalore rural
- Jawahar Navodaya Vidyalaya, Gajanur
- Jawahar Navodaya Vidyalaya (JNV), Mudugal, Raichur, Karnataka
- Jawahar Navodaya Vidyalaya, Mandya
- Jawahar Navodaya Vidyalaya, Panchavati
- JNV Dharwad - Jawahar Navodaya Vidyalaya, Dharwad, Karnataka
- Kalakshetra Foundation, Chennai
- Kandla Port Trust
- Kendriya Vidyalaya CRPF, Amerigog, Guwahati, Assam
- Kendriya Vidyalaya No.1, Jipmer Campus, Puducherry
- Kendriya Vidyalaya No.2, Kota, Rajasthan
- Kendriya Vidyalaya Sangathan (KVS)
- Khuda Bakhsh Oriental Public Library

- Kolkata Port Trust
- Lakshmibai National University of Physical Education, Gwalior
- Lala Ram Swarup Institute of Tuberculosis and Respiratory Diseases
- Lalit Kala Akademi, National Academy of Fine Art, New Delhi
- Madras Institute of Development Studies (MIDS)
- Maharsi Sandipani Rashtriya Veda Vidya Pratishtan, Ujjain, Madhya Pradesh
- Mahatma Gandhi Antarrashtriya Hindi Vishwavidyalaya
- Malaviya National Institute of Technology, Jaipur (MNIT)
- Marine Engineering and Research Institute (MERI), Kolkata
- Marine Products Export Development Authority (MPEDA)
- Maulana Abul Kalam Azad Institute of Asian Studies (MAKAIAS)
- Maulana Azad Education Foundation
- Maulana Azad National Institute of Technology, Bhopal
- Maulana Azad National Urdu University
- Military Engineering Service (MES)
- Morarji Desai National Institute of Yoga (MDNIY)
- Mormugoa Port Trust
- Motilal Nehru National Institute of Technology (MNNIT), Allahabad
- Mumbai Port Trust
- National Academy of Sciences
- National Accreditation Board for Testing and Calibration Laboratories (NABL)
- National AIDS Control Organisation (NACO), Department of AIDS Control
- National Anti-Doping Agency (NADA)

- National Assessment and Accreditation Council
- National Atmospheric Research Laboratory (NARL)
- National Bal Bhavan
- National Book Trust (NBT), India
- National Brain Research Centre (NBRC)
- National Centre for Antarctic and Ocean Research (NCAOR)
- National Centre for Cell Sciences (NCCS)
- National Council for Promotion of Sindhi Language (NCPSL)
- National Council for Promotion of Sindhi Language (NCPSL), New Delhi
- National Council for Promotion of Urdu Language (NCPUL)
- National Council of Educational Research and Training (NCERT)
- National Council of Rural Institutes, Hyderabad
- National Council of Science Museums (NCSM)
- National Culture Fund (NCF)
- National Dairy Research Institute, Karnal, Haryana
- National Foundation for Communal Harmony (NFCH)
- National Gallery of Modern Art (NGMA), New Delhi
- National Handicrafts and Handlooms Museum (Crafts Museum)
- National Institute for Empowerment of Persons with Multiple Disabilities (NIEPMD)
- National Institute for Entrepreneurship and Small Business Development (NIESBUD)
- National Institute for Micro, Small and Medium Enterprises
- National Institute for the Mentally Handicapped (NIMH)
- National Institute for the Orthopaedically Handicapped (NIOH), Kolkata

- National Institute of Agricultural Extension Management (MANAGE)
- National Institute of Agricultural Marketing (NIAM)
- National Institute of Ayurveda
- National Institute of Design (NID)
- National Institute of Electronics and Information Technology, Delhi
- National Institute of Electronics and Information Technology, Kohima, Nagaland
- National Institute of Electronics and Information Technology - NIELIT (formerly DOEACC Society)
- National Institute of Electronics and Information Technology - NIELIT, Srinagar, Jammu (DOEACC Society)
- National Institute of Financial Management (NIFM)
- National Institute of Homoeopathy (NIH)
- National Institute of Hydrology (NIH), Roorkee
- National Institute of Immunology (NII)
- National Institute of Mental Health and Neuro Sciences (NIMHANS)
- National Institute of Naturopathy (NIN)
- National Institute of Ocean Technology
- National Institute of Open Schooling (NIOS)
- National Institute of Pharmaceutical Education and Research (NIPER)
- National Institute of Plant Genome Research, New Delhi
- National Institute of Public Cooperation and Child Development (NIPCCD)
- National Institute of Rehabilitation Training and Research (NIRTAR)
- National Institute of Rock Mechanics (NIRM)
- National Institute of Rural Development (NIRD)
- National Institute of Technology, Calicut
- National Institute of Technology, Hamirpur

- National Institute of Technology, Jamshedpur
- National Institute of Technology, Karnataka (NITK)
- National Institute of Technology, Kurukshetra
- National Institute of Technology, Rourkela
- National Institute of Technology, Srinagar
- National Institute of Technology, Tiruchirappalli
- National Institute of Technology, Warangal
- National Institute of Unani Medicine (NIUM), Bangalore, Karnataka
- National Institute of Urban Affairs (NIUA)
- National Meat and Poultry Processing Board
- National Museum Institute (NMI)
- National Playing Fields Association of India (NPFAI)
- National Power Training Institute (NPTI), Faridabad, Haryana
- National Remote Sensing Agency (NRSA)
- National School of Drama
- National Service Scheme (NSS)
- National Tuberculosis Institute (NTI), Bangalore
- National Water Development Agency (NWDA)
- Nava Nalanda Mahavihara, Nalanda, Bihar
- Navodaya Vidyalaya Samiti (NVS)
- Nehru Memorial Museum & Library (NMML), New Delhi
- New Mangalore Port Trust
- North Central Zone Cultural Centre (NCZCC)
- North Eastern Hill University (NEHU), Shillong, Meghalaya
- North Eastern Indira Gandhi Regional Institute of Health and Medical Sciences (NEIGRIHMS)
- North Eastern Institute of Ayurveda and Homoeopathy (NEIAH), Shillong, Meghalaya

- North Eastern Regional Institute of Science and Technology (NERIST)
- North Eastern Space Applications Centre
- North East Zone Cultural Centre, Dimapur, Nagaland
- North Zone Cultural Center, Sheesh Mahal, Patiala
- Ocean Science and Technology Cell (OSTC)
- Pandit Deen Dayal Upadhyaya Institute for the Physically Handicapped (PDDUIPH)
- Paradip Port Trust
- Pondicherry University
- Port Health Organisation, Visakhapatnam
- Post Graduate Institute of Medical Education and Research, Chandigarh
- Prasar Bharati, Broadcasting Corporation of India
- Press Council of India (PCI)
- Raja Rammohun Roy Library Foundation (RRRLF)
- Rajiv Gandhi Centre for Biotechnology (RGCB)
- Raman Research Institute, Bangalore, Karnataka
- Rampur Raza Library
- Rashtriya Ayurveda Vidyapeeth
- Rashtriya Mahila Kosh (RMK)
- Rashtriya Sanskrit Sansthan
- Repatriates Co-operative Finance and Development Bank Limited
- Saha Institute of Nuclear Physics (SINP), Kolkatta
- Sahitya Akademi
- Sainik School Bhubaneswar, Odisha
- Sainik School Ghorakhal, Nainital, Uttarakhand
- Sainik School Kapurthala, Punjab
- Sainik School Rewari, Haryana
- Salar Jung Museum, Hyderabad, Andhra Pradesh
- Salim Ali Centre for Ornithology and Natural History (SACON), Coimbatore, Tamilnadu

- Sangeet Natak Akademi
- Sant Longowal Institute of Engineering and Technology (SLIET)
- Sardar Vallabhbhai National Institute of Technology, Surat
- Sardar Vallabhbhai Patel International School of Textiles & Management, Coimbatore, Tamil Nadu
- Satyajit Ray Film and Television Institute
- Satyendra Nath Bose National Centre for Basic Sciences
- Securities Appellate Tribunal, Mumbai
- Semi-Conductor Laboratory
- Society for Applied Microwave Electronic Engineering and Research (SAMEER)
- Software Technology Parks of India (STPI)
- Sree Chitra Tirunal Institute for Medical Sciences and Technology (SCTIMST)
- State Institute of Education Technology, Bhubaneswar
- State Institute of Education Technology, Hyderabad
- State Institute of Education Technology, Lucknow
- State Institute of Education Technology, Patna
- Syama Prasad Mookerjee National Institute of Watersports (NIWS)
- Tariff Authority for Major Ports (TAMP)
- Tata Institute of Fundamental Research (TIFR)
- Tata Memorial Centre (Hospital) (TMC)
- Technology Information, Forecasting and Assessment Council (TIFAC)
- Telecom Equipment and Services Export Promotion Council (TEPC), New Delhi
- Telecommunication Engineering Centre, New Delhi
- Tezpur University
- Tuticorin Port Trust
- Universal Service Obligation Fund (USOF)

- University Grants Commission (UGC)
- University of Delhi
- University of Hyderabad, Andhra Pradesh
- Variable Energy Cyclotron Centre (VECC)
- Victoria Memorial Hall, Kolkata
- Vigyan Prasar Science Portal
- Visakhapatnam Port Trust (VPT)
- Visva-Bharati, Santiniketan
- Visvesvaraya Industrial and Technological Museum, Bangalore
- Visvesvaraya National Institute of Technology (VNIT), Nagpur
- V. V. Giri National Labour Institute (VVGNLI)
- Zonal Cultural Centres (ZCC)

Similarly, there are several autonomous bodies, institutes, organizations attached and subordinate offices in ministries and departments which come under the purview of the State Governments. For example, the list of autonomous bodies, institutes and organizations under the Kerala Government can be accessed from the link **http://www.kerala.gov.in/index.php?option=com_content&view=article&id=1734&Itemid=2 318**

EDUCATIONAL INSTITUTIONS

- At present, there are sixteen Indian Institutes of Technology (IITs) viz. at Bombay, Delhi, Kanpur, Kharagpur, Madras, Guwahati, Roorkee, Hyderabad, Patna, Bhubaneshwar, Ropar, Jodhpur, Gandhinagar, Indore, Mandi and Varanasi
- There are twelve Indian Institutes of Managements (IIMs) viz. at Ahmedabad, Lucknow, Bangaluru, Kolkata, Indore, Kozhikode, Shillong, Rohtak, Raipur, Ranchi, Tiruchirappalli and Kashipuri
- There are thirty National Institutes of Technology. The list can be accessed from **http://mhrd.gov.in/nit**

- Indian Institute of Science at Bangaluru
- There are five Indian Institutes of Science Education and Research (IISER) viz. at Kolkata, Pune, Mohali, Bhopal and Thiruvananthapuram
- There are four Indian Institute of Information Technology (IIITs) viz. at Allahabad, Gwalior, Jabalpur and Kanchipuram
- There are four National Institute of Technical Teachers Training and Research (NITTTR) viz. at Kolkata, Chandigarh, Chennai and Bhopal
- There are 40 central universities. The list can be accessed on **http://mhrd.gov.in/central_univ_eng**
- There are 251 State Universities out of which University Grants Commission makes budget allocation for 123 universities
- Other centrally aided institutions like
    - School of Planning & Architecture (SPA), New Delhi
    - School of Planning & Architecture (SPA), Bhopal
    - School of Planning & Architecture (SPA), Vijayawada
    - Central Institute of Technology, Kokrajhar
    - Sant Longowal Institute of Engineering & Technology (SLIET), Longowal, Punjab
    - North Eastern Regional Institute of Science & Technology (NERIST), Itanagar
    - Indian School of Mines University (ISMU), Dhanbad
    - National Institute of Industrial Engineering (NITIE), Mumbai
    - National Institute of Foundry & Forge Technology (NIFFT), Ranchi

There are several educational institutions which are formed under Central/State enactments. These institutions and other State Government institutions also publish recruitment for various posts from clerical to professors. The recruitment to various posts is done by the institutes themselves. For some posts qualification of

NET is required. Candidates can access their respective websites to get the details of recruitment procedures.

Recruitment for the post of Professors/Associate Professors/Assistant Professors (Group A Post) in National Institute of Technology (NITs) is done as per the NIT Faculty Recruitment Rules, 2011 which can be accessed on **http://www.nitrr.ac.in/downloads/forms/admin/MRR_Faculty.pdf.**

REGULATORY BODIES

There are several regulatory commissions in India. They can be categorized as:

1. **Electricity Regulatory Commission** – eg. Maharashtra Electricity Regulatory Commission (MERC), Delhi Electricity Regulatory Commission (DERC)
2. **Insurance Regularity Commission** like Insurance Regulatory Development Authority (IRDA)
3. **Telecom Regulatory Commission** (TRAI)
4. **Financial Regulatory Commission** like Securities and Exchange Board of India (SEBI), Foreign Investment Promotion Board (FIPB)

    The list of other regulatory bodies can be accessed from **http://archive.india.gov.in/govt/studies/annex/8.1.1.pdf.**

    The recruitment to these commissions is done by notifications published on their respective websites and various dailies. Candidates can access their respective websites to get the details of recruitment procedures. Even the recruitment notifications are displayed on the various job related sites already discussed earlier.

RESEARCH INSTITUTIONS

There are numerous research institutes in India in different fields. Some of them are owned by the Government while some are partially or fully aided by the Government. These institutes function under different ministries/departments of the Government. The list of the institutes is shown in the table below. The recruitment to these research institutes are also regularly published in the newspapers as well as on their websites.

Institute	Location
All India Institute of Medical Sciences (AIIMS)	New Delhi
All India Institute of Medical Sciences (AIIMS)	Mandi (HP)
All India Institute of Speech and Hearing (AIISH)	Mysore
Aryabhatta Research Institute of Observational Sciences	Nainital
Birbal Sahni Institute of Palaeobotany	Lucknow
Bose Institute	Kolkata
Central Drug Research Institute	Lucknow
Central Electronics Engineering Research Institute	Pilani
Central Food Technological Research Institute	Mysore
Central Glass and Ceramic Research Institute (CGCRI)	Kolkata
Central Institute for Cotton Research	Nagpur
Central Institute of Agricultural Engineering	Bhopal
Central Institute of Brackish Water Aquaculture	Tamil Nadu
Central Institute of Educational Technology	New Delhi
Central Institute of Fisheries Education	Mumbai
Central Institute of Fisheries, Nautical and Engineering Training	Kochi
Central Institute of Fresh Water Aquaculture	Bhubaneswar

Institute	Location
Central Institute of Indian Languages	Mysore
Central Institute of Plastics Engineering & Technology	Chennai
Central Institute of Psychiatry	Ranchi
Central Institute of Medicinal and Aromatic Plants	Lucknow
Central Institute of Road Transport (CIRT)	Pune
Central Leather Research Institute	Adyar, Chennai
Central Institute of Technology Kokrajhar (CIT)	Kokrajhar
Central Mine Planning & Design Institute Limited	Ranchi
Central Research Institute for Dryland Agriculture	Hyderabad
Central Sheep & Wool Research Institute	Avikanagar
Central Soil Salinity Research Institute	New Delhi
Centre for Cultural Resources and Training (CCRT)	New Delhi
Centre for Development Studies	Thiruvananthpuram
Centre for Excellence in Basic Sciences	Mumbai
College of Defence Management	Secunderabad
Film and Television Institute of India	Pune
Fluid Control Research Institute	Kanjikode
Foreign Service Institute	New Delhi
Harcourt Butler Technological Institute	Kanpur
Harish Chandra Research Institute (HRI)	Allahabad

Institute	Location
Indian Agricultural Research Institute (IARI)	New Delhi
Indian Association for the Cultivation of Science (IACS)	Kolkata
Indian Diamond Institute	Surat
Indian Institute of Architects	Mumbai
Indian Institute of Astrophysics	Bangalore
Indian Institute of Chemical Biology (IICB)	Kolkata
Indian Institute of Chemical Technology	Hyderabad
Indian Institute of Ecology and Environment	New Delhi
Indian Institute of Engineering Science and Technology (IIEST)	Shibpur
Indian Institute of Foreign Trade (IIFT)	New Delhi
Indian Institute of Forest Management (IIFM)	Bhopal
Indian Institute of Forestry Research and Education	Dehradun, Shimla, Ranchi, Jorhat, Jabalpur, Jodhpur
Indian Institute of Information Technology (IIIT)	Gwalior, Allahabad, Jabalpur, Kanchipuram, Tiruchirappalli, Chittoor, Guwahati, Kota, Vadodara, Thiruvananthapuram
Indian Institute of Management	Ahmedabad, Bangalore, Kozhikode, Indore, Lucknow, Kashipur, Calcutta, Raipur, Ranchi, Rohtak, Udaipur, Tiruchirappalli
Indian Institute of Information Technology	Allahabad
Indian Institute of Information Technology and Management	Gwalior

Institute	Location
Indian Institute of Mass Communication (IIMC)	New Delhi
Indian Institute of Petroleum	Dehradun
Indian Institute of Plantation Management	Bangalore
Indian Institute of Pulses Research	Kanpur
Indian Institute of Remote Sensing (IIRS)	Dehradun
Indian Institute of Science (IISc)	Bangalore
Indian Institute of Science Education and Research (IISER)	Kolkata, Pune, Mohali, Bhopal, Thiruvananthpuram
Indian Institute of Social Welfare and Business Management	Kolkata
Indian Institute of Soil Science	Bhopal
Indian Institute of Space Science and Technology (IIST)	Thiruvananthpuram
Indian Institute of Spices Research	Kozhikode
Indian Institute of Sugarcane Research	Lucknow
Indian Institute of Technology (IIT)	Kharagpur, Kanpur, Mumbai, Chennai, Delhi, Guwahati, Bhubaneswar, Roorkee, Ropar, Hyderabad, Gandhinagar, Jodhpur, Patna, Mandi, Indore, Varanasi
Indian Institute of Tourism and Travel Management	Gwalior
Indian Institute of Tropical Meteorology	Pune
Indian Institute of Natural Resins and Gums (Indian Lac Research Institute)	Ranchi

Institute	Location
National Institute Of Technical Teachers Training and Research	Chennai
International Institute for Population Sciences (IIPS)	Mumbai
Indian School of Mines	Dhanbad
Indian Statistical Institute	Bangalore, Kolkata, Delhi
Indian Veterinary Research Institute	Bareilly
Indira Gandhi Institute of Development Research	Mumbai
Indira Gandhi Centre for Atomic Research (IGCAR)	Kalpakkam
Institute for Studies in Industrial Development	New Delhi
Institute of Defence Studies and Analyses	New Delhi
Institute of Economic Growth	New Delhi
Institute of Food Security	Gurgaon
Institute of Genomics and Integrative Biology (IGIB)	New Delhi
Institute of Mathematical Sciences (IMSc)	Chennai
Institute of Physics (IOP)	Bhubaneswar
Institute for Plasma Research (IPR)	Gandhinagar
Institute of Rural Management	Anand
Institute of Secretarial Training and Management	New Delhi
Institute for Studies in Industrial Development	New Delhi
International Institute for Population Sciences	Mumbai
Jawaharlal Nehru Centre for Advanced Scientific Research (JNCASR)	Bangalore
Kendriya Hindi Sansthan	Agra

Institute	Location
Lakshmibai National Institute of Physical Education (LNIPE)	Gwalior
Maulana Abul Kalam Azad Institute of Asian Studies	Kolkata
Morarji Desai National Institute of Yoga	New Delhi
National Academy of Agricultural Research Management	Rajendranagar
National Academy of Agricultural Sciences	New Delhi
National Academy of Construction	Hyderabad
National Academy of Customs, Excise and Narcotics (NACEN)	Kolkata
National Botanical Research Institute (NBRI)	Lucknow
National Civil Defence College	Nagpur
National Dairy Research Institute	Karnal (Haryana)
National Defence College of India	Delhi
National Environmental Engineering Research Institute	Nagpur
National Institute of Agricultural Extension Management	Hyderabad
National Institute of Agricultural Marketing	Jaipur
National Institute of Construction Management and Research	Mumbai
National Institute of Criminology and Forensic Science	New Delhi
National Institute of Design	Ahmedabad

Institute	Location
National Institute of Disaster Management	New Delhi
National Institute of Homoeopathy	Kolkata
National Institute of Hydrology	Belgaum, Roorkee
National Institute of Mental Health & Neuro Sciences	Bangalore
National Institute of Open Schooling	Noida
National Institute of Technology (NIT)	Goa
National Institute of Oceanography (NIO)	Goa
National Institute of Ocean Technology	Chennai
National Institute of Pharmaceutical Education and Research	Mohali, Ahmedabad, Raebareli, Hyderabad, Guwahati, Hajipur, Kolkata
National Institute of Rural Development	Hyderabad
National Institute of Science Communication (NISCOM)	New Delhi
National Institute of Science Communication and Information Resources	Delhi
National Institute of Science Education and Research (NISER)	Bhubaneswar
National Institute of Technology	Agartala, Allahabad, Bhopal, Kozhikode, Durgapur, Hamirpur, Jaipur, Jalandhar, Jamshedpur, Kurukshetra, Shillong, Nagpur, Patna, Raipur, Rourkela, Silchar, Srinagar, Surat, Surathkal, Tiruchirappalli, Warangal, Yupia

Institute	Location
National Institute of Urban Affairs	New Delhi
National Institute of Water Sports	Goa
National Museum Institute	New Delhi
National Power Training Institute	Faridabad
National Sugar Institute	Kanpur
National Tuberculosis Institute	Bangalore
Netaji Subhas National Institute of Sports (NSNIS)	Patiala
Physical Research Laboratory (PRL)	Ahmedabad
Raman Research Institute (RRI)	Bangalore
Saha Institute of Nuclear Physics	Kolkata
Sanjay Gandhi Post Graduate Institute of Medical Sciences	Lucknow
S.N. Bose National Centre for Basic Sciences (SNBNCBS)	Kolkata
Sher-i-Kashmir Institute of Medical Sciences	Srinagar
State Institute of Public Administration and Rural Development	Agartala
Sant longowal institute of Engineering and technology (SLIET)	Sangrur
Sant longowal institute of Engineering and technology (SLIET)	Sangrur
Satyajit Ray Film and Television Institute	Kolkata
Tata Institute of Social Sciences	Mumbai
Tata Institute of Fundamental Research (TIFR)	Mumbai, Hyderabad

Institute	Location
V. V. Giri National Labour Institute	New Delhi
Directorate of Forest Education (DFE)	Dehradun
Indira Gandhi National Forest Academy (IGNFA)	Dehradun
Indian Institute of Horticulture Research (IIBR)	Goa
Indian Institute of Hotel Management	Goa
National Institute of Animal Welfare	Faridabad
Variable Energy Cyclotron Centre	Kolkata
Bhabha Atomic Research Centre	Mumbai

REGISTERED SOCIETIES OF GOVERNMENT

There are several organizations and institutions which function under the administrative control of various ministries and departments and are registered as societies under the Society Registration Act, 1860. Recruitment to these societies is done by the Society themselves. Some of them are indicated below:

1. Central Board for Workers' Education Registered Society under the Ministry of Labour
2. National Council of Safety in Mines, Dhanbad Registered Society under the Ministry of Labour
3. National Labour Institute Registered Society under the Ministry of Labour
4. Council of Scientific and Industrial Research Society under the Ministry of Science & Technology 5. Indian Council of Agricultural Research - A Society controlled by the Government under the Ministry of Agriculture
6. Sports Authority of India - A Society controlled by the Government under the Ministry of Youth Affairs and Sports

7. National Council for Hotel Management and Catering Technology, New Delhi registered under Societies Registration Act, 1860 under the Ministry of Tourism
8. Institute of Hotel Management, Catering and Nutrition, New Delhi registered under Societies Registration Act, 1860 under the Ministry of Tourism
9. Institute of Hotel Management, Catering Technology and Applied Nutrition, Mumbai registered under Societies Registration Act, 1860 under the Ministry of Tourism
10. Institute of Hotel Management, Catering Technology and Applied Nutrition, Chennai registered under Societies Registration Act, 1860 under the Ministry of Tourism
11. Institute of Hotel Management, Catering Technology and Applied Nutrition, Chennai registered under Societies Registration Act, 1860 under the Ministry of Tourism
12. Institute of Hotel Management, Catering Technology and Applied Nutrition, Goa registered under Societies Registration Act, 1860 under the Ministry of Tourism
13. Institute of Hotel Management, Catering Technology and Applied Nutrition, Bangalore Registered under Societies Registration Act, 1860 under the Ministry of Tourism
14. Institute of Hotel Management, Catering Technology and Nutrition, Lucknow registered under Societies Registration Act, 1860 under the Ministry of Tourism
15. Institute of Hotel Management, Catering and Nutrition, Ahmedabad registered under Societies Registration Act, 1860 under the Ministry of Tourism
16. Institute of Hotel Management, Catering and Nutrition, Ahmedabad registered under Societies Registration Act, 1860
17. Institute of Hotel Management, Catering Technology and Applied Nutrition, Bhubanewar registered under Societies Registration Act, 1860 under the Ministry of Tourism
18. Institute of Hotel Management, Catering Technology and Applied Nutrition, Jaipur registered under Societies Registration Act, 1860 under the Ministry of Tourism

19. Institute of Hotel Management, Catering Technology and Applied Nutrition, Bhopal registered under Societies Registration Act, 1860 under the Ministry of Tourism
20. Institute of Hotel Management, Catering Technology and Applied Nutrition, Srinagar Registered under Societies Registration Act, 1860 under the Ministry of Tourism
21. Institute of Hotel Management, Catering Technology and Applied Nutrition, Guwahati registered under Societies Registration Act, 1860 under the Ministry of Tourism
22. Institute of Hotel Management, Catering Technology and Applied Nutrition, Gwalior registered under Societies Registration Act, 1860 under the Ministry of Tourism
23. Institute of Hotel Management, Catering Technology and Applied Nutrition, Thiruvananathapuram registered under Societies Registration Act, 1860 under the Ministry of Tourism
24. Institute of Hotel Management, Catering and Nutrition, Chandigarh registered under Societies Registration Act, 1860 under the Ministry of Tourism
25. Institute of Hotel Management, Catering Technology and Applied Nutrition, Gurdaspur registered under Societies Registration Act, 1860 under the Ministry of Tourism
26. Institute of Hotel Management, Catering Technology and Applied Nutrition, Shimla registered under Societies Registration Act, 1860 under the Ministry of Tourism
27. Institute of Hotel Management, Catering Technology and Applied Nutrition, Patna registered under Societies Registration Act, 1860 under the Ministry of Tourism
28. National Power Training Institute, Faridabad registered under Societies Registration Act, 1860 under the Ministry of Power
29. Indian Institute of Advanced Study, Shimla registered under Societies Registration Act, 1860 under the Ministry of Human Resource Development

30. Kendriya Vidyalaya Sangathan, New Delhi registered under Societies Registration Act, 1860 under the Ministry of Human Resource Development
31. Navodya Vidyalaya Samiti, New Delhi, registered under Societies Registration Act, 1860 under the Ministry of Human Resource Development
32. Indian Council of Medical Research, Ansari Nagar, New Delhi registered under Societies Registration Act, 1860 under the Ministry of Health & Family Welfare
33. Film and Television Institute of India, Pune registered under Societies Registration Act, 1860 under the Ministry of Information and Broadcasting
34. Satyajit Ray Film and Television Institute, Calcutta registered under Societies Registration Act, 1860 under the Ministry of Information and Broadcasting
35. Indian Institute of Astrophysics Autonomous body registered under the Societies Registration Act, 1860 under Department of Science and Technology
36. National Rural Roads Development Agency Autonomous body registered under Societies Registration Act, 1860 under the Ministry of Rural Development
37. National Horticulture Board registered under the Societies Registration Act, 1860 under the Ministry of Agriculture
38. Small Farmers Agriculture Business Consortium registered under the Societies Registration Act, 1860 under the Ministry of Agriculture
39. National Institute for Agricultural Extension and Management Autonomous Organisation registered under Societies Registration Act, 1860 under the Ministry of Agriculture
40. National Institute of Health and Family Welfare Autonomous Body/Society under Societies Registration Act 1860 under the Ministry of Health and Family Welfare
41. All India Institutes of Speech and Hearing Autonomous Body registered as a Society under the Societies Registration

Act, 1860 under the Ministry of Health and Family Welfare
42. Central Institute of Plastics Engineering and Technology, Autonomous Institute registered under the Societies Act of 1860 under the Ministry of Chemicals & Fertilizers
43. National Institute of Public Finance and Policy (NIPFP) registered under Societies Act of 1860 under the Ministry of Finance Department of Revenue.

LOCAL BODIES AND PANCHAYATS

The rural areas of the country come under the Panchayati Raj Institutions while the urban areas come under Municipalities and Corporations.

Panchayati Raj is divided into three levels i.e. Village (Gram) level, Block (Taluka) level and District (Tehsil) level.

For the purpose of running Panchayats in villages, a Sarpanch along with other members are elected. They are responsible for the administration of the village. They plan and implement schemes which are necessary for the economic and social development of the villages. A Zila Panchayat Chief who is an IAS officer is elected by the Panchayat.

A Municipal Corporation is formed in the place with large population like metro cities. A Mayor and a Sabhashad are elected to look into the administration.

Municipality is formed in the place with population more that a lakh. The whole place is divided into wards and a member is elected from each ward and a chairman is elected separately.

A city council is formed in a place with a population of few thousands.

The recruitment to Local Bodies like Municipalities and Panchayats for officers and staff are done by the respective State Governments. Every State has a dedicated website for Panchayats where information about the structure, hierarchy and recruitment details are hosted. Some of them are:

www.biharpanchayat.gov.in
www.panchayat.gujarat.gov.in
www.odishapanchayat.gov.in
www.rajpanchayat.gov.in
http://www.lsg.kerala.gov.in/en/index.php

There are some websites which are dedicated to a particular district of a State. These websites also host information about various job openings within the district. Apart from that the recruitment notifications are regularly published in the local newspapers and Employment News. The details of recruitment can be accessed from the respective websites and local newspapers.

Similarly there are hundreds of municipal corporations throughout the country. Recruitment across various cadres are done by the municipal corporations themselves. The notifications for various posts are published on the respective websites of the corporations as well as in the local news papers.

PRASAR BHARTI

Public broadcasters like Doordarshan and All India Radio come under the Ministry of Information and Broadcasting. There are several recruitments in these organisations which are published on the official websites like http://allindiaradio.gov.in/Oppurtunities/Recruitment/Pages/Simple.aspx

Vide press release dated 28.03.2013, Prasar Bharti stated that efforts are being made to set up a recruitment board for recruitment in Prasar Bharti. In the first major recruitment drive after a long gap, Staff Selection Commission held a combined entrance test for recruitment of various posts in Prasar Bharti. The details can be seen from http://prasarbharati.gov.in/NR/rdonlyres/1A0FEE21-8F52-4B4B-BC10-495A1DF2AE18/20357/NewsReleaseason28032013.pdf.

INDIAN JUDICIARY

There is one Supreme Court, 24 High Courts and numerous subordinate courts. The High Courts are the principal civil courts of original jurisdiction in each state and union territory. However, a High Court exercises its original civil and criminal jurisdiction only if the subordinate courts are not authorized by law to try such matters for lack of pecuniary, territorial jurisdiction. High courts may also enjoy original jurisdiction in certain matters if so designated specifically in a state or federal law.

However, the work of most High Courts primarily consists of appeals from lower courts and writ petitions in terms of Article 226 of the constitution. Writ jurisdiction is also original jurisdiction of High Court. The precise territorial jurisdiction of each High Court varies. The appeal order is the following: tehsil-kotwali-criminal/civil courts - district - high court - supreme court.

Each state is divided into judicial districts presided over by a District and Sessions Judge. He is known as a District Judge when he presides over a civil case, and a Sessions Judge when he presides over a criminal case. He is the highest judicial authority below a High Court judge. Below him, there are courts of civil jurisdiction, known by different names in different states. Under Article 141 of the Constitution, all courts in India (which includes High Courts) are bound by the judgments and orders of the Supreme Court of India by precedence.

There are several posts in the courts where recruitment is done by the recruitment cell of the court itself. Some of the websites are indicated below to find the recruitment notifications:

Supreme Court of India

http://supremecourtofindia.nic.in/recruitment.htm

High Courts

Every High Court has its own website where recruitment notifications are published online. The same is published in the local newspapers and Employment news. Some of the suggested websites are:

www.bombayhighcourt.nic.in/recruitment.php
www.highcourtchd.gov.in

www.gujarathighcourt.nic.in
www.orissahighcourt.nic.in/recruitment.asp

DISTRICT COURTS

There are more than 300 districts courts in the country. The recruitment is done by the courts themselves and is published in the local news papers and websites. The details of the websites can be searched on the internet. Alternatively, the candidates can also register to any job related website to get an update on the latest recruitment notification.

JAICO PUBLISHING HOUSE
Elevate Your Life. Transform Your World.

ESTABLISHED IN 1946, Jaico Publishing House is home to world-transforming authors such as Sri Sri Paramahansa Yogananda, Osho, The Dalai Lama, Sri Sri Ravi Shankar, Robin Sharma, Deepak Chopra, Jack Canfield, Eknath Easwaran, Devdutt Pattanaik, Khushwant Singh, John Maxwell, Brian Tracy and Stephen Hawking.

Our late founder Mr. Jaman Shah first established Jaico as a book distribution company. Sensing that independence was around the corner, he aptly named his company Jaico ('Jai' means victory in Hindi). In order to service the significant demand for affordable books in a developing nation, Mr. Shah initiated Jaico's own publications. Jaico was India's first publisher of paperback books in the English language.

While self-help, religion and philosophy, mind/body/spirit, and business titles form the cornerstone of our non-fiction list, we publish an exciting range of travel, current affairs, biography, and popular science books as well. Our renewed focus on popular fiction is evident in our new titles by a host of fresh young talent from India and abroad. Jaico's recently established Translations Division translates selected English content into nine regional languages.

Jaico's Higher Education Division (HED) is recognized for its student-friendly textbooks in Business Management and Engineering which are in use countrywide.

In addition to being a publisher and distributor of its own titles, Jaico is a major national distributor of books of leading international and Indian publishers. With its headquarters in Mumbai, Jaico has branches and sales offices in Ahmedabad, Bangalore, Bhopal, Bhubaneswar, Chennai, Delhi, Hyderabad, Kolkata and Lucknow.

SINCE 1946

www.ingramcontent.com/pod-product-compliance
Lightning Source LLC
Chambersburg PA
CBHW020745160426
43192CB00006B/253